The Pattern of Judgment
in the *Queste* and *Cleanness*

# The Pattern of Judgment
# in the *Queste* and *Cleanness*

Charlotte C. Morse

University of Missouri Press

Columbia & London, 1978

Library of Congress Cataloging in Publication Data

Morse, Charlotte C., 1942–
    The Pattern of Judgment in the *Queste* and *Cleanness*.

    1. La Queste del Saint Graal. 2. Cleanness (Middle
English poem) I. Title.
PQ1475.M67        809′.1        77–25158
ISBN 0–8262–0242–X

To the memory of my grandmothers

Mattie Harris Sanford Turner (1884–1966)

Eugenia Virginia Blair Cook (1887–1974)

## List of Abbreviations

| | |
|---|---|
| CCCM | Corpus christianorum. Continuatio mediaevalis (Turnhout, Belg.: Brepols) |
| CCSL | Corpus christianorum. Series latina (Turnhout, Belg.: Brepols, 1955) |
| CFMA | Les Classiques français du moyen âge |
| CSEL | Corpus scriptorum ecclesiasticorum latinorum (Vienna: F. Tempsky, Hoelder-Pichler-Tempsky) |
| EETS | Early English Text Society (London) |
| o.s. | original series |
| n.s. | new series |
| SC | Sources chrétiennes (Paris: Éditions du Cerf) |

# Acknowledgments

Under the pressure of studying for the Ph.D. oral examination at Stanford, more than ten years ago, I perceived that if vessels in *Cleanness* are viewed as analogies to men, the poem is aesthetically and intellectually coherent. Once I had completed my dissertation, I began to pursue the implications of that perception. The pursuit led me to Grail texts, biblical criticism, theological inquiry, social history, and art history. At every turn, friends, colleagues, and students have generously listened, advised, read, criticized, and sympathized.

The first to hear and respond were friends and professors at Stanford: Penelope B. R. Doob, V. A. Kolve, R. W. Ackerman, and Roger Dahood, who also read Chapter 1 in recent months. To these folks, I owe my original confidence.

My colleagues at Yale University helped to determine the scope of my work and contributed to it in ways direct and indirect. To Fred J. Nichols and Edward J. Mendelson, I owe the most subtle debt: we talked, mused, and argued continually for six years; both have read parts of this manuscript in various stages. John Freccero not only taught me about Dante, he also encouraged me to expand my work to the Grail texts, and wholeheartedly supported my earliest endeavors. The faculty of the medieval seminar in the History, Arts and Letters program, especially Jeremy du Quesnay Adams, Walter Cahn, and Steven Ozment, have over the years shared in my research and formulation of ideas. The students of that seminar have greeted my work enthusiastically and provided their own sharp insights into the texts: I would like especially to thank Richard Carr and Sheila Steiner. The Master and Fellows of Morse College provided me with a special kind of intellectual community and taught me many things; but I mention here, for the sake of brevity, only those who contributed directly to my work on this book: Asger Aaboe, Victor Ehrlich, the late Jacob Finkelstein, Hugh Stimson, and, above all, E. G. Stanley, who read and commented on the entire manuscript.

Those who read a manuscript perform an inestimable service,

vii

not to be confused with responsibility for what the book says. Stephen A. Barney, Joan S. Bennett, Rachel Jacoff, John Leyerle, and Jaroslav Pelikan read an early version of the manuscript in whole or in part. Marie Borroff, Fred Robinson, and Brian Stock read later versions and, together with E. G. Stanley and the readers for the Press, provided helpful guidance toward a final manuscript. Boyd M. Berry and Beate Hein Bennett of Virginia Commonwealth University have tested the beginning and ending. Mark Booth, Jeffrey Henderson, and Maria Borroni have helped to minimize errors of one kind and another.

To those named above, to my former husband, M. Mitchell Morse, to unnamed colleagues from my days at Yale, I feel a special gratitude for making the intellectual context in which I worked so rich and lively. Yale University generously supported my work through a Morse Fellowship, an A. Whitney Griswold grant, and superb libraries.

C.C.M.
27 January 1978

# Contents

# 1

## Introduction

In the French prose romance *La Queste del Saint Graal* (ca. 1220) and in the English alliterative poem *Cleanness* (ca. 1375), vessels—altar vessels or the Grail—figure as analogies of righteous men. The authors of the *Queste* and *Cleanness* both suggest that man is like a vessel, a *vas*, a ship, a temple, a cup. Like any of these vessels, man may be filled with good or evil, with "precious aromatic spices" or with "stinking rot," with righteousness or with sin;[1] unlike ordinary vessels, man chooses his own content through his response to the grace of Christ, which allows man, through penance, to exchange rot for spices. Both the French prose romance and the English biblical poem call on their audiences to repent. Both understand Christian reform as a reordering of love. Both interpret universal history and the actions of men with concepts drawn from Christian biblical commentary and homiletic literature. Although the *Queste* and *Cleanness* are quite unlike, an analysis of certain images and ideas common to both is fundamental to a right understanding of either.

Critics usually praise both the *Queste* and *Cleanness* for the stylistic skill their authors display in handling French prose or the alliterative line, in plotting an episode or laying out a description, but they rarely claim that these are intellectually complex and coherent texts. If, however, we begin to explore how vessel imagery functions in these texts as part of the call to repentance, we perceive that the texts are both complex and coherent. I hope to show this complex coherence by explaining the concepts that largely govern the significance of character and event in the *Queste* and *Cleanness*.

Religious figures in the *Queste*, monks and hermits, interpret

1. See Caesarius of Arles, *Sermones*, 70, CCSL 103:295 (see "List of Abbreviations" p. vi).

1

the knights' adventures to the knights, and the poet in *Cleanness* directly exhorts his audience to repent; neither text leaves interpretation entirely to its audience. Indeed the hermits are so skillful at glossing and advising that the *Queste* almost seems to insist on interpreting itself, so that one might wonder what more can be said. The hermits, however, never really give us anything but interpretations of specific events and particular dreams. They do not reveal what principles underlie the whole. *Cleanness* has exasperated some readers with its seeming incoherence and the poet's puzzling insistence that filth of the flesh makes God angry as other sins do not, though the primary message of the poem, that men should repent, is not obscure.

The authors of the *Queste* and *Cleanness* confront a question of overwhelming importance to a medieval Christian audience: how does a man gain entry to the eschatological banquet, to God's wedding feast? They answer, as doctrine requires, that he does so by penance, the sacrament through which a man exchanges his condition of sin for a condition of righteousness. The progress from sin to penitence translates into narrative art as plot, as Lancelot's case illustrates. Lancelot sets out on the quest with Gawain, chief among the sinners, but through penance finally achieves companionship with Galahad, the type of purity. Lancelot goes through three major stages in his penance: first, recognition of his own sinfulness in the episode of the sick knight; second, confession of his adulterous and idolatrous love of the queen; and third, active penance signaled by the discipline of adhering to an ascetic diet and wearing a hair shirt. In *Cleanness*, Nebuchadnezzar typifies the Christian penitent. First, he disregards God; then, after suffering a period of divinely imposed madness that is both punishment and expiation, he regains his wits and his throne.

Both texts contrast sinners and the righteous in a series of exempla that demonstrate the pattern of God's judgments on men. Taking his examples from biblical history, the *Cleanness* poet shows that the bond between God and man becomes more defined when the Age of Nature passes into the Age of the Written Law. The rough outside altar becomes an elaborate temple with many vessels, the crafting of the vessels becomes a sign of the increasingly elaborated and individualized nature of the bond between God and man. In the stories of the Flood and of Sodom and Gomorrah, the destruction and death that foreshadow the Last Judgment fall upon whole populations; in the story of the Temple vessels, invading armies deliver death in Jerusalem and Babylon to specific individual sinners, the kings Sedecias and Belshazzar. The poet sees history as a succession of compacts between God and man in which, as age succeeds age, physical requirements gradually become unimportant and spiritual ones all important. The "found" altar of the Age of Nature becomes the crafted vessel of the Age of the Written Law, and the vessel's design is an expression of the spiritual commitment of its makers; by implication, under the Christian dispensation, every man becomes the craftsman of the spiritual vessel of himself.

Because the knights who return from the Grail quest still have time to repent or to sin, the author of the *Queste* judges them conditionally as sinners or reprobates. Their histories in the quest illustrate the pattern of judgment: Hector and Gawain earn conditional damnation, and Lancelot and Bors achieve conditional salvation. The author of the *Queste* perceives in the story of the Fall a model pattern for analyzing sin: Adam and Eve's disobedience leads them to the discovery of sexual sin, a private sin, and their children to the discovery of murder, a public and social sin. The histories of the Grail knights themselves and the stories that they hear from earlier Judeo-Christian history show that men repeat this pattern of sinning over and over, first sexual sin, then murder. Salvation is possible because of man's capacity to overcome both sins through grace, as Galahad and Perceval do.

In interpreting men and history from an eschatological point of view, the authors of the *Queste* and *Cleanness* employ a set of related concepts centered on the vessel as an image of man. Men are compared implicitly to vessels in the Old Testament exemplum of the potter and his vessel (Jer. 18:2–6, 19:10–11; Isa. 29:15–16), and explicitly in the description of Paul in Acts 9:15 ("vas electionis"). This comparison was extended by medieval commentators who read the tabernacle and Temple "vasas Domini" as allegories of faithful Christians (for "vasa Domini," see 2 Par. 36:7; Isa. 52:11; Jer. 27:16). Adopting the biblical and exegetical tradition and perceiving man either as a vessel of filth or sin or as a vessel of cleanness or grace, the authors of the *Queste* and *Cleanness* show sinners proceeding from adultery and idolatry to murder and sacrilege and the righteous proceeding from purification to community, banquet, and marriage.

The call to repentance, issued by both the *Queste* and *Cleanness*, invites some comment. At no other period in Western history have writers so widely agreed upon the way in which literature ought to justify its own existence as they did in the twelfth, thirteenth, fourteenth, and, in some countries, the fifteenth centuries. Writers great and small, preachers, and poets agreed that the justification for their work lay in urging their audiences to repent. One of the greatest poems to make a call to repentance is, of course, Dante's *Commedia*; Robert Mannyng's *Handlyng Synne* belongs to the more common genres of penitential literature, the preachers' and confessors' manuals.

The cultural obsession, as we might call it, with penance began in twelfth-century France where the most intelligent Western theologians since Augustine thought, wrote, preached, and taught. They defined the nature and number of the sacraments and worked out a rational theology for them; from these thinkers came a theology of the sacrament of penance that prevailed, largely unchanged, until the mid–twentieth century. Inheritors of the Gregorian reforms of the eleventh century, they extended the spirit of reform in a new direction, toward a vigorous concern with the spiritual welfare of the laity, rather than focusing on reform of religious life in the monasteries and of the higher orders of the regular clergy. They and their successors in the Church, the reforming bishops and preachers, were responding to pressures from the laity, who wanted to be involved in the life of the Church. These theologians were attempting to give direction to energies that sometimes provoked the laity into heretically taking over the direction of their own spiritual affairs. As reformers, the theologians of the High Middle Ages considered the sacrament of penance the primary method of reaching the laity.

Which came first, the interest of theologians in penance or of the laity in penitential activity? Which had the greater impact on society and on literature? These are difficult questions to answer; but they are interesting and important questions to ask, and answers to them inevitably implicate the scholar—historian or critic— in theories on the causes of mass social behaviors and on the origins of cultural change. A serious problem confronting medievalists who would answer these questions is the lack of a comprehensive social history of penitential activities, such as crusades, pilgrimages, confraternities, and messianism. The literature surveying the development of the sacrament of penance is highly developed, and even the literature studying the implementation of reforms in penance made by the Fourth Lateran Council in 1215 has recently grown handsomely. Inevitably, then, current answers to questions of influence are likely to concentrate on the impact of the work of the theologians and bishops, on the influence of the Church as an institution upon the individual lay person.

As long as we do not forget the social background, the involvement of the laity in penitential activity, I think it reasonable to argue that the Church's institutional promotion of penance had a substantial influence on literature, at least in the two quite different categories of penitential literature. Manuals and handbooks of confession were brought into being under the patronage of the Church, but even the "higher" literature of penance, such as the *Queste* and *Cleanness* and even the *Commedia,* depended on the authority of the Church for justification in a theoretical sense and on the literature of the Church for the concepts and interpretations of man and history that they embody in fiction. However popular it may have been, this "higher" literature is intellectually sophisticated. As the primary sponsor of literacy and intellectual thought in the Middle Ages, a sponsorship more loosely exercised through the universities of the later Middle Ages than through the monasteries in the early Middle Ages, the Church doubtless had a more direct influence on literature than had the activities of the laity; but the latter encouraged and gave relevance to the literature. The continuing devotion of the laity in the High Middle Ages to penitential activity helped to guarantee the audience's interest in fiction that urged penance.

In an institutional sense, the Fourth Lateran Council marked a turning point in the Church's official support of private penance, pastoral reform, and penitential literature. John Baldwin, in *Masters, Princes, and Merchants,* identifies the theologians who pressed for reform in the late twelfth century with Peter the Chanter and his circle; this group was largely responsible for formulating the program of pastoral and lay reform adopted by the Fourth Lateran Council. Several of the resulting canons promulgated by Innocent III concern parish clergy, their education and morals; the imperative need for these canons came from the passage of canon 21, which for the first time *required* annual confession (participation in the sacrament of penance) of all Christians above the age of discretion, thus authorizing the practice of private penance as the way for ordinary Christians to participate in the life of the Church. Private penance, in contrast to public penance, seems to have developed originally in the Celtic Church and to have spread into northern Europe through the work of Anglo-Saxon missionaries; in private penance, the sinner confesses in private to his parish priest, whose skill in spiritual healing must be like that of the doctor in healing the body (an analogy explicit in canon 21) and whose own life should serve as a model to his parishioners.[2] To guide parish priests, the moral reformers, mostly Frenchmen and Englishmen, several of them bishops and responsible for carrying out the reforms of the Fourth Lateran, produced or commissioned in the late twelfth and thirteenth centuries a new literature for the direction of priests and laity. Unlike the old penitential tariffs that set a fixed penance for a particular sin, the new manuals encouraged confessors to consider a penitent's condition and intentions, not just his actions, in determining satisfaction and absolution; this development encouraged the study of character and increased the character types available to narrative fiction. The new manuals also often served as preaching manuals and were divided into sections dealing with, for example, the Lord's Prayer, the Ten Commandments, the sacraments, and the seven deadly sins. The manuals indicated what laymen were expected to know, and exempla illustrating these matters began to appear in them. The reformers' goal was nothing short of mass spiritual education.

With the passage of canon 21 and the emergence of a more or less official confessional literature associated with the sacrament of penance, the Church adopted a generally accepting attitude toward narrative fiction. The adoption of canon 21 implied the sanctioning of fiction that urged repentance. Even the scrupulous could feel free to write or to read works such as Dante's *Commedia*, Langland's *Piers Plowman*, the *Queste*, and *Cleanness*.

The attitude of the Church to imaginative literature varied considerably during the Middle Ages. Because all imaginative literature competes, at least theoretically, with the Bible and threatens its primacy, rigorists tended to reject all imaginative literature. Explicitly Christian literature, such as hymns, saints' lives, the poetry of biblical paraphrase, and meditations on holy subjects,

2. For the text of canon 21, see Joannes Dominicus Mansi, ed., *Sacrorum conciliorum, nova et amplissima collectio*, 22:1007–10.

was usually, however, granted a right to existence because of its subject matter; but concentrating on the rhetorical beauties of these works rather than on their content was dangerous, as Augustine pointed out.[3]

Augustine's literary theory, more fully developed than that of most later writers, offers support both to rigorists and to those of more liberal attitudes, as we shall see. Fundamentally, Augustine's literary theory distinguishes Christian from secular literature, truth from lie. In *Confessiones*, for example, Augustine laments his early love for the *Aeneid*, which brought him to weep over Dido's suicide for love of Aeneas, a mere fiction, while he thought not at all of the reality of his own spiritual condition of being dead to God.[4] The fictive, lying nature of the *Aeneid* becomes Augustine's chief objection to it. For Augustine, as for many other Fathers, the truth of biblical narrative is the primary attribute distinguishing it from other narratives. Any literature not grounded in true biblical narrative is, in Augustine's theory, a dangerous waste of time or an outright invitation to evil.

Augustine was greatly concerned about the effect of literature on its audience, as his rhetorical treatise *De doctrina christiana* illustrates; however, in this treatise he discusses only Christian literature, especially sermons. Like classical orators, Augustine identifies three levels of style: low, moderate, and grand. Unlike classical theorists who relate style to content, Augustine refers the decorum of stylistic choice to theoretical purpose. Any verbal communication necessarily contains three elements: a speaker, that which is spoken, and a hearer. By relating style to purpose, Augustine shifts the emphasis in his treatise from the content to the hearer (see *De doc. chrs.*, 4.8–11.22–26, where Augustine recommends clarity as a virtue, an indication of the importance of the audience in his theory). Like Cicero, Augustine recognizes three purposes of rhetoric: to teach, to delight, and to move (*De doc. chrs.*, 4.12.27). Augustine regards moving or persuading an audience to reform their lives as the highest and most difficult achievement of the Christian orator, and to this end he recommends the grand style. He judges his own success in the grand style, in per-

3. Augustine, *De doctrina christiana* (*On Christian Doctrine*), 4.5.7, 4.14.30–31 (hereafter cited as *De doc. chrs.*).
4. Augustine, *Confessiones* (*The Confessions of St. Augustine*), 1.13. 20–21 (hereafter cited as *Conf.*). See also *Conf.*, 3.2.2–4.

suading an audience, not by the applause but by the tears of the
audience (*De doc. chrs.*, 4.24.53). More generally, he concludes:

> Sunt et alia multa experimenta, quibus didicimus, homines
> quid in eis fecerit sapientis granditas dictionis, non clamore
> potius quam gemitu, aliquando etiam lacrimis, postremo
> vitae mutatione monstrasse. (There are many other
> experiences through which we have learned what effect the
> grand style of a wise speaker may have on men. They do not
> show it through applause but rather through their groans,
> sometimes even through tears, and finally through a
> change in their way of life.) *De doc. chrs.*, 4.24.53

Although Augustine recognizes that tears may not always lead to
active reform, he is not, as Aelred of Rievaulx and Peter of Blois
(active 1160–1200) were to be, suspicious of tears shed in response
to Christian literature.

Far more, Augustine fears the power of literature to move an
audience to desire and imitate evil rather than God. The great
danger is that rhetoric may be used to promote evil (*De doc. chrs.*,
4.2.3), as in Homer and the stories of classical gods (*Conf.*, 1.16.25–
26); and it was this danger that concerned writers of the later Middle Ages, though it did not trouble Aelred of Rievaulx or Peter
of Blois in the twelfth century.

Aelred and Peter are particularly interesting to us, since the
*Queste* belongs to Arthurian literature and both Aelred and Peter
refer to Arthurian literature while expressing rigorist attitudes
toward imaginative literature. Ironically, moreover, the author of
the *Queste* identifies religious figures in his narrative with the
white monks, the Cistercians, though less than a century earlier,
in 1142–1143, the Cistercian Aelred took the view in his *Speculum
caritatis* that Arthurian stories were frivolous. Both Aelred and
Peter substitute the example of Arthurian narrative for the *Aeneid*
to illustrate the vanity of secular literature. In the *Speculum
caritatis* Aelred discusses the effects of literature on the spiritual
life. A novice is trying to evaluate the tears he shed while he was
still in the world, out of compassion for Christ. Aelred argues that
such tears, if they led to no active commitment to the love of God,
to no spiritual reform, are as vain as the tears shed over the heroes
of tragedies and vain songs. The novice admits the truth of Aelred's
argument by acknowledging that he had been equally moved to

tears by the fables of "nescio quo. . . Arthuro."[5] In a late twelfth-century treatise on confession, Peter of Blois substantially repeats Aelred's argument, adding to it the names of "Ganganno" (Gawain?) and "Tristanno."[6]

Aelred doubts the value of even Christian literature to move an audience and has no patience with secular literature at all, but he does not explicitly worry about the possibility that literature might lead an audience to outright evil, as Augustine did. So did Dante, and the most famous medieval illustration of the dangers of fiction comes from *Inferno*, canto 5, where Dante shows the effect of Arthurian romance on Paolo and Francesca. They respond to the Lancelot and Guinevere story (from the *Prose Lancelot*, which precedes the *Queste* in the Vulgate cycle) not passively, but actively. Enraptured by these fictional heroes, they imitate the lie and find themselves forever wafted by the breeze of their vanity, forever separated from each other's embrace, and condemned to embrace nothingness. Their case demonstrates the danger of misunderstanding the nature of secular fiction.[7] Like Aelred and Peter, Dante makes Arthurian literature his primary example of secular fiction, where in a similar argument Augustine had used Virgil's *Aeneid*. In making Dido merely an inhabitant of that circle where Paolo and Francesca reap the eternal reward of their vain passion, Dante is probably alluding to Augustine while at the same time acknowledging a shift in literary taste.

Late medieval penitential writers accept an Augustinian theory of literature. They judge the significance of literature by its capacity to affect an audience, not by its intrinsic beauty or craft (matters of secondary though often real importance to them). But

5. Aelred of Rievaulx, *Speculum caritatis*, 2.17.49–51, CCCM 1:89–90.

6. *Liber de confessione sacramentali*, in *Patrologia latina* 207: 1088–89. Unaware of Peter's dependence on Aelred, Erich Auerbach translates and discusses this passage in *Literary Language and Its Public in Late Latin Antiquity and in the Middle Ages*, pp. 303–6. On the relationship of Peter of Blois to Aelred, see R. W. Southern, "Peter of Blois: A Twelfth Century Humanist?" in *Medieval Humanism and Other Studies*, p. 123; in the note on manuscripts of Peter's work appended to this essay, Southern observes that the work in which the Arthurian reference occurs originally formed part of Peter's letter collections, appearing in manuscripts dated ca. 1195.

7. See Renato Poggioli, "Tragedy or Romance? A Reading of the Paolo and Francesca Episode in Dante's *Inferno*"; and Dante Alighieri, *The Divine Comedy*, 2:79–95.

they reverse Aelred's verdict. Writing for lay audiences, theoretically more difficult to persuade to penance than monastic audiences, penitential writers embrace fiction for whatever help it may provide. Like Augustine, they assume that passive affective response often leads beyond itself to a reform of life. These writers return, at least implicitly, to an Augustinian optimism about the effects of rhetorical art and compose not only sermons and commentary but also a wide variety of narratives, from simple exempla to classical stories with allegorical interpretations and narratives with Christian implication. All these become acceptable media for addressing Christian audiences.

Instead of following Aelred and Peter in disparaging Christian literature because it can have the same effects as secular literature, the penitential writers revalue secular literature by grounding it in Christ, either by recasting the story so that it contains a Christian reading or by imposing a Christian allegorical interpretation on it. The *Queste* author uses both strategies, shaping events into a morality-drama plot and introducing the religious—monks, hermits, and nuns—to interpret events. Writing within a generation of Peter of Blois's death, the author of the *Queste* displays a markedly different attitude toward the value of Arthurian stories, as had Robert de Boron and the author of the *Perlevaus*, both of whom christianize the Grail quest. All of these writers accept the popularity of Arthurian stories as an advantage and as a challenge to their ability to make Arthurian narrative serve God. They are at once preservers and destroyers, shaping an old story to a new end.

The *Cleanness* poet, unlike the *Queste* author, was using familiar biblical material and thus did not have the problem of theoretically unsuitable matter. He did, though, need to make his invitation to repent compelling. In part he did this by rearranging the biblical material into an unfamiliar order, a strategy that encourages us to think about the reason for such a reordering, to discover the interpretation of man and God implicit in *Cleanness*. The intellectual and much of the aesthetic appeal of the poem lies in discovering arguments to account for the order of the material. The central message of the poem, that man should repent in order to prepare for the heavenly wedding feast, does not, however, depend on sophisticated critical interpretation. The liveliness of the poet's exhortations and the verisimilitude of his exempla provide the audience with a vivid picture of the real consequences of sin and of righteousness. The poet compels his audience, irrespective of the more subtle aspects of his art and theology, to acknowledge the benefits of penance.

Since Augustine, the Western Church has understood Christian reform to be a reordering of love, a point that writers of penitential manuals often obscure but that is central to the *Queste* and *Cleanness*. Literally, through penance one reshapes one's desire and redirects the desire to a new end—for example, from food and earthly love to Christ—so that one may come to the eschatological wedding feast as Christ's bride. From the twelfth century, in devotional literature and fiction, love became the primary concern of writers examining subjective human responses. As elaborated primarily by Bernard of Clairvaux, Cistercian mysticism, expressing the soul's love for God, took physical images and made them spiritual by referring them to God. Writers of romance tended to reliteralize the language of love by making the lady its object and allowing physical imagery to signify physical rather than spiritual things. The case of love imagery is, then, similar to that of other medieval images, like armor, which is spiritually interpreted by Paul in Eph. 6:11-17 ("Put you on the whole armour of God") and then made literal again by the medieval crusaders. Such images in medieval literature oscillate between spiritual and literal interpretations, the one begetting the other in seemingly endless succession. The author of the *Queste* turns human love back to divine love in his story, again spiritualizing what had been made literal by his fellow writers of romance. Through Beatrice, Dante makes human love the avenue to divine love. The *Cleanness* poet attempts an even more unusual feat, to harmonize human and divine love without renouncing either. His poem is not a romance, yet his treatment of love derives from the romances.

# 2

## The Paradigm of the Vessel as an Image of Man

The image of the vessel lies at the conceptual center of the *Queste* and *Cleanness*. In the *Queste*, Galahad and the Grail appear on Pentecost at Arthur's court as a challenge to the knights to conform to them, the vessels containing God. In the middle part of *Cleanness* the poet makes the analogy of vessels to men explicit in order to introduce the story of Nebuchadnezzar's theft of the Temple vessels; like these vessels, God's chosen people are dedicated to him. This passage retrospectively interprets earlier parts of the poem and links its beginning and end.

By defining man as a vessel or container, the authors of the *Queste* and *Cleanness* invite us to attend to what man may contain. They distinguish the content of the sinner from that of the righteous man and explain how a sinner may exchange his content for that of the righteous. The separation of sinners from the righteous reflects the pattern of judgment; to effect a change from sin to righteousness, the authors recommend the sacrament of penance.

To illumine that distinction between sinners and the righteous, I must explicate the paradigm of the vessel, which is illustrated on the opposite page. By holding the book upside down, you may see the pattern of the sinner's life, which directs him toward hell. According to this pattern, the sinner first commits a sin that signifies his turning away from God and toward the world. Usually that sin is sexual; by it, man pollutes himself. The contents of his vessel then are impure and unclean, and this ontological state finds expression in consequent acts, usually murder. The spilling of blood publicizes the polluted state of the sexual sinner, who effects a sacrilege that pollutes the land through the spilling of semen and blood. In extraordinary circumstances, a man may maintain himself unpolluted after baptism, the sacrament that removes the stain of Original Sin. More often, man pollutes the vessel of himself and

# The Paradigm of the Vessel as an Image of Man

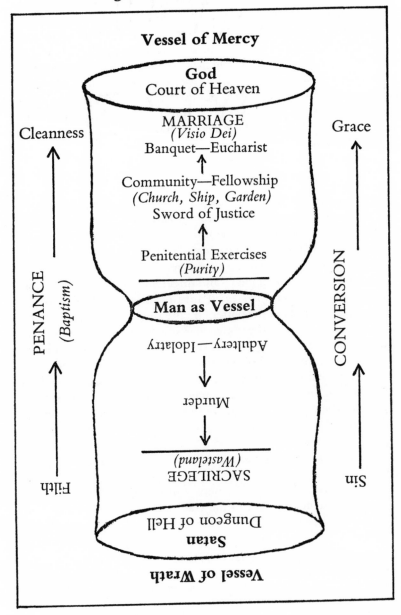

can regain the ritual state of purity only by penance. Turning himself toward God, the sinner must undergo penance and then, in
consequent acts, particularly communion, manifest his cleansed
soul. In what follows, I shall first trace the biblical and exegetical
bases for thinking of man as a vessel, then trace the features of the
paradigm of the vessel, looking first at commentary on how sexual
sins, idolatry, and murder pollute the vessel and result in sacrilege.
Then I shall consider how a polluted vessel might, according to
the tradition, be ritually cleansed through the sacrament of penance and how this second ontological state flowered in a curiously
refined sexuality of communion.

## Vessels as Images of Man

Passages in the Bible that use the vessel as an image of man or
as an analogy to man cluster around two themes: judgment and
service or sacrifice. *Vessel of wrath* and *vessel of mercy*, the terms
used to identify the two states described in the pattern of judgment, derive from a hortatory passage in which Paul promises
rewards to the vessels of mercy and threatens destruction to the vessels of wrath (Rom. 9:20–23). Paul's exhortation alludes to the
prophetic exempla of the potter and the vessel (Jer. 18:2–6, 19:10–
11; Isa. 29:15–16). As the potter may break a faulty vessel, so may
God break a sinful man. Several early manuscript illuminations of
Adam's creation seem also to reflect this conception of man as an
earthen vessel: they show God shaping a human figure of clay who
is Adam (*adamah*, or earth).[1] Augustine popularized Paul's metaphors of the vessel by using them in his *De civitate Dei* to identify
the citizens of the city of man and the city of God, cities with a
primarily eschatological reality. Emphasis in the use of these metaphors falls on the end point of human life and history, the Judgment.

In speaking of the proper nature of Christian life in history,
prior to judgment, the Pauline tradition draws the analogy between the vessel and man because the vessel is an instrument of
service (2 Tim. 2:20–21). Medieval commentary applies this anal-

1. See H. L. Kessler, "*Hic Homo Formatur*: The Genesis Frontispieces
of the Carolingian Bibles"; Wilhelm Köhler, *Die karolingischen Miniaturen*, vol. 1, *Die Schule von Tours*, pp. 109–20; and Ernst Robert Curtius, "God as Maker," in *European Literature and the Latin Middle
Ages*, pp. 544–46.

ogy to gloss many biblical passages concerned with vessels of the
tabernacle and the Temple, with vessels of service and sacrifice,
and often in moral allegorizing identifies the vessels as men.[2] The
idea of cleanness attaches itself to the idea of the vessel as man in
glosses on Isa. 52:11, as the twelfth-century English treatise called
*Vices and Virtues* attests; Reason explains that the vessel is man
himself and that man bears God in his heart: " 'Makieð ʒew clane
ðe bereð godes faten!' Clanse þine hirte for ðan þe hie owh to
benne godes fatt" ("Make yourselves clean who bear God's vessels!"
Cleanse thy heart, because it ought to be God's vessel).[3] By identifying the vessels of the tabernacle with the faithful, as Gregory
the Great did in commenting on Job 32, interpreters of the Mass
were able to explain what men brought to the unbloody sacrifice
of the Eucharist: a pure heart.[4] Paul provides authority for this
interpretation in his letter to the Romans, in which he begs them
to "present your bodies a living sacrifice, holy, pleasing unto God,
your reasonable service," and then explains how to live a holy
life (Rom. 12:1 ff.). The interpreters of the Mass perceived an
analogy between the communicant, the vessel bearing a pure heart,
and the paten and the chalice, vessels bearing the Body and the
Blood of Christ. If the analogy failed, that is, if the communicant
was not pure, then the sacrament was not efficacious; in the *Queste*,
when the analogy of a knight to the Grail breaks down, the knight

2. See *Glossa ordinaria*, in *Patrologia latina* (hereafter cited as *PL*),
114:635; Caesarius of Arles, in *Sermones*, 70, CCSL 103:295–96, succinctly combines this metaphor with the themes of cleanness and filth
and of judgment (see "List of Abbreviations" p. vi).

3. *Vices and Virtues*, pp. 122–23. Gregory the Great identifies these
vessels with the souls of men, whom the priest brings as living vesels to
the temple of eternity, in *Liber regulae pastoralis*, 2.2, in *PL* 77:27; cf.
*Gregorianum*, in *PL* 193:454. Ranulph Higden suggests this text, Isa.
52:11, as a model text for a sermon to the lower clergy; see G. R. Owst,
*Preaching in Medieval England*, p. 249.

4. See Gregory the Great, *Moralia in Job* (*Morals on the Book of Job*),
23.11.20, in *PL* 76:264 (hereafter cited as *Moralia*); cf. *Gregorianum*, in
*PL* 193:453. On the offering of the pure heart and the Christian's sacrifice, see Augustine, *De civitate Dei* (*The City of God*), 10.3–6, 20.25–26
(hereafter cited as *De civ. Dei*). The notion of the sacrifice of the pure
heart is widespread; see Amalarius of Metz, *Liber officialis*, 3.48–51, in
*Opera liturgica omnia*, 2:318–320; discussed extensively by O. B. Hardison, Jr., in *Christian Rite and Christian Drama in the Middle Ages*, pp.
35–79.

is not able to see the Grail. This analogy of man to vessel can be used to interpret Paul's warning to the Corinthians that whoever eats the bread or drinks the chalice of the Lord unworthily eats and drinks damnation to himself (1 Cor. 11:27–29). Most Mass liturgies repeat this warning. Ultimately, since Christian thinking in the Middle Ages is oriented to the End, the themes of service and sacrifice lead to Judgment. God judges the service or sacrifice man offers; God decides whether the analogy man presumes to exist between himself and the chalice does exist.

Medieval thought often worked by a process of continuous analogy, discovering both in its description of things and in its interpretation of history abstract patterns in order to demonstrate analogous structures in all of creation. The medieval method of associating different things under the category of the vessel illustrates this process. Considered abstractly, a vessel may be any physical object that can contain something: a bowl, a cup, a dish, a platter, a ship, or a chest or a building or a man. Among some vessel images important to a discussion of the *Queste* and *Cleanness* are the Garden of Eden or the garden enclosed, Noah's ark, the Ark of the Covenant, the temple, the church, the chalice or the paten, and the hall or lodging—all images conventionally associated with each other in medieval biblical commentary. These images can also be understood as analogies to man or metaphors for him. They are traditionally linked in patristic and, later, in biblical commentary; Hugh of St. Victor in *De arca Noe morali* uses several of them:

> Ingredere ergo nunc si secretum cordis tui, et fac habitaculum
> Deo, fac templum, fac domum, fac tabernaculum, fac arcam
> testamenti, fac arcam diluvii, vel quocunque nomine appel-
> les, una est domus Dei. In templo adoret psalma Creatorem,
> in domo veneretur filius patrem, in tabernaculo honoret
> miles regem, in testamento auscultet assecla praeceptorem,
> in diluvio imploret naufragus gubernatorem. (Enter your
> own inmost heart, and make a dwelling-place for God.
> Make Him a temple, make Him a house, make Him a
> pavilion. Make Him an ark of the covenant, make Him an
> ark of the flood; no matter what you call it, it is all one
> house of God. In the temple let the creature adore the
> Creator, in the house let the son revere the Father, in the
> pavilion let the knight adore the King. Under the covenant,

let the disciple listen to the Teacher. In the flood, let him
that is shipwrecked beseech Him who guides the helm.)[5]

Hugh connects all these images by regarding them as receptacles
and compares each to the human heart, like them a receptacle of
God, at least potentially. He is alluding to typologies familiar to
anyone who knows Latin or popular biblical commentary of the
Middle Ages. All of Hugh's biblical vessel images—the ark, the
tabernacle, the temple—point toward the Church.

Since Christ identifies his human body with the Temple (John
2:19b–21; see also Mark 14:58; Matt. 26:61), and since Paul identifies the human body with the Church (1 Cor. 3:16–17; cf. 12:12–
14, 27), all of those biblical vessel images that are types of the
Church become also associated with the human body of the faithful, corporately and individually. In the Latin Church, Augustine
and Bede made famous the interpretation of the dimensions of
Noah's ark (300x50x30, Gen. 6:15) as the proportions of the human
body.[6] Just as the Ark of the Covenant contained the witnesses to
the covenant, the golden urn of manna, Aaron's rod, and the
tables of the Law; just as a church houses the testament of the new
covenant, its Scriptures, and the bread and wine that are the Body
and Blood of Christ, so too may each individual Christian be
thought of as the receptacle of God or of Christ as the God-man
or as the Word of the Scriptures. The image of the hall or lodging,
which Hugh associates with types of the Church, lends itself to the

5. Hugh of St. Victor, *De arca Noe morali,* 1.2, in *PL* 176:621–22, and
translated in *Selected Spiritual Writings,* p. 51. On the typological connection of the ark (*navis,* ship) to the church (with its nave) in theory and
in art, see Hartmut Boblitz, "Die Allegorese der Arche Noahs in der
frühen Bibelauslegung," and Joachim Ehlers, *"Arca significat ecclesiam:*
Ein theologisches Weltmodell aus der ersten Hälfte des 12. Jahrhunderts." On the Church voyaging East, see Joseph A. Jungmann, *The
Mass of the Roman Rite,* 1:254, and Hugo Rahner, "Antenna crucis,
III." On the Church as Ship of Faith, an allegory related to ark-Church
typology, see G. R. Owst, *Literature and Pulpit in Medieval England,*
pp. 68–76; for the classical tradition that influences this allegory, see
Hugo Rahner, "Odysseus at the Mast." For the typologies of the taber-
nacle-Church and the Temple-Church, see Bede, *De tabernaculo,* CCSL
119A:1–139, and *De templo,* CCSL 119A:141–234; his commentaries were
sources for a twelfth-century genre of treatises on the tabernacle, a literature surveyed by Henri de Lubac in *Exégèse médiévale,* vol 1, pt 2, pp.
403–18.

6. Augustine, *De civ. Dei,* 15.26; Bede, *Hexaemeron,* 2, in *PL* 91:88–89.

familiar tone of much late medieval piety that humanizes Christ.
For example, medieval Christians responded to Christ's plaintive
exclamation, "The foxes have holes and the birds of the air
nests; but the Son of man hath not where to lay his head" (Matt.
8:20), by offering him a resting place in themselves. That resting
place may be thought of as lying in the community of Christians
or in the individual.

The great model to the individual Christian is the Virgin Mary,
"Vas caelestis gloriae,/ Templum nostri redemptoris,"[7] who physically bore Christ in her body. For example, Clare of Assisi in a
letter to Agnes of Bohemia compares Agnes to Mary:

> Ipsius dulcissime matri adhereas, que talem genuit filium,
> quem celi capere non poterant, et tamen ipsa parvulo
> claustro sacri uteri contulit. . . . Sicut ergo virgo virginum
> gloriosa materialiter, sic et tu. . . . casto et virgineo corpore
> spiritualiter semper portare potes, illum continens, a quo
> tu et omnia continentur. (Cling to His most sweet Mother
> who begot a Son Whom the heavens could not contain; and
> yet she carried him in the little cloister of her holy womb. . . .
> As therefore the glorious Virgin of virgins carried Him in her
> body, so without shadow of doubt thou canst carry Him
> in a spiritual way in thy chaste and virginal body. . . . thou
> wilt contain Him by whom thou and all things are
> contained.)[8]

Paradoxically, Agnes is the bride of Christ, whom she contains
and by whom she is contained.

Medieval commentaries on the Song of Songs identify the bride
of Christ as either the Church or the Virgin Mary, who becomes a
figure for the Church. Through the Virgin the idea of marriage to
God, which is the ultimate goal for a Christian, becomes closely
associated with vessel imagery.

The logic relating vessel images in the *Queste* and *Cleanness* is
of two kinds: the logic of analogy and the logic of equipollent
images. I have already alluded to the first in discussing the Mass.

---

7. *Analecta hymnica medii aevi*, 54:407, no. 263. For a useful catalogue
of Marian types, see Betty Al-Hamdani, "The Burning Lamp and Other
Romanesque Symbols for the Virgin that Come from the Orient."

8. Walter Seton, "The Letters from Saint Clare to Blessed Agnes of
Bohemia," pp. 516–17; Ignatius Brady, trans., *The Legends and Writings
of Saint Clare of Assisi*, p. 94.

Other instances of it occur when the authors imagine receptacles within receptacles, for example, Noah in the ark in *Cleanness*, the Grail companions on Solomon's ship, or Gawain and Hector in the temple in the *Queste*. If the analogy of one receptacle to another fails in God's eyes, then the two receptacles—for example, man and ship—must be separated; if the analogy holds, then the two may remain, one containing the other, without fear of injury or division.

In formal logic, equipollency describes an extended way of analogizing that is common in patristic exegesis. Equipollent arguments consist of a series of statements equivalent to each other, notated $A=B=C=D$, hence $A=D$.[9] If for these letters we supply images that take the same predicate, we discover that two images never explicitly equivalent to each other become so by their relationship to intermediate images. For example, *if* vessel (Grail)= body of Christ=ship of faith=body of man (Galahad), because all contain Christ, *then* vessel=body of man. This final equation is considered true, whether or not the writer has established an explicit equivalence between the particular vessel and the particular man. An appreciation of the logical interconnectedness of container images—vessels—is necessary to an understanding of the *Queste* and *Cleanness* because these texts seldom overtly state the equivalence of one vessel image to another.

The vessel, as a metaphor for man, holds central place in the paradigm: the vessel becomes significant through its content. As man chooses the alternative of sin or of purity, the vessel of his body or the vessel that represents him is filled with corruption or righteousness. The choice becomes a permanent reality in man's death when his soul attains its eternal fate of hell or heaven; his individual history may be related by analogy or contrast to the history of his people. Life, or history, is thus like a sentence in that the significance of either becomes clear only with closure. This heavy emphasis on closure is characteristic of Christian rather than Old Testament theology. Christ's interpretation of Old Testament themes, such as the kingdom, the day of the Lord, and marriage, gives Christianity an eschatological bent, as medieval theologians normally recognized. I will now examine "the shapes a bright container can contain," the contents of man—the vessel—which determine his fate: life or destruction.

9. See R. W. Southern, *St. Anselm and His Biographer*, pp. 22–24.

## The Vessel of Wrath: Adultery, Idolatry, and Murder

The first shape in the bright container that I will consider is the shape of sin, especially of sexual sin. The emphasis on sexual sin in *Cleanness* and the *Queste* reflects early Church analyses of sin, rather than the tradition of the seven deadly sins that dominated late medieval penitential theory and relegated lechery to one of the lesser but also most ineradicable tendencies to sin. The reasons for following the early Church's emphasis on actual sexual sin were probably several. The Old Testament connection of sexual sin with idolatry made it possible for Christian writers to treat sexual sin as a figure for almost all sins. Furthermore, the sexual sinner contrasts directly with the Christian ideal of dedicated virginity. That ideal, often called spiritual marriage, leads us back to the word *vas*, which describes the role of the bride in both divine and human relationships. In the spiritual marriage, the bride contains God's grace, Christ, and the elements of the Eucharist all at once. As we have already noted, traditional commentaries frequently refer to the bride—the faithful Christian—as a vessel. Just as the bride's containment of grace makes possible a fruitful marriage in the spiritual order, so, in human marriage, the woman as vessel contains the man's semen to make possible a fruitful marriage in the natural order. Canonists and Scholastic theologians use the phrase *vas debitum* (the fit vessel, the vessel owed the marriage debt [cf. 1 Cor. 7:3]) to denote the vagina; for example, Alexander of Hales defines uncleanness as sexual sins that result "in pollutione extra vas debitum (in pollution outside the fit vessel)."[10] Sexual sin, much of which involves a misuse of the *vas debitum*, becomes, then, an appropriate figure for sin in general: in sinning, man misuses himself, the vessel of God. For medieval Christians, like the author of the *Queste* and the *Cleanness* poet, a poetic logic, centered in the word *vas*, grows out of the Old Testament association of sexual sin with idolatry.

The roots of this tradition of interpreting sexual sin as a figure for sin in general lie in the Old Testament prophets and the Deuteronomic reviser, who make marriage a metaphor for the covenant. When they accuse Israel of fornication and adultery, they

10. Alexander of Hales, *Summa theologica*, 2-2.3.4.2.1.7.9.3; see also 2-2.3.5.2.1.8.3. For further corroboration of this sense of *vas debitum*, see John T. Noonan, Jr., *Contraception*, pp. 224–27, and Thomas N. Tentler, *Sin and Confession on the Eve of the Reformation*, pp. 186–208.

introduce marriage as a metaphor for the covenant relationship between God and Israel. The Canaanite cults commonly practiced cult prostitution, so the prophets associated Israel's idolatry with sexual sin; the Hebrew word *zanah*, which means both *to fornicate* and *to worship idols*, reflects this reality. Hosea, the first to speak of the covenant between God and Israel as if it were a marriage and to portray Israel's infidelity to God as adultery, articulates most of the themes associated with this kind of adultery, such as idolatry and barrenness. Following God's instructions, Hosea makes his marriage a demonstration of God's marriage to Israel by taking to wife a woman who is "filled with the spirit of whoredom" (Heb. *'esheth zenunim*), a phrase that suggests he takes his wife from among the Hebrew women involved in the Canaanite practice of ritual prostitution: "Vade, sume tibi uxorem fornicationum, et fac tibi filios fornicationum: quia fornicans fornicabitur terra a Domino" (Go, take thee a wife of fornications: and have of her children of fornications: for the land by fornication shall depart from the Lord), Hos. 1:2.[11] Jerome and the medieval commentators who follow him did not, however, recognize cult prostitution as an aspect of Israel's idolatry; they often took sexual sin in a transposed sense (in Hos. 1:2b, *fornicabitur* means *stray away* [through fornication]).

In his commentary on Hosea, Jerome acknowledges the literal meaning of the Hebrew *zanunim*: "multas fornicationes sonat" (it means many fornications).[12] He tends, however, to allegorize the story of Hosea by reading its pattern into contemporary Old Testament history or into Christian history. The human example of a man who marries a prostitute or an adulteress (see Hos. 4) illustrates God's rescue of Israel from an idolatrous Egypt and his mercy toward her later infidelities and also illustrates Christ's acceptance of the gentiles: "De Salvatoris et Ecclesiae typo in praefatiuncula diximus, quod sumpserit sibi uxorem fornicariam, quae prius idolis serviebat" (We have spoken of this in the preface

11. See Gerhard von Rad, *Old Testament Theology*, vol. 2, *The Theology of Israel's Prophetic Traditions*, pp. 140–41, who says that *'esheth zenunim* means "a woman who took part in Canaanite fertility cults," and James Luter Mays, *Hosea*, pp. 25–26. For a somewhat different view, see Abraham Heschel, *The Prophets*, p. 52, n. 8.

12. Jerome, *In Osee prophetam*, 1.1.2, CCSL 76:8 (hereafter cited as *In Osee*, with my translations). Note that for Jerome the verb *fornicor* has a transposed sense, meaning *to depart, to stray away*.

as a type of Christ and the Church, because he [Hosea, like Christ] took to himself a wife of fornications, who formerly served idols), *In Osee*, 1.1.2. This sentence contains in brief the most essential elements of Jerome's exegesis of the covenant as marriage and the sins against it as idolatry accompanied by sexual sin. For Jerome, as for other Christian commentators, the association of sexual sin and idolatry is a strong one.

Paul offered further authority for the Christian association of idolatry and sexual sin. In Rom. 1:18–27 Paul echoes the Book of Wisdom: "For the beginning of fornication is the devising of idols: and the invention of them is the corruption of life" (Wisd. 14:12). Idolatry, Paul argues, leads to sexual sin, especially to sodomy, or homosexuality, a sin prominent in *Cleanness*, and finally results in all kinds of ill-tempered behavior, such as avarice, envy, and murder. The pollution, or sacrilege, that idolatry involves on a spiritual level is physically manifested in sexual sin and murder, in the spilling of semen and blood.

Old Testament evidence also exists for associating idolatry with murder: in a few instances the prophets refer to the custom of child sacrifice (e.g., Ezek. 16:36–38, 23:37–39; Jer. 7:31). Modern biblical scholarship suggests that the custom of child sacrifice represents a brief phase in Israel's idolatry, but orthodox antagonists of the heretics of the High Middle Ages frequently accuse heretics of child sacrifice. These accusations, which seem to modern scholars unfounded, indicate the tendency of medieval writers to use Old Testament models to imagine the faults of heretics (idolaters).[13]

In Christian commentary, the basic, literal sense of idolatry—the worship of man-made objects, such as statues of deities—was generalized to include anything man-made and extended to include any created thing, as opposed to the uncreated Judeo-Christian God. For example, Jerome extends the concept of idolatry to heresy because, like idols of sticks and stones, the dogmas of heretics are man-made. The heretics serve these idols, "quae de suo corde finxerunt" (which they have made from their own heart), with an artfully lying rhetoric, just as faithless Israel decks herself out with artful contrivance, with golden earrings and pearl necklaces, to make herself pleasing to foreign gods; as Jerome explains,

13. See Walter W. Wakefield and Arthur P. Evans, eds. and trans., *Heresies of the High Middle Ages*, nos. 3 and 9, for orthodox descriptions of child sacrifices that, allegedly, were made by the heretics.

"Non. . . habent curam simplicis rusticitatis quae meretricia orna-
menta non quaerit; sed artificis elegantisque mendacii, ut ama-
toribus suis diabolis et daemoniis placeant" (they have no love
for simple rusticity which does not seek the ornaments of whores,
but a love for ingenious and elegant lies that they may be pleasing
to their lovers, devils and demons), *In Osee*, 1.2.13. In the case
of idolaters or heretics, the gods they worship are made by themselves and must be considered either as offspring or as self-images;
so, that by loving their gods, idolaters and heretics either commit
incest or a kind of sodomy. Dante probably understands Brunetto
Latini's sodomy in a similar fashion in *Inferno* 15: Brunetto was in
love with his own words, which expressed a faith in the classical
and humanist ideal of fame, and hence he loved in a way that produced no spiritual offspring, that bore no fruit for the kingdom
of heaven.[14]

Indeed, the heretics are accused of virtually all sexual crimes.
With their rhetoric, of which Jerome speaks in the passage above,
the heretics entice others to join them and take to themselves those
who were once faithful to God, which, as Gregory the Great explains, is adultery:

> Sicut is qui adulterium facit carnem alienae conjugis sibi
> illicite conjungit, ita omnes haeretici, cum fidelem animam
> in suum errorem rapiunt, quasi conjugem alienam tollunt,
> quia videlicet mens Deo spiritaliter inhaerens et ei
> quasi in quodam amoris thalamo conjuncta, cum perversis
> persuasionibus ad pravitatem dogmatis perducitur, quasi
> aliena conjux a corruptore maculatur. (As he that commits
> adultery joins to himself unlawfully the flesh of another
> man's wife, so all heretics, while they carry off the faithful
> soul into their own error, are as it were bearing off another's
> wife, in this way, because the soul which is spiritually
> wedded to God and joined to Him as if in a kind of bride-
> chamber of love, when by wicked persuasions it is led on
> into corruptness of doctrine, is as it were like the wife of
> another defiled by the corrupter.)[15]

14. For the general sense of this interpretation of Brunetto Latini's
sin as sodomy, I am indebted to John Freccero of Yale University. On
the related issue of heresy as the worship of man-made doctrine, see de
Lubac, *Exégèse médiévale*, vol. 1, pt. 2, pp. 99–128, 153–81.

15. Gregory the Great, *Moralia*, 16.70.74, in *PL* 75:1156; Bede compares Origen's fall into heresy with the seduction of Solomon, Samson,

Charges of sexual sin frequently accompany charges of heresy in
the Middle Ages. The Sodomites, whom the *Cleanness* poet takes
to be types of heretics, reveal their willingness to commit the sin
against nature when they attempt to entice the angels to become
their lovers.

Augustine, whose definition of idolatry is broader than Jerome's,
follows Paul in defining the idolater as one who worships and
serves the creature rather than the Creator (Rom. 1:25). To explain the difference between the service owed to the Creator and
that proper to the creature, Augustine argues that men may use the
things of the world, such as food, drink, and sex, but should reserve
their love for God, lest they take a mediate good for the Ultimate
Good.[16] Augustine illustrates this distinction between use and en-
joyment with an exemplum that, by virtue of its fictional terms,
becomes a commentary on idolatrous love. First he invites us to
imagine a lover who made for his betrothed a ring that she then
loved so much more than she loved him that she did not want to
see him again. In human terms the exemplum seems to be about
idolatry: the betrothed loves the ring. But interpreting the relationship involving the beloved, the lover, and the ring to represent
the relationship of man, God, and the things of the world, suggests
that the sin is adultery. When a man loves a human lover more
than he loves God, loves a creature more than the God who created it, then his love is adulterous ("nonne tuus amor adulterinus
deputabitur?" [*In epis. Joannis*, 2.11]). Just so, in the *Queste*,
Lancelot's love for Guinevere is idolatrous and adulterous.

The late medieval Church had at its disposal not only the new
penitential literature with its analysis of the seven deadly sins,
but also interpretations of sin made by the early Church with its
theory of capital, or mortal, sins, a theory that, by the fourth century, was fully developed. Adultery, idolatry, and murder always

---

and David by women, implying a correspondence between adultery (Old
Law) and heresy (New Law), in *Super parabolas Salomonis*, 1.7, in *PL*
91:964; cited in de Lubac, *Exégèse médiévale*, vol. 1, pt. 1, p. 263.

16. Augustine, *Commentaire de la première épître de S. Jean (Tractatus in epistolam Joannis ad Parthos)*, 2.12 (hereafter cited as *In epis.
Joannis*); for a translation see *Augustine: Later Works*. See also Augustine, *De doctrina christiana (On Christian Doctrine)*, 1.3–5.3–5; and *De
civ. Dei*, 12.8.

figured in the list of capital sins on the authority of the Ten Commandments and Acts 15:20, 28–29.[17] When Tertullian in his heretical Montanist phase denied to the Church the power to remit
these three sins, he helped to insure their prominence. The Church,
however, generally claimed the power to absolve these sins, but
required public penance for them.[18] For example, Augustine says
in *De fide et operibus* that while lesser sins may be compensated by
almsgiving, the deadly sins of unchastity, idolatry, and homicide
must be punished by excommunication until they are cured by
"poenitentia humiliore."[19]

Tertullian suggests the rationale underlying the category of
mortal sins (he sometimes adds fraud and false witness to idolatry,
sexual sin, and homicide) when he calls them "violations of the
temple of God,"[20] in other words, acts that pollute man, the temple and the vessel of God. In the early centuries of the Church, the
sins declared mortal were thought to pollute the sinner and to
make him utterly unclean in a way that lesser sins did not.[21] By
example or through involvement with the faithful, such a sinner
might spread his contamination. In effect, the sinner commits a
kind of sacrilege upon himself and makes himself a danger to the
Christian community through his uncleanness. Honorius Augustodunensis explicitly extends the application of the crime of sacrilege from the church building to the individual Christian, who
is spiritually the temple of God: he argues that adultery, heresy

17. See Bernhard Poschmann, *Penance and the Annointing of the
Sick*, p. 47; and Watkins, *History of Penance*, pp. 11–14, who cites as
authorities, with texts, Irenaeus, Tertullian, Cyprian, Pacian, Augustine,
Jerome, Fulgentius, and Ambrosiaster. Later Judaism also tended to
select idolatry, fornication, and murder as the worst offenses among the
seven sins outlawed by the Noachian commandments; see *Theological
Dictionary of the New Testament*, s.v. πόρνη, 6:590 (hereafter cited as
*Theol. Dict. NT*). See also A. Büchler, *Studies in Sin and Atonement in
the Rabbinic Literature of the First Century*, pp. 292–99.

18. See Poschmann, *Penance and the Annointing of the Sick*, pp. 35–
49.

19. Augustine, *De fide et operibus*, 19, in *PL* 40:220. On public penance from the fourth to the sixth centuries, see Poschmann, *Penance
and the Annointing of the Sick*, pp. 81–121.

20. Tertullian, *De pudicitia*, 19.25, CCSL 2:1323.

21. E.g., a homily attributed to Caesarius of Arles, which clearly suggests that by capital sins a man corrupts himself, in *PL* 39:2229–30.

(idolatry), and homicide pollute the temple of God, whether that temple be physical or spiritual.[22]

Within the tradition linking adultery, idolatry, and homicide as violations of the temple of God, one kind of sexual sin, defined differently from adultery or fornication, has a place of special prominence in literary texts such as *Cleanness* and the much earlier *De planctu naturae* by Alain de Lille. This sin, the sin against nature, encompasses all kinds of sexual intercourse that violate the normal pattern of human male and female coupling. It was often thought to accompany sins of fornication or adultery, which are sins because the two people involved have no sanction for their coupling and hence do not want offspring: the sin against nature prevents offspring. An understanding of medieval analysis of this sin is crucial to the interpretation of *Cleanness*, which presents the sin against nature as the chief offense committed before God by both the Flood generation and the Sodomites.

As Alain de Lille suggests in *De planctu naturae* and as John T. Noonan, Jr., points out in *Contraception: A History of Its Treatment by the Catholic Theologians and Canonists*, for a sin to be against nature, it is necessary to view nature as a prescriptive concept. In Alain's poem the goddess Natura presides over created nature to see that God's first command, to "increase and multiply, and fill the earth" (Gen. 1:28), is fulfilled. Of all created beings, only man fails to do her work and gives her cause for lament. Natura's work is accomplished so long as man respects the generative purpose of sexual union and does not, in the very form of the act, frustrate its end. Alain's Natura analogizes her work to the orderliness of grammar and syntax; the perversion of her sexual order, like the perversion of language, is the work of idolaters and heretics. Natura's analogy no doubt owes something to Jerome, Gregory, and others who, as we have noticed, link the rhetoric of heretics to sexual sin. But for Natura, sexual sin is, in itself, an act of idolatry. Called upon to explain the effects of impure love, Natura tells of the daughters of idolatry who come in its train and who are not human offspring, but vices. Like the *Queste* and *Cleanness*, Alain's *De planctu naturae* associates sexual sin and idolatry and, like them, assumes that sexual sin leads inevitably into other

22. Honorius Augustodunensis, *Gemma animae*, 1.170, in *PL* 172:596–97.

sins.[23] Alain's work concludes with a curse upon whoever defies the order of Natura: "A supernae dilectionis osculo separetur" (let him be separated from the kiss of heavenly love).[24]

The medieval canonists and theologians whom Noonan surveys and analyzes share Alain's severe attitude toward the sin against nature. Noonan attributes the early Church's need to establish a standard of nature to its contemporary cultural context. The Christians were seeking a middle way between the Gnostics, whose abhorrence of marriage expressed itself either in asceticism or in sexual promiscuity (often accompanied by a desire to avoid children), and the pagans, whose search for sexual pleasure led them into a riot of sexual activity. Believing that God had created nature, the Christians found Stoic philosophy sympathetic: Stoicism set nature as the pattern by which to measure what is fit and what is unfit and found natural those processes, functions, and actions from the natural world that showed what man should be.[25] For example, Stoicism took the behavior of animals (with certain exceptions, like the hyena, thought to enjoy sex for its own sake) and the more obvious function (taken to be self-evident) of a bodily organ to be "natural." The Wife of Bath refuses to declare what the more obvious function of human genitalia is, as between purgation and engendering, but even she does not openly quarrel with the theory that procreation is the natural purpose of sexual intercourse (*Wife of Bath's Prologue*, lines 115–34). The medieval standard of nature makes very little sense when it is removed from the cultural context in which it developed; the appeal to what is natural, as Noonan concludes, served a pedagogic function in expressing what man ought to be, and this function was developed by the Christians largely in reaction to paganism and Gnosticism. The Stoics approved marriage and sex for the purpose of procreation but not for pleasure, and the Christians adopted their phi-

23. Alain de Lille, *De planctu naturae*, pp. 484–91. See also *PL* 210: 461–65. For recent criticism of Alain's *De planctu naturae*, see Winthrop Wetherbee, *Platonism and Poetry in the Twelfth Century*, pp. 188–211, and his earlier article, "The Function of Poetry in the *De planctu naturae* of Alain de Lille."

24. Alain de Lille, *De planctu naturae*, p. 521 (*The Complaint of Nature*, p. 94), also in *PL* 210:482.

25. Noonan, *Contraception*, pp. 74–76, 239–46.

losophy to combat pagan immorality and Gnostic abhorrence of marriage.

Thomas Aquinas, who provides a résumé of standard medieval theory, explains that natural law came into being with God's creation. It is discernible in creation itself, independent of divine revelation or of human law; hence, it is available to all men. The Christian authority for natural law is found in Rom. 1–2, where Paul assumes that gentiles may discover the law of justice from the visible creation; here, Paul is obliquely alluding to the Noachian commandments (since all men descend from Noah, the rabbis regarded these as universal law).[26] From the basic law of nature, that one seeks the good and shuns evil, Thomas derives three basic precepts: that it is natural to preserve one's own life, that it is natural to preserve one's species by procreation, and that it is natural to live within an ordered society.[27] Since the third precept is dependent on the second, which Thomas relates especially to man, the weight of his discussion falls upon the law of procreation. Procreation is the primary and most obvious activity of all living beings, the means of perpetuating natural existence; it has the status of prescriptive law.

That the designation *sin against nature* should refer in medieval usage to sexual sin attests to the centrality of the procreative obligation under the natural law. The laws later introduced into history by Moses and Christ, the written law and the "law" of grace, may modify (or, to use Christ's term, fulfill) the natural law but may not violate its principles. Adultery, for example, becomes a sin under the written law. Because the stories of the Flood and Sodom occur in the Age of Nature, when natural law was the only law, the *Cleanness* poet properly makes the sin against nature the cause of God's wrath when he retells these stories.

Since nature was the standard by which actions were judged, and since procreation was judged to be the natural purpose of the

26. See W. D. Davies, *Paul and Rabbinic Judaism*, pp. 114–17. The just pagan is one who perceives the order of justice implicit in creation. Paschasius Radbertus uses this theory of the law visible in the creation to explain how all men from the beginning of history have been invited to the heavenly wedding feast, see *PL* 120:742.

27. Thomas Aquinas, *Summa theologica* (*Summa Theologica*), 1–2. 91.2, 1–2.94 (hereafter cited as *ST*). See also F. C. Copleston, *Aquinas*, pp. 219–35; and idem, *A History of Philosophy*, vol. 2, *Mediaeval Philosophy, Augustine to Scotus*, pp. 398–411.

sexual act, then any form of intercourse that hindered or avoided procreation was unnatural and hence a sin. And only one form of insemination was widely recognized by medieval writers, that in which the man lies above the woman and deposits his seed in the *vas debitum* (fit vessel). Not only, then, did unnatural sex refer to homosexuality, or sodomy, but to all forms of sexual intercourse except the prescribed form. Noonan cites Bernard of Pavia who defines the "extraordinary pollution" resulting from intercourse in an unnatural way as "all pollution which is not done within the vessel fit by nature, that is, within the vulva, whether it be done in some other vessel or outside" (*Summa of Decretals*, 4.14.7).[28] The natural, normal form of the sex act was quite precisely defined by the theologians and canonists.

To understand how the sin against nature offends God, we have only to look to Thomas Aquinas, who expresses the standard view of Scholastic philosophy on this point, a view that the *Cleanness* poet evidently shares. Thomas's view develops from influential twelfth-century authorities in law and theology who agreed that the sin against nature is a horrible evil. Gratian in his *Decretum* (ca. 1140) and Peter Lombard in his *Sentences* (ca. 1155), the basic texts for later medieval canon lawyers and theologians, attribute to Augustine an extended comparison of sexual sins: incest with one's mother is worse than adultery, which is worse than fornication; but worst of all is the sin against nature "ut si vir membro mulieris non ad hoc concesso voluerit uti" (as when a man wishes to use a member of his wife not conceded for this).[29] The justification for such an extreme view of unnatural sex depended on medieval assumptions about the givenness of the natural order, which, as Thomas explains, God himself established: "Ordo naturae est ab ipso Deo. Et ideo in peccatis contra naturam, in quibus ipse ordo naturae violatur, fit iniuria ipsi Deo, Ordinatori naturae" (The order of nature is from God Himself: wherefore in sins contrary to nature, whereby the very order of nature is violated, an injury is done to God, the Author of nature), *ST*, 2–2.154.

28. Noonan, *Contraception*, p. 224; see also pp. 222–27, 260–73; and Tentler, *Sin and Confession on the Eve of the Reformation*, pp. 168–70, 186–208.

29. Gratian, *Decretum*, C. 32, q. 7, c. 11; for a translation see Noonan, *Contraception*, p. 174. See also Peter Lombard, *Sententiarum libri quatuor*, 4.38.5, column 423.

12. Other sexual sins transgress the law of reason developed by man "ex praesuppositione tamen naturalium principiorum" (on the presupposition, however, of natural principles), *ST*, 2–2.154. 12. In Thomas's theory only the sin against nature offends God fundamentally and directly.

In developing his theory of the sin against nature, Thomas found support for his position in Augustine's *Confessiones*. There Augustine approves God's wrathful response to the sin against nature because this sin not only destroys human society but also subverts the relationship of man to God:

> Flagitia, quae sunt contra naturam, ubique ac semper destestanda atque punienda sunt, qualia Sodomitarum fuerunt. quae si omnes gentes facerent, omnes eodem criminis reatu divina lege tenerentur, quae non sic fecit homines, ut se illo uterentur modo. violatur quippe ipsa societas, quae cum deo nobis esse debet, cum eadem natura, cuius ille auctor est, libidinis perversitate polluitur. (Vicious deeds that are contrary to nature, are everywhere and always detested and punished, such as were those of the men of Sodom. Even if all nations should do these deeds, they would all be held in equal guilt under the divine law, for it has not made men in such fashion that they should use one another in this way. For in truth society itself, which must obtain between God and us, is violated, when the nature of which he is author is polluted by a perverted lust.)[30]

Thomas quotes this passage in *ST*, 2–2.154.12, the article in which he demonstrates that the sin against nature, as distinct from other sexual sins, directly offends God.

Other sexual sins, which Thomas refers to reason, threaten the family and human society. Reason regulates which women are forbidden to a man as his sexual partner so that the human social order may be preserved, and in treating sexual sins that offend reason Thomas is particularly concerned about the integrity of the family. Fornicators bent on their own pleasure do not consider the possibility of children or want to accept responsibility for their care. Adulterers not only disregard the welfare of potential children, but also injure the husband. Nature, however, provides the underlying principle on which all man's reasonable decisions de-

30. Augustine, *Confessiones* (*The Confessions of St. Augustine*), 3.8.15.

pend, and again Thomas explains that the sin against nature is the heaviest sin:

> Genere pessima est principii corruptio, ex quo alia depen-
> dent. Principia autem rationis sunt ea quae sunt secundum
> naturam; nam ratio, praesuppositis his quae sunt a natura
> determinata, disponit alia secundum quod convenit. . . .
> Quia ergo in vitiis quae sunt contra naturam transgreditur
> homo id quod est secundum naturam determinatum circa
> usum venereum, inde est quod in tali materia hoc peccatum
> est gravissimum. (Worst of all is the corruption of the
> principle on which the rest depend. Now the principles of
> reason are those things that are according to nature, because
> reason presupposes things as determined by nature, before
> disposing of other things according as it is fitting. . . . since
> by the unnatural vices man transgresses that which has been
> determined by nature with regard to the use of venereal
> actions, it follows that in this matter this sin is gravest of
> all.) *ST*, 2–2.154.12

The assumption that unnatural sex threatens the very foundation of God's order makes it a sin worthy of the most severe judgment. Nothing else good is possible when the foundation of goodness is violated.

In the passages quoted above, Thomas and Augustine imply that the law of nature established by God represents the first covenant between God and man. The sin against nature, then, has the same significance under the law of nature as adultery and idolatry have under the written law and the law of grace. The *Cleanness* poet's interpretation of biblical history respects the division of history into the three ages of law by assigning the sin against nature to offenders of the natural law and assigning adultery and idolatry to offenders of the written law.

Making adultery, or sexual sin, the principal literal sign of the broken covenant indicates that it is the chief sin against God. If the covenant between God and man is thought of as a marriage, then there is a pleasing theoretical neatness in assigning such gravity to the literal sin of adultery; but, historically, the charge of sexual sin in the later Middle Ages usually became serious—a matter deserving the death penalty—only if it was combined with the charge of heresy. The tendency of polemicists in the second great period of heretical activity (from the late twelfth century to the

Reformation) to charge heretics with sexual sin and sometimes
murder, usually child sacrifice, provided the authors of the *Queste*
and *Cleanness* with a literature of current interest that kept alive
the early Church's analysis of sin.[31] Like the antiheretical polemicists, both *Cleanness* and the *Queste* treat sexual sin as an extreme-
ly grave offense: it is the sign of the broken covenant.

## The Concept of Sacrilege

Having polluted the vessel of himself through sexual sin, idolatry, and/or murder, the sinner also commits sacrilege; that is, he
spreads the taint of his ontological condition to what he touches.

Sacrilege, according to Thomas Aquinas, is a failure to pay the
reverence owed to a sacred thing or person (*ST*, 2–2.99.1). He has
in mind the theft of church vessels, the shedding of blood or the
spilling of semen in a church, and the burial of pagans or infidels
in consecrated ground, all of which are examples of sacrilege commonly recognized in Scholastic theology and medieval canon law.[32]
In each of these examples a holy thing or place is polluted by contact with the profane or unclean. Until it is cleansed and rededi-
cated, the polluted thing or place is no longer holy, nor can it
serve as a point of contact with the holy, with God.

Thomas and the canonists take a limited, pragmatic, and legal-
istic position in their discussions of sacrilege, in contrast to many
of the Church Fathers and to medieval fiction writers; but all
medieval thinking on this issue has its roots in the Old Testament.[33] God demands in his covenant with Moses that his people
be holy, even as he is holy. To the Deuteronomic reviser and to the

31. See Wakefield and Evans, *Heresies of the High Middle Ages*, pp.
21, 25–26, 38–39, 46, 56–67 and texts nos. 3, 6, 8, 9, 11, 14, 15, 37, 38, 42, 45,
51, and 55 for charges of sexual misconduct against heretics; see no. 49 for
a denial of such a charge against the Cathari. For evaluations of the
legitimacy of such charges, see Noonan, *Contraception*, pp. 179–93; Robert E. Lerner, *The Heresy of the Free Spirit in the Later Middle Ages*, pp.
1–34; and Gordon Leff, *Heresy in the Later Middle Ages*.

32. See Gratian, *Decretum*, C. 17, q. 4, c. 4, 5, 12, 13, 18, 21; D. 1, c. 19–
20, 27–28, de cons.; and D. 68, c. 3. For a useful guide to canon law literature on the pollution of the Church, see Lucius Ferraris, "Ecclesia, art.
iv," in *Prompta bibliotheca canonica, juridica, moralis, theologica*, 3:
409–22.

33. On the biblical idea of the polluted land, see Büchler, *Studies in
Sin and Atonement*, pp. 212–16.

prophets, to be holy is to keep the covenant, to love God, the husband of Israel. This interpretation of the covenant, as we have noted, was a response to the nature of the competing Canaanite fertility cults, which worshipped Baal gods and involved cult prostitution. In turning away from her God, then, Israel literally involves herself in the pollution of spilled semen. She attributes her goods—her crops, her cattle, her offspring—to the favor of the Baal gods. To show her the error of her ways, God makes the land desolate. In making the prophecy of desolation, the prophets drew on ancient Hebrew tradition, on the stories of the Flood and especially of Sodom: when God intervened in the past to show his anger, he had always devastated the land, and he would do so again. The example of Sodom was appealing both because the sin of its people was sexual and because it was a city like the cities to which the prophets preached.

The prophets also represented Israel as a vineyard or garden subject to ruin, a figure that referred to the special relationship of God to man in the garden in Genesis, a relationship that God offered to reestablish with Israel through the covenant. The figure of Israel as garden also offered the prophets a way to counter the claims of the Canaanite fertility cults. Isaiah, for example, prophesies that by breaking the covenant Israel will make herself a ruined garden (Isa. 1:7–9, 29–30). The people are God's vineyard, but when they yield wild grapes (that is, rebel against the covenant) God prophesies a barren landscape; his grace will not descend upon the people (cf. John 15:5–6), and the land itself will reflect the people's sterility:

> And now I will shew you what I will do to my vineyard.
> I will take away the hedge thereof, and it shall be wasted: I
> will break down the wall thereof, and it shall be trodden
> down. And I will make it desolate. It shall not be pruned and
> it shall not be digged: but briers and thorns shall come up.
> And I will command the clouds to rain no rain upon it.
> (Isa. 5:5–6)

The abominations of men defile the land, according to the prophets, and the prophets attribute the wasting of the land to God.

The wasteland, then, signifies a sinful people, whose sins pollute and infect the land and make it barren or chaotic. In the Grail romances, the wasteland—the Gaste Forêt—seems more chaotic than infertile: its disorder serves no human needs. It offers neither physical nor spiritual food. In the *Queste* the Gaste Forêt represents the fallen world; infected by Original Sin, it can only be redeemed by holy men and women and then only partially. In *Cleanness* wastelands result from God's vengeance on sinners and, in the case of Sodom particularly, the wasteland becomes a warning of what God's judgment on sin will be.

Both the *Queste* and *Cleanness* reflect Christian interpretations of sacrilege in that both texts focus on the capacity of the individual to pollute himself, to make a wasteland of himself. For example, one of the hermits reproves Lancelot by describing him as having been a garden of virtues in his youth but having wasted himself through lechery, "la voie qui gaste cors et ame si merveilleusement que nus nel puet tres bien savoir qui essaié ne l'a."[34] The logic underlying this reproof depends upon Christian interpretations of vessel images, especially that of the garden.

Christianity centers all these images in the individual believer who, through faith and grace, remakes the garden within himself; who becomes a temple; whose body is the sacred vessel bearing Christ. Acts that pollute the individual believer become, then, the most intense kind of sacrilege, especially if these acts involve physical as well as spiritual pollution. Sexual sin is sacrilege because it pollutes the body—temple or vessel—of the believer. Paul provides the basis for this patristic and literary interpretation when he uses the image of the temple to explain to the Corinthians what being washed, sanctified, and justified by Christ ought to mean:

> But the body is not for fornication, but for the Lord; and the
> Lord for the body. . . . Know you not that your bodies are
> the members of Christ? Shall I then take the members
> of Christ and make them the members of an harlot? God
> forbid! Or know you not that he who is joined to a harlot is
> made one body? For they shall be, saith he, two in one
> flesh. But he who is joined to the Lord is one spirit. Fly
> fornication. Every sin that a man doth is without the body;
> but he that committeth fornication sinneth against his own
> body. Or know you not that your members are the temple

34. *La Queste del Saint Graal*, p. 126 (hereafter cited as *Q* by page number).

of the Holy Ghost. . . . Glorify and bear God in your body.
(I Cor. 6:13b, 15–20; cf. 3:16–17)

Chaucer's Parson explicitly interprets sexual sin as sacrilege when
he compares adultery to the theft of a church vessel, a legally recognized instance of sacrilege:

> This [adultery] is a fouler thefte than for to breke a chirche
> and stele the chalice; for this avowtiers breken the temple
> of God spiritually, and stelen the vessel of grace, that is the
> body and the soule, for which Crist shal destroyen hem,
> as seith Seint Paul. (*Parson's Tale*, line 878)

Under the concept of the Church as the body of Christ—every
Christian is himself the body of Christ and all Christians together
form the body of Christ—the joining of even one Christian to a
harlot can be interpreted as affecting the whole Church, as Rabanus Maurus argues: the fornicator pollutes the Church because
he is the temple of God; defiling himself, he defiles the Church.[35]
Through the one Christian who represents in himself the Church
and who brings himself into intimate contact with a harlot, the
whole Church is stained.

Scholastic theology and medieval canon law, for practical reasons, restrict the application of the charge of sacrilege to those
Christians in the most holy state of dedicated virginity, but the
principles for understanding sacrilege remain constant. As Gratian explains, because they result in the pouring out of semen or
blood, sexual sin and murder committed within the church pollute
it (D. 1, c. 27–28 *de cons.*). Similarly, when Gratian extends the
crime of sacrilege to people, blood and semen are agents of pollution, but the only people against whom such crimes can be committed are clerics (C. 17, q. 4, c. 21, regarding injury to a cleric) and
consecrated virgins:

> Sciendum est omnibus, quod Deo sacratarum feminarum
> corpora per votum propriae sponsionis et verba sacerdotis
> Deo consecrata esse templa scripturarum testimoniis
> conprobantur, et ideo violatores earum sacrilegi, ac iuxta
> Apostolum filii perditionis esse noscuntur. (Let it be known
> to all, that bodies of women dedicated to God through

35. Rabanus Maurus, *Homilia*, 142, in *PL* 110:418–21. See *Theol.
Dict. NT*, s.v. "ἅγιος, 1:88–115, for Paul's idea of the Christian community.

vows of their own solemn promise and the words of the priest
are sanctioned as temples consecrated to God by the witness
of scriptures, and therefore violators of them commit
sacrilege, and according to the Apostle they are known as
sons of perdition.) C. 27, q. 1, c. 37; my translation

Thomas is even more explicit in recognizing one form of sexual
sin as sacrilege: "Si autem abutatur virgine Deo sacrata, inquantum est sponsa Christi, est sacrilegium per modum adulterii" (Intercourse with a virgin consecrated to God, inasmuch as she is the
spouse of Christ, is sacrilege resembling adultery), *ST*, 2–2.154.10.
As a spouse of Christ, the virgin is a figure of the Church or the
temple. Quoting Isidore, Gratian argues that fornication is the
greatest crime "quia per carnis immunditiam templum Dei violat"
(because it violates the temple of God through uncleanness of the
flesh).[36] Isidore's language implies that fornication is sacrilege, but
Gratian does not define the sexual sins of ordinary Christians as
sacrilege, presumably because to charge every sexual sinner with
sacrilege was impractical and lessened the distinction between
ordinary Christians and those specially dedicated to God.

A somewhat different problem, that of corrupt priests, led
Thomas and others to resist theories arguing that pollution spread
from the unclean to the clean, except in the restricted cases where
holy persons, places, or things were contaminated by blood, semen,
or some other physical as well as spiritual irreverence. To combat
heretics who refused to acknowledge the authority of the Church's
duly appointed ministers because some were obviously corrupt,
the Church argued that sacraments administered by unclean
priests are nevertheless efficacious for those who participate worthily. The unclean priest cannot defile the Body and Blood of Christ,
although, like any unworthy communicant who is polluted with
sin, the unclean priest eats damnation to himself.[37] To guard the
sacraments and to protect those innocent of sacrilegious intent
from being affected by the defilement of others, the Church developed a rebound theory of pollution, which argued that a pol-

36. Isidore, *Sentences*, 2.39, in *PL* 83:642; Gratian, *Decretum*, C. 32,
q. 7, c. 15. My translation.

37. See Master Vacarius, *Liber contra multiplices et varios errores*,
prologue, in Ilarino da Milano, *L'Eresia di Ugo Speroni nella confutazione del Maestro Vacario*, pp. 476–77.

luted person corrupts the use of sacred things or sacred rites only as to himself.

Both the New Testament and the distinctions of Aristotelean philosophy lent authority to a theoretical analysis of sacrilege that limited the spread of pollution. In criticizing Pharisaic ablution ritual, Christ had emphasized human intention as the determinant of pollution, an emphasis that was picked up in the medieval rebound theory of sacrilege:

> Not that which goeth into the mouth defileth a man; but
> what cometh out of the mouth, this defileth a man. . . . Do
> you not understand that whatsoever entereth into the mouth
> goeth into the belly and is cast out into the privy? But the
> things which proceed out of the mouth come forth from
> the heart; and those things defile a man. For from the heart
> come forth evil thoughts, murders, adulteries, fornications,
> thefts, false testimonies, blasphemies. These are the things
> that defile a man. (Matt. 15:11, 17–20a)

In his statement of the rebound theory of sacrilege, Thomas relies on the Aristotelean distinction that "honor is in the person who honors and not in the one who is honored"; Thomas argues that irreverence to a sacred thing lies in the one who is irreverent, so that the irreverent person violates the sacred thing so far as he himself is concerned, but does not violate the sacred thing itself (*ST*, 2–2.99.1).

The tendency of the Church to interpret the sin of the heretic or idolater as analogous to sexual sin and to accuse the heretic of sexual sin respects the connection of adultery and idolatry to sacrilege. Ideally, the heretic should be physically as well as spiritually polluted, and to suggest that he is polluted and an agent of pollution leads Rupert of Deutz into wordplay on *adultery*:

> "Oculus, inquit, adulteri observat caliginem" (Job. 24:15).
> id est sicut adulter per tenebras in carnali coitu non prolem
> quaerit, sed voluptatem; sic haereticus in hypocrisi
> adulterat, Dei verbum, quia videlicet non spirituales Dei
> filios gignere sed suam scientiam praedicando desiderat
> ostentare, et quasi alienam conjugem tollit, dum fidelem
> animam in suum errorem allicit. ("The eye of the adulterer,"
> he says, "watches for darkness" [Job 24:15], that is, just as
> the adulterer during the darkness does not seek offspring in

> sexual intercourse, but pleasure; so the heretic adulterates
> the word of God in his pretended sanctity, because he
> does not desire to beget spiritual sons of God but rather
> to show off his own knowledge by preaching, and as it were
> he takes away the wife of another, while he attracts the
> faithful soul into his own error.)[38]

Adultery pollutes adulterers because it not only involves physical pollution but also violates the spiritual bond of marriage. When it is a figure for idolatry, as in the *Queste* and *Cleanness*, it combines physical and spiritual pollution, which, from a medieval point of view, is the most intense form of pollution, just as the combination of physical with spiritual cleanness is the most intense form of purity.

The *Queste* and *Cleanness* illustrate the pollution of the broken covenant through sexual sin and idolatry by using the correlative of the wasteland, which represents a condition of chaos and death within and without. The way out of the wasteland, as the *Queste* demonstrates in the stories of Lancelot, Perceval, Bors, and Galahad, and as *Cleanness* demonstrates through the examples of Noah, Abraham, Lot, and Nebuchadnezzar, lies in faith, cleanness, and courtesy.

## The Vessel of Mercy: Ritual Purity

To journey out of the wasteland, to leave sin and its destructive consequences, man must enter into a state of cleanness. A Christian enters this state through baptism and reenters it through penance. The ritual cleansing of baptism or penance has both religious and ethical significance for medieval Christian thinkers, who tend not to separate ritual (the forms and ceremonies through which man makes contact with God) from ethics, as is evidenced in the general belief that only a man in a state of ritual purity can do good works (this belief was, however, a point of controversy in discussions of the virtuous pagan). Medieval Christians generally regard sins, wrongdoings that make a man filthy spiritually and sometimes physically, as offenses against both religion (ritual) and ethics. In order for a sinner to right himself in relationship to God and to human society, he must undergo a ritual that at once

---

38. Rupert of Deutz, *Commentarius in Job*, 24.15, in *PL* 168:1066. Cited in de Lubac, *Exégèse médiévale*, vol. 1, pt. 2, p. 115. My translation.

cleanses him (makes him ritually, physically pure) and signifies to him and to others a reformed conscience, a conscience that wills to do good and not evil. The ritual purification allows the sinner to begin his life again, to start afresh on the pilgrimage to God. For the *Queste* author and the *Cleanness* poet, ritual purity is a prerequisite to the *visio Dei*, the goal of total happiness (beatitude) toward which they move, and it is necessary for the accomplishment of good works along the way. The knights on the Grail quest, the poet, and his audience seek to fulfill the condition of the sixth Beatitude, "Blessed are the clean in heart," so that its conclusion, "for they shall see God," may apply to them. Before we can consider the *visio Dei*, we must first understand cleanness and penance as medieval theologians did.

The State of Cleanness

In the *Queste* the concept of cleanness seems to be treated simply, to be equated (both sexually and spiritually) with virginity; in *Cleanness*, apparently different meanings of the word have led some critics to argue that the poem lacks coherence. The *Cleanness* poet establishes the word *cleanness* as synonymous with *sexual purity* in the stories of the Flood and Sodom and demonstrates its broader moral significance through the story of Belshazzar and the Temple vessels. Precisely how the poet links the earlier stories to the later, I will explain in Chapter 4; but to show the closeness of the relationship between the limited and the broad moral and spiritual senses of cleanness will provide a ground for that discussion.

The word *clean* (*clani-, OE clǣne, OF pur, monde; L mundus; Gr kathoros) appears to have a basic meaning of *clear or pure*.[39] In Old English it translates a related group of Latin words, *mun-*

39. This discussion of the word *clean*, which translates the Latin words *mundus* and *purus*, the Old French word *net* and the Greek word καθαρός, is based on the following reference works: *The Oxford English Dictionary; Middle English Dictionary; An Anglo-Saxon Dictionary* and *Supplement; Thesaurus linguae latinae; Französisches etymologisches Wörterbuch,* s.v. nitidus, horridus; *Altfranzösisches Wörterbuch; Dictionnaire de l'ancienne langue française; Nouveau Dictionnaire étymologique; Theol. Dict. NT; A Greek-English Lexicon of the New Testament and Other Early Christian Literature;* and *A Patristic Greek Lexicon.* See also Leo Charles Yedlicka, *Expressions of the Linguistic Area of Repentance and Remorse in Old French,* pp. 160–65.

*dus, purus, castus,* and *innoxius.* Through the contact of Old English with Latin Christianity, then, the word *clean* takes on a complex range of meanings, which refer both to spiritual and physical conditions. If in early Old English usage the word *clǣne* connoted a bright or shining condition, as it probably did prehistorically and as it did in Middle English, then it was a particularly apt word for translating the Latin *mundus,* which was used to describe the state of the blessed who are to be in glory, a condition also associated with brightness and shining light through the biblical accounts of the glory of the Lord manifested in the Ark of the Covenant and in the transfiguration of Christ. The English word in the context of Christian thought is, in fact, a richer and more suggestive word than either *mundus* or *purus* or the Old French *net.* The Old French antonyms *net* and *ort* describe the physical conditions of being washed clean or of being covered with ordure; transposed to a spiritual sense, the antonyms *net* and *ort* describe the ontological conditions of righteousness or of sinfulness. To return to the main argument, *clean* in Middle English describes a state of spiritual perfection. The merely physical states defined in Middle English by the word *clean*—such as being unadulterated, free from dirt or disease, shapely, bright or gleaming—often become outward signs of an inward state, that of being free from the pollution of sin.

The transferred or spiritual meanings that the English word *clean* picked up from the contact of Old English with Latin Christianity can be understood through a consideration of the concept in Judeo-Christian ritual. *Cleanness* belongs to a set of ritual concepts, all of which are associated with sacrifice, the center of ritual. This set of concepts—cleanness, wholeness, and holiness—describes the condition of things or creatures (in the Old Testament, of produce and beasts) appropriate for sacrifice. In the New Testament, as we noted earlier, Paul exhorts the faithful to present their bodies as a "hostiam viventem, sanctam, Deo placentem" (Rom. 12:1). Christianity spiritualizes the sacrifice by inviting the individual believer to think of himself, of his heart or mind, as an offering and apply to himself the conditions that in the Old Testament applied to the things and beasts of sacrifice.

The way the Old Testament understands cleanness, wholeness, and holiness provides a basis for comprehending the spiritualization of these concepts in Christian thought. The Law prescribes what is clean and what is unclean. The purpose of having a category of cleanness is clear: since God is clean, all things offered to him must be clean; if man offers anything unclean, God rejects the offering. The concept of purity is closely related to those of wholeness or completeness and of holiness, which as a word means *to be set apart*.[40] The Law requires that all beasts offered for sacrifice, except in the case of the firstborn, must be clean and must also be perfect, whole, and without blemish; it requires that priests be men without physical imperfection. Wholeness, like cleanness, is a way of defining the integrity of an offering or of a minister in the service of God. Cleanness is not, however, a synonym for holiness. Rather it is a precondition of holiness. The category of the common or profane includes both the clean and the unclean: whatever is both common and unclean is utterly opposed to holiness and therefore opposed to God. Under the Law, that which is clean and profane (the rest of the harvest, after the offering of firstfruits, for example) can be put to ordinary use.

In Christianity, which celebrates only one sacrifice, that of the Mass in which the communicant offers himself to Christ and receives Christ in return, the ultimate objective of every Christian is to belong to the category of the clean and holy so that he may avoid being made deathly sick by an unworthy communication. Medieval Christianity, however, made distinctions between the faithful that correspond to the two categories of clean and holy and of clean and profane. In the former category were all those who dedicated themselves wholly to God, vowing themselves to virginity or chastity for his sake, preserving themselves clean, whole, and holy for him. In the latter category were all those who, like the married, participated in the affairs of the world. That the ultimate goal of all Christians was to belong to the higher category of the clean and holy probably explains why so many men and women, both in life and in literature—for example, Guinevere and Lancelot at the end of the *Mort Artu*—entered a monastery to die in holy orders. Holiness, for the medieval Christian, was a state to

40. See *Theol. Dict. NT*, s.v. 'αγιος; Norman H. Snaith, *The Distinctive Ideas of the Old Testament*, pp. 21–50; H. Ringgren, *The Prophetical Conception of Holiness*; and Mary Tew Douglas, *Purity and Danger*, pp. 41–57.

strive for, a state both of mind and body in which the individual sought to dedicate himself to God, to abandon wholly the world and its cares.

Christ in *Cleanness* and Galahad (who is a type of Christ the perfect sacrifice) in the *Queste* illustrate the Christian ideal of cleanness, wholeness, and holiness. To keep company with them is possible only for those like them. They are most like Christ who dedicate themselves sexually pure and whole to God. Because Christianity also recognizes marriage as legitimate, those who dedicate themselves to God only through spiritual purification are also like Christ, though in a lesser degree, since they are not sexually pure and whole. In other words, in a ritual context, a condition that combines both spiritual and physical qualifications (dedicated virginity) is better than one that meets only spiritual qualifications (chaste marriage), while mere physical qualification has no significance. This hierarchy of degrees of cleanness corresponds to the standard medieval interpretation in John 14:2 that the many mansions of heaven promised by Christ indicate that heaven holds places for the more and less perfect.

According to Christian thought, uncleanness is a failure to conform to Christ, a failure generally understood in a spiritual sense: Christ is without sin, so to be with sin is to fail to conform to him. Old Testament Law usually distinguishes unclean from clean, imperfect from whole, on physical grounds; Christianity takes physical signs, such as sickness, to be indicators of a spiritual state, but recognizes that these signs may be inaccurate. Medieval Christian imaginative literature, however, usually makes a physical state a sign of a spiritual condition. In a broader spiritual sense, cleanness is freedom from sin in all its manifestations; but often in medieval literature, sexual purity is the sign by which an author indicates a character's spiritual perfection, his freedom from sin.

Things or persons in the two extreme conditions of holiness or uncleanness are sources of power and danger to those in contact with them. This principle is most strikingly illustrated in *Cleanness* and the *Queste* in cases of contact with holiness. Early in the Grail adventures Galahad violently repels Lancelot and Perceval because they are not yet conformed to him. In *Cleanness* Christ has the tattered guest thrown out. Contact with holiness may cause sickness or death. So it does to Core (Korah) and his company when they burn incense before God's altar (Num. 16:1–35), an incident echoed in the *Queste* account of those who sat in Josephes's seat at the Grail Table and were swallowed up as in an earthquake, presumably because they could not match Josephes's cleanness and holiness (Q, 76; cf. Q, 8–9). In 1 Cor. 11:29, Paul promises death to those who eat the sacrament of Christ's Body and Blood unworthily: the *Cleanness* poet interprets Belshazzar's sin of drinking from the Temple vessels, for which he is struck down by the wrath of God, to be similar to unworthy communication. When, at the end of the *Queste*, Lancelot goes closer to the Holy Grail than one at his level of spiritual progress may go, he is stunned and lies in a coma one day for each of his years of sin, yet he wakes to report the sweetness of his vision of the Grail. Because he does not actually communicate, he does not die; but his experiences of sweetness and sickness typify the two destinies between which he must yet choose. By penance, he has satisfied the condition of cleanness that is prerequisite to any vision of the Grail, but he has not yet advanced into a state of holiness that corresponds to the nature of the Grail as the *visio Dei*.

## Baptism and Penance: Cleansing Sacraments

Baptism and penance, sometimes called the second baptism, are purification rites through which the individual Christian changes his ontological condition of filth to a condition of cleanness so that he may worthily participate in the eucharistic sacrifice, the rite through which he offers his heart to God and receives God in return. The *Queste* and *Cleanness* recall their audiences to God by urging repentance. The Grail romances present Lancelot's penance as an example that implicitly invites the audience to imitate him. The *Cleanness* poet not only offers his audience stories that foreshadow baptism and penance, stories of the Flood and of Nebuchadnezzar's madness, but he also directly urges his audience to penance. The theology of the two penitential sacraments is related (penance renews baptism); but in the later Middle Ages, since infant baptism was a common practice, penance was the relevant sacrament to urge upon an ordinary audience.

Baptism, the initial Christian sacrament of purification, redeems Original Sin and all of a man's personal sins. It marks a man's entrance into the Christian covenant and it is unrepeatable. Through it, the Christian dedicates himself to Christ, that is, he becomes clean and holy, a man separated to God: he dies to the world. His cleansing in the waters of baptism does not merely effect the purification from sexual pollution, leprosy, or rotting flesh that was bestowed by the ritual ablutions of the Old Testament. Rather, by the grace of Christ the waters remove the stains of sin, which is a spiritual concept and may or may not involve physical pollutions of the body.

Once cleansed by this rite of initiation into the covenant, a man enters into the full responsibility of fulfilling that covenant, of fulfilling the law of love that Christ expresses in the two great commandments: "Thou shalt love the Lord thy God with thy whole heart and with thy whole soul and with thy whole mind" and "Thou shalt love thy neighbour as thyself" (Matt. 22:37, 39; cf. Deut. 6:5, Lev. 19:18). Christ emphasizes the inward orientation of the human heart by making an attitude of love and willing obedience the center of his teaching. He abrogates the necessity of fulfilling a prescribed set of laws, replacing them with the law of love, an apparently simple standard by which to judge actions. To some degree, the Church reintroduced prescriptive law by setting out specifically the implications of the law of love, for example, declaring at the so-called Council of Jerusalem (Acts 15) that adultery, idolatry, and murder are forbidden to Christians. More generally, however, love contains all the virtues and expresses itself in virtuous actions; love contrasts itself to all vices and vicious deeds (see Gal. 5:19–25). Not only does love encompass all the virtues named in the New Testament, but, when medieval writers give a spiritual dimension to the language of courtesy by using it to apply to man's relationship to a person of the Trinity or to the Virgin, then the virtues they name, such as "debonairtee" or "courtesy," also become attached to the Christian concept of love. In fact, the *Cleanness* poet uses *courtesy* as a synonym of *charity*.

One who sins after baptism falls out of the covenant: walking in the way of love is impossible to the impure and the unclean. Purity is a precondition for love in the Christian sense, a state attainable only through divine grace and available only to those who meet God's initial offer of grace with faith in God's redeeming power. Faith and purity, then, are closely related in Christian thought: fulfillment of the covenant is conditional upon them.

The difficulty of avoiding sin after baptism made penance in some form a practical necessity in Christianity. The medieval

Church ordinarily understood sin as a spiritual sickness, a disease to be cured by penance.[41] Christ's healing miracles, his cures of the menstruous woman, lepers, and madmen, all of whom were considered unclean under the Old Law, were generally understood as a sign that all sinners might be healed by faith in Christ.

Penance achieved its status as a sacrament of the Church in the twelfth and thirteenth centuries with the development of the theology of the sacraments. The Fourth Lateran Council accepted the, by then familiar, ritual of private penance as the proper form of the sacrament. In discussing penance, theologians of this period found biblical authority for penance in the miracle of Lazarus, whom Christ raised from the dead, and in Christ's healing of the ten lepers.[42] They describe the confessor's duty to be "inter lepram et lepram discernere."[43] In other words, the confessor must decide and declare who is clean, by virtue of contrition and confession, and who is unclean, even though for Christians the disease is not literally leprosy but sin. He must see through the outward signs of sin (or lack of them) to the spiritual reality of the soul and pronounce absolution on those who truly repent, thus reinstating them into a condition of spiritual health.

To become a penitent, a sinful Christian first has to acknowledge his sins to himself in sorrow; he must undergo an inward conversion from his life of sin to a life in Christ. In this state of contrition he must seek out a priest (normally his parish priest) to whom he can confess his sins. After charging the penitent to make satisfaction for his sin, by restoring goods wrongfully gotten, for example, or by undergoing some form of ascetic discipline, the priest absolves the penitent, thus reconciling him to God and

41. See canon 21 of the Fourth Lateran Council, in Joannes Dominicus Mansi, ed., *Sacrorum conciliorum*, 22:1010.

42. See Paul Anciaux, *La Théologie du sacrement de pénitence au XIIe siècle*, pp. 169–72, 224 n. 3, 240, 265–66, 276, 428–29, 447, 496, and 496 n. 1.

43. Anciaux, *Théologie*, p. 585, quoting from Peter of Roissy's *Manuale de mysteriis*; see also pp. 38–39, 169–72, 275–353, and 610–12. My description of penance follows twelfth-century, and thirteenth-century Franciscan, theology, which emphasizes contrition and gives a problematical answer to the priest's use of the keys and to the function of absolution, from the point of view of sacramental theology. For a detailed discussion of the medieval theology of penance, see Poschmann, *Penance and the Annointing of the Sick*, pp. 155–93; see also Tentler, *Sin and Confession on the Eve of the Reformation*, pp. 3–27.

to the Church (in many twelfth- and thirteenth-century theories, the penitent's contrition reconciled him to God; the priest's absolution declared this reconciliation and reconciled the penitent to the Church).

Penance, like baptism, involves an absolution: in penance the cleansing is effected by the penitent's tears and acts of expiation and by the priest's words. As a ritual it is less dramatic than baptism: much of the "actio poenitentiae" is performed in private and requires that the penitent submit himself to introspective self-examination with the help of a priest. To respond flexibly to individual penitents, confessors had to analyze a sinner's personal circumstances and his actions, both of which are important elements in narrative fiction, which thrives on particular acts and individualized characters. The ritual of penance, then, is allied not to drama, but to narrative. As the body of literature written to guide confessors grew, it included not only expository treatments of sins, but also illustrative narratives, a development that seems a natural and inevitable consequence of the twelfth- and thirteenth-century conception of penance. Penance has its place in the narratives of *Cleanness* and the *Queste*, it is the way to begin again on the journey to God.

## Christian Banquet: Rite of Fellowship and Rite of Marriage

The *visio Dei*, the goal of the knights in the Grail quest and of the *Cleanness* poet, cannot be expressed in human language; even Dante fails to be able to render the experience except indirectly (see *Paradiso* 33). It is, however, prefigured in the sacrament of the Eucharist, the Christian banquet that unites men in the fellowship of the altar table and joins each man to God.[44] *Cleanness* begins with a description of the Eucharist; the *Queste* ends with celebrations of the Grail mass, which is a heightened and mystical form of the Eucharist.

The Eucharist, like the Old Testament peace offering, is a meal shared by the Christian congregation, but its significance is more

44. See Baldwin of Ford, Archbishop of Canterbury (d. 1190), *Le Sacrement de l'autel (Tractatus de sacramento altaris)*, 2.4.3, SC 94:352–55, 362–69. Cistercian commentary on the Eucharist emphasizes both the unity with Jesus and the fellowship of the Church, see Camille Hontoir, "La Dévotion au Saint Sacrement chez les premiers Cisterciens (XIIe–XIIIe siècles)," pp. 132–41.

complex. The sharing of food in the eucharistic banquet not only signifies the fellowship of the congregation, but through Christ it actually makes the congregation into a united body, the Church. Participation in Christ, then, and not membership in any particular tribe or people, is the common bond of the Christian community.

The Eucharist dramatically embodies the intimacy of the relationship between God and man in Christianity. Like the holocaust and the peace offerings of the Old Law, it is both an offertory celebration (the bodies of the faithful being vessels in which they bring their hearts to God) and a celebration of Christ's sacrifice of himself for man, both a joyous and a somber occasion. Through this sacred meal God provides sustenance to the faithful so that they can continue to keep their covenant with Christ by walking in the way of love.

More than that, this feast unites Christ and man, since in eating the Body and Blood the communicant actually makes God a part of his own body, or, to speak in precise and theological language, man becomes part of Christ, incorporated into Christ, literally one body with Christ.[45] This one body was understood to signify a mystic or spiritual reality, the union made in the mystical marriage of Christ and his Church. This spiritual union, generally understood by reference to Pauline texts on marriage ("the husband is the head of the wife, as Christ is the head of the Church" [Eph. 5:22 ff.]) and on the body of Christ (which is the Church [see 1 Cor. 6:15]), is thus analogous to human marriage in which two people become one flesh through sexual intercourse. The act of eating becomes a sign of the spiritual union just as sexual intercourse is a sign of the union in human marriage.

In exploring the analogy between eating the Eucharist and sexual intercourse, the acts that consummate marriage on the divine and human levels, respectively, I do not claim that any medieval writer explicitly articulated this analogy. However, some writers did, unselfconsciously, come close to an explicit analogy because they so often talked of spiritual realities in human terms. Their habits of speech seem to be reflected in certain contrasts in the *Queste* and *Cleanness*. All the Grail knights give up sexual

---

45. Hugh of St. Victor, *De Sacramentis christianae fidei (On The Sacraments of the Christian Faith)*, 2.8.5, in *PL* 176:465 (hereafter cited as *De sacr.*). Hugh's point is conventional.

intercourse when they enter the Grail quest, although of the sinners only Lancelot understands the significance of the requirement of sexual purity: he gives up the queen in order to feed upon a vision of the Grail. Perceval withstands a temptation to sexual intercourse and instead feeds upon the Living Bread. In *Cleanness* Abraham and Lot share meals with the angels (the Trinity), while the men of Sodom want to have unnatural sexual intercourse with the angels.

The basis for any analogy between eating and sexual intercourse lies in ordinary physical reality: in both acts, in the case of women, the body is penetrated by something outside itself. Christian theology treats every believer like a woman in that the believer becomes a bride of Christ and as a believer receives, not seed in the ordinary human sense, but grace. The Eucharist, which culminates in the act of communication, celebrates the union of Christ with his Church, his faithful. By the act of eating his Body and his Blood, the faithful become "one flesh," as Christ himself makes clear in his insistence on the physical act of eating:

> Except you eat the flesh of the Son of man and drink his
> blood, you shall not have life in you. He that eateth my flesh
> and drinketh my blood hath everlasting life; and I will
> raise him up in the last day. For my flesh is meat indeed;
> and my blood is drink indeed. He that eateth my flesh and
> drinketh my blood abideth in me; and I in him. (John
> 6:54–57)

The act of eating the Eucharist and bringing about a new spiritual life corresponds to the act of human intercourse that begins a new human life.

Hugh of St. Victor makes the analogy between eating and sexual intercourse almost explicit in his discussion of the institution of the sacrament of marriage and his description of the office of matrimony. Marriage, he says, consists "in consensu foederis socialis" (in the consent of the social pact), which is a sign of the spiritual society between God and the soul. The office of matrimony, he says, consists "in copula carnis" (in the copulation of the flesh), which does not, in fact, find its spiritual correlative until the Incarnation of Christ, when God assumes flesh so that he may be united to his Church (*De sacr.*, 1.8.13). The Eucharist, which cele-

brates the Incarnation of Christ and his sacrifice of himself in his
human nature, is in fact the sacrament that in a literal sense effects
the marital union of Christ the bridegroom to the Church his
bride, a union that signifies the mystical body of Christ, of which
"Crist hys þat heued. . . Þe lymes þat folk i-vere" (Christ is that
head. . . the limbs that folk all together). Here William of Shoreham conventionally applies the Pauline concepts of marriage and
the body of Christ, which make "cryst and his derlynges [Bride-
groom and Bride] O body."[46] Hugh of St. Victor concludes his exposition of marriage and its office by comparing the office of human marriage to the relationship of God and man:

> In quo officio masculo quidem (qui superior erat) datum
> est quod propagandum fuisset de suo seminare, feminae
> autem concipere et parere, ut in eadem similitudine demon-
> straretur quod in illa invisibili societate anima rationalis
> nullatenus fructificare posset, nisi prius semen virtutis a
> Deo conciperet. (In this office, indeed, it was given to man,
> who was superior, to engender from his own what was to be
> propagated but to woman to conceive and to bear, so that
> in this same similitude it might be shown that in the invisible
> society the rational soul could in no way bear fruit unless
> it first received the seed of virtue from God.) De sacr., 1.8.13

Hugh does not explain precisely what he means by "semen virtutis," but he probably means something very like what Catherine
of Siena means by "il seme della grazia." She is fond of the seed
image and takes "il seme della grazia" to be the image of likeness
to God, lost through Adam's sin and restored to man by Christ
through the sacraments.[47] The grace God grants to man, as Hugh
explains, allows him to be fruitful in good works, which are the
spiritual offspring of the divine marriage. The tendency of Hugh
to extend the description of the divine marriage to account for its
offspring, as one might describe human marriage by its fruit in
human offspring, offers support for a comparison of the two chief

46. William of Shoreham, "De septem sacramentis," lines 622–23, in
Poems, p. 23.
47. Catherine of Siena, Libro della divina dottrina 23 (cf. 12), pp. 45–
47 (cf. 28–30). The image semen is, in fact, an equipollent image, and can
mean verbum Dei (Scripture or Christ) or Christ; see Rabanus Maurus,
De universo, 6.1, in PL 111:174; and Jerome, In Osee, 1.1.10.11.

acts by which the two kinds of marriage are, as it were, consummated. To describe the spiritual offspring of the divine marriage is, in fact, a commonplace.

That the analogy between eating and sexual intercourse, between the reception of two kinds of seeds, is an implicit assumption in medieval Christian thinking can be corroborated in other ways. Ambrose, for example, discusses the Eucharist in language borrowed from the Song of Songs and its commentaries, interpreting the epithalamium for the bridegroom and bride as a marriage song for Christ and the Church: the implication is that the act of communicating is analogous to sexual intercourse.[48] In his commentary on the Song of Songs, Bernard of Clairvaux, being more careful than some commentators, makes the difference between the two marriages apparent in his analogy: "Nam si carnale matrimonium constituit duos in carne una, cur non magis spiritualis copula duos coniunget in uno spiritu?" (For if marriage according to the flesh constitutes two in one body, why should not a spiritual union be even more efficacious in joining two in one spirit?).[49] Both are unions, one of flesh, one of spirit. As Paul seems to do in Eph. 5, Bernard uses the attributes of human love and marriage to enrich the idea of spiritual marriage. Commenting on Cant. 1:1, "Let him kiss me with the kiss of his mouth," Bernard identifies the speaker as the bride and explains why the title of *bride* is especially appropriate for the soul seeking God:

> Quae vero osculum postulat, amat. Excellit in naturae donis affectio haec amoris, praesertim cum ad suum recurrit principium, quod est Deus. Nec sunt inventa aeque dulcia nomina, quibus Verbi animaeque dulces ad invicem exprimerentur affectus, quemadmodum sponsus et sponsa: quippe quibus omnia sunt communia, nil proprium, nil a se divisum haventibus. Una utriusque haereditas, una mensa, una domus, unus thorus, una etiam caro. (But the one who asks for a kiss, she is a lover. Among all the natural endowments of man love holds first place, especially when it is directed to God, who is the source whence it comes. No sweeter names can be found to embody that sweet interflow

48. See Ambrose, *De mysteriis*, 7.39–41, 9.55–57, and idem, *De sacramentis*, 5.2–3.5–17, CSEL 73:105–6, 113–15, 61–65.

49. Bernard of Clairvaux, *Sermones super Cantica canticorum (On the Song of Songs)*, 8.9 (hereafter cited as *Serm. Cant. cant.*).

of affections between the Word and the soul, than bride-groom and bride. Between these all things are equally shared, there are no selfish reservations, nothing that causes divisions. They share the same inheritance, the same table, the same home, the same marriage-bed, they are flesh of each other's flesh.) *Serm. Cant. cant.*, 7.2

The fellowship shared by husband and wife, as Bernard and Paul describe it, corresponds in most respects to the fraternity that ought to exist among men: but instead of sexual intercourse, the sharing of a common feast becomes the mark of fraternal union.

The history of medieval spirituality offers another reflection of the analogy between eating and sexual intercourse. In the thirteenth and fourteenth centuries devout women especially revered the Body and Blood of Christ—the Corpus Christi—and were more insistent than their male counterparts in desiring frequent reception of the Eucharist.[50] Perhaps this fervent devotion was not accidental, but an instance of language affecting history. These women wanted to be brides of Christ and could think of themselves filling the role specified for the bride in the commentaries on the Song of Songs and similar mystical treatises, a role that, by the accident of their gender, applied to women in a more literal sense than to men. One of the earliest of these women was Marie d'Oignies (d. 1213), whose biographer Jacques de Vitry reports her response to Christ's statement, offensive to the Jews, promising life to them who ate his Body and drank his Blood (John 6:54):

> Non erat ei durus hic sermo sicut Judaeis; sed suavis: quippe qui omnem delectationem et omnem saporis suavitatem in ejus perceptione, non solum interius in animo, sed etiam in ore ejus mellifluo sentiebat: et plerumque sub pueri specie, sub mellis sapore, cum aromatum odore, in puro et exornato cordis thalamo, Dominum suum feliciter admittebat. (This saying was not hard to her as it was to the Jews, but sweet. Indeed she who felt every delight and every

50. See Édouard Dumoutet, *Le Christ selon la chair et la vie liturgique au moyen-âge*, pp. 113–44; Jean Leclercq, François Vandenbroucke, and Louis Bouyer, *The Spirituality of the Middle Ages*, pp. 243–50, 356–64. The devotion of women to Christ is assumed by the (early?) thirteenth-century author of the *Ancrene Wisse*, pp. 20–21, 135. The life of Catherine of Siena (d. 1380) by Raymund of Capua describes her as frequently taking communion, which troubled even her confessor; see *Acta sanctorum*, April, 3:861–986, esp. 893, 903–4.

sweetness of taste in taking him, not only in her soul within, but even in her mouth flowing with honey, happily admitted her Lord many times in the shape of a boy, under the taste of honey, with the smell of spices, in the pure and adorned marriage-chamber of her heart).[51]

By communicating in the Eucharist, these women imitated the act of the Virgin Mary, the first bride of Christ, whose womb was the marriage chamber where divinity and flesh first joined. In addition, they made their hearts vessels, marriage chambers for Christ.

Those who effectively join themselves to Christ through the Eucharist belong to the Church of the just (the elect), which has an eschatological implication: at the time of the Last Judgment, at the Resurrection of the Bodies, this Church will join the churches of purgatory and heaven to become one universal Church in glory. The Pauline warning that he who communicates unworthily eats damnation certainly made some theologians reluctant to urge communication more frequently than a few times a year, for fear that the preparation of the faithful, through penance, might be inadequate. Worthy communication in the Eucharist, the kind of participation desired by the faithful, offered a foretaste of the joy of the eschatological wedding feast, the unending celebration of the marriage of Christ and his Church.

The parable of the wedding feast, recorded in both Matt. 22: 2–14 and Luke 14:16–24, illustrates the covenant of love, its demands, its glory, and its danger, and offers a human analogy to the eschatological state of the blessed, who feast perpetually on the *visio Dei*, seeing God face to face. Matthew gives weight to the eschatological implications of the parable feast; while Luke, who does not connect the feast to the wedding motif, emphasizes its covenant aspects by showing in detail the pattern of invitation and response. The two versions were often conflated in medieval sermons and poetry, as they are in *Cleanness*.

Medieval commentary on the parable of the wedding feast (Matthew) and the great supper (Luke) tends to ignore differences in the two versions and to allegorize the elements of the parables consistently. While neither the *Queste* author nor the *Cleanness* poet allude directly to these allegorical interpretations of the parable,

51. *Acta sanctorum*, June, 5:568. My translation. Rabanus Maurus allegorizes *thalamus* as the uterus of the Virgin and as the hearts of the saints, *De universo*, 7.5, in *PL* 111:192.

some at least of the elements in these interpretations seem to have influenced the way the *Cleanness* poet developed analogies to the parable and the way the *Queste* author imposed the pattern of the parable on the lives of his characters. Since both writers probably knew the commentary tradition, let me summarize.[52]

Matthew's version of the parable, which identifies the feast as a wedding celebration, influences commentary on Luke's great supper: most commentators refer the feast in both versions to the Incarnation, which is, as they explain, the beginning of the nuptials between Christ and his Church, for which the womb of the Virgin provided the marriage chamber (*thalamus*). The food prepared for the feast is usually said to be the Scriptures or the Body of Christ or both. This alternation or combination of interpretations reflects the traditional assimilation of Christ as Word to Christ as the Living Bread descended from heaven (John 1:1, 6:41). As Scripture (the Word of God) or as sacramental bread and wine, Christ provides spiritual nourishment. Commentators often compared the "fractio hostiae" to the "apertio Scripturae," the fraction of the Host in the Mass to the opening of the Scriptures: both are revelations of Christ, the Word of God.[53]

The plot of the parable begins when the king (God) or the man (Christ or God) directs his servants to call guests to the feast. The commentators identify the servants first as patriarchs and prophets and later as apostles who have invited God's people into the covenant of Christ (prospectively, in the case of the Old Testament servants, through prophesies of Christ). The first guests scorn the invitation. In Luke's version they offer the excuses that, under the Law, permitted a man to stay home from the army: having just

52. This summary of medieval exegesis on the parable of the wedding feast is based on the following sources, which, unless otherwise noted, are commentaries on Matthew: Hilary, in *PL* 9:1041–44; Jerome, in CCSL 77:199–202; Augustine, *De consensu evangelistarum*, 2.51, in *PL* 34:1145 and *Sermones*, 112, in *PL* 38:643–47; Gregory the Great, *Homiliae in evangelia*, 2.36, 2.38, in *PL* 76:1265–74, 1281–93; Bede, in *PL* 92: 95–96; Christianus Druthmarus, monk of Corbie, in *PL* 106:1438–41; Rabanus Maurus, in *PL* 107: 1053–58; Paschasius Radbertus, in *PL* 120:739–49 (a particularly full and interesting interpretation); *Glossa ordinaria*, in *PL* 114:885; Rupert of Deutz, *De Trinitate et operibus ejus: De Sancto Spiritu*, 3.11, in *PL* 167:1651–52; Thomas Aquinas, *Catena aurea in quator Evangelia*, 1:316–21, 2:206–9; and Nicholas of Lyra, *Moralia super totam biblium*.

53. Henri de Lubac, *Corpus Mysticum*, pp. 80–82.

bought a farm or five yoke of oxen or having just married. The commentators offer moral readings of these excuses, associating such activities with various vices, such as pride, covetousness, and undue delight in earthly pleasures. The excuses given in Matthew are briefer, but similarly treated. To identify those who refuse the invitation (quite apart from their excuses), the commentators resort to historical allegory: those who refuse are the Jews. Sometimes they are both Jews and heretics. Those who accept when the invitation is made again are the gentiles.

In different ways Matthew and Luke pass judgment on those who refuse, judgments with eschatological import. When the host in Luke declares that none of the guests who refused will taste his supper, he means that none of them will be admitted to fellowship in Christ or to paradise. Matthew's parable is longer and more complex, in his version those who first refuse kill the king's servants and are in turn destroyed by his armies: so, said the commentators, again reading the parable as historical allegory, did the Jews kill Christ and his followers, which led to God's using the Roman armies of Vespasian and Titus to destroy the Temple and to disperse the Jews. This historical episode, like the destruction of Sodom and Gomorrah and the exile of the Jews to Babylon, two of the stories recounted in *Cleanness*, foreshadows the Last Judgment. Matthew, however, reserves his directly eschatological judgment for the guest who comes to the feast with the second and third groups of invited guests but does not wear a wedding garment. The wedding garments worn by the other guests represent, according to most commentators, a combination of innocence (cleanness) and charity; the commentators particularly emphasize charity, or good works, which are the fruit of the true Christian's innocence and grace. The tattered guest demonstrates his faith by responding to the king's invitation but shows an incomplete understanding of and commitment to its implications: he is without good works, imperfectly repentant, still a sinner whose sins make him a filthy and unfit guest. That the guests at the feast include both the clean and the filthy indicates that they represent the Church on earth, which includes both good and bad Christians.[54] The fate of the tattered guest serves as a warning to the earthly Church.

54. On the composition of the Church on earth, see Augustine, *De civ. Dei*, 1.35, 18.48–49; and Otto of Freising, *Chronicon*, prologues 5, 7, pp. 218–19, 295–96; Otto concludes that in his age there are not two

Matthew lets the weight of judgment in his version of the parable fall on the tattered guest: similarly, the judgments in the
*Cleanness* poet's narratives fall most heavily on those who, like
the tattered guest, pretend that to belong to God's order of creation places no obligation on them. The king in the parable commands his servants to bind the hands and feet of the ill-clothed
guest and cast him into the outer darkness: "There shall be weeping and gnashing of teeth" (Matt. 22:13). "There," as the commentators unanimously agree, is hell. The inner darkness, the
blindness of sin, precedes the outer darkness; but "there," in the
outer darkness of hell, the inner and outer realities are one.

"Many are called, but few are chosen" (Matt. 22:14): this dire
warning moves both the *Queste* author and the *Cleanness* poet to
deliver through the medium of fiction instruction in what it means
to be called and in what is necessary to be chosen. The wages of sin
is death, the everlasting night of the soul; but the alternative is
paradise, the everlasting celebration of the wedding feast, the
*visio Dei*. The contrast the *Queste* author and the *Cleanness*
poet make between these two destinies contains an implication of
urgency because they assume that they and each member of their
audiences has to choose a destiny, to choose heaven or hell.

---

cities, but only one, the city that is the Church and that contains both
elect and reprobate.

# 3

## The *Queste del Saint Graal* and Malory's *Tale of the Sankgreal*

The Vulgate cycle *Queste* and Sir Thomas Malory's translation of it, *The Tale of the Sankgreal*, interpret history through the paradigm of the vessel. They measure the significance of the lives of King Arthur's knights by standards that determine meaning in all historical time (from the Fall to the Last Judgment), standards that are summarized by the paradigm of the vessel. The *Queste* and the *Sankgreal*, then, offer a metahistorical vision, in the context of which the histories of individual knights become exemplary. They illustrate the pattern of judgment as well as the plot implicit in the sacrament of penance.

Few members of the *Queste*'s audience could hope to do better than Lancelot does, were they engaged in the quest for the Grail themselves. In fact, the quest for the Grail is an analogue of the Christian life; understood in that way, Lancelot's penance becomes an example for the audience to apply to itself. He becomes an Everyman figure.[1] This interpretation of the *Queste* and the *Sankgreal* involves a revision of the usual estimate of Lancelot's role in the *Queste* and implies a more sympathetic relationship between the *Sankgreal* and the *Queste* than many critics acknowledge.

Through their adventures in the Grail quest, King Arthur's knights have opportunities to choose between remaining as they are or changing. Lancelot changes. Gawain does not. Gawain al-

1. Several critics recognize this observation without exploring its implications—see Rosemond Tuve, *Allegorical Imagery*, p. 419; Albert Pauphilet, *Études sur la Queste del Saint Graal*, pp. 127–30, 133–34; and R. T. Davies, "Malory's Lancelot and the Noble Way of the World." Edmund Reiss, in *Sir Thomas Malory*, pp. 123–55, emphasizes Lancelot's partial success and his structural importance to the adventures of fulfillment.

ways refuses to confess, but Lancelot confesses and pursues a Christian life; and Malory makes the contrast between them explicit in one of the hermit's reproofs to Gawain near the end of the quest. Change is not, of course, required of the faithful, but proof through trials is. The steadfast Bors and the innocent Perceval are "proved in the fire" as they confront difficult situations that require them to make difficult choices. Though tempted, Perceval does not actually fornicate with his damsel in distress, but in recognition of his proneness to error he submits himself to a rigorous penance. Bors confesses as he begins his adventures, which test his capacity to keep the faith through an active fulfillment of its demands. Galahad perfectly fulfills every adventure reserved for him.

The author of the *Queste* solves the narrative problem of recounting the story of a number of characters in the usual way of thirteenth-century romance, by a strategy that scholars call "interlace" (*entrelacement*) or interweaving.[2] Once the knights depart from Arthur's court, the tale follows the wanderings of first one knight or group of knights and then another, reporting on those who undergo penance and those who refuse, until the three companions, Bors, Perceval, and Galahad, meet to go to Corbenic and then Sarras for the Grail masses. Eugène Vinaver finds an analogue for this kind of narrative both in the art of weaving—an analogy also made by medieval writers to describe writing[3]—and in the intricate designs in Romanesque illuminated capitals. The term *interlace* was adopted in response to a critical need for a vocabulary to describe a kind of narrative that Aristotle and his many, sometimes unselfconscious, disciples simply do not describe, as Vinaver wittily points out in *The Rise of Romance*.[4] The *Queste* is a simple example of this kind of narrative, since there are relatively few

2. See Ferdinand Lot, *Étude sur le Lancelot en prose*, pp. 17–28; Eugène Vinaver, *Malory*, pp. 24–25, 31, 34, and idem, *The Rise of Romance*, pp. 68–98.

3. See John Leyerle, "The Interlace Structure of Beowulf," pp. 4–7. Though it was perhaps not well known in the Middle Ages, one poem, the "Ciris," from the *Appendix Vergiliana*, ed. R. Ellis (1907; reprint, Oxford: Clarendon, 1957), contains an elaborate comparison of weaving and making poetry, lines 9, 21–41.

4. Vinaver, *Rise of Romance*, pp. 68–73; see also Larry D. Benson, "Sir Thomas Malory's Le Mort Darthur," pp. 91–107. Benson surveys recent Malory criticism, much of which is concerned with the problem of unity in the *Morte Darthur*, a problem that leads critics to comment incidentally on the *Sankgreal*.

major characters (or threads) and we follow each thread for a considerable distance before it disappears to come to the surface again further on; Malory often loosened the interlace design of the narratives he was translating, but he follows the loose interlace of the *Queste* exactly.

### The History of Lancelot: Key to the Relationship of the *Sankgreal* to the *Queste*

From a certain point of view, then, Lancelot is the hero of these quest romances.[5] Because Lancelot is a habitual sinner, his test, which involves renouncing the queen and committing himself to penance, is especially hard. He is less steady in his judgment than the other good knights and he cannot avoid making mistakes: yet he perseveres in his new life and finally sees a vision of the Grail. That he has rarely been acclaimed a hero of the *Queste* may be a fault of our critical vocabulary. What we have no names for we tend not to see, and we do not have any convenient vocabulary to describe a hierarchy of heroes.[6] Whatever the reason for Lancelot's insufficient reception by the critics, it must be redressed if we are to give a just account of the relationship of the *Sankgreal* to the *Queste*.

Vinaver avers that Malory treats Lancelot indulgently and obscures his failure in the Grail quest;[7] in fact, Malory is one of the best interpreters of the *Queste* and of Lancelot's heroism in relation to Galahad's. As Étienne Gilson has ably argued, Galahad has the characteristics of a saint;[8] he is as perfect as any man with

5. Charles Moorman argues that Lancelot is the protagonist but not the hero in "*The Tale of the Sankgreall*: Human Frailty," in R. M. Lumiansky, ed., *Malory's Originality*, p. 196.

6. C. S. Lewis, in a widely quoted review of *Sir Thomas Wyatt and Some Collected Studies* by E. K. Chambers, notes this problem and suggests Mark-Lancelot-Galahad as the hierarchy of heroes in the *Morte Darthur*. A. B. Ferguson notes in *The Indian Summer of English Chivalry*, pp. 42–58, that the knight turned religious was a stock figure, even in the fifteenth century; hence, for the knights to fall into a hierarchy of heroes according to their spiritual status should not seem odd.

7. Vinaver, *Malory*, pp. 70–84; Thomas Malory, *The Works of Sir Thomas Malory*, pp. lxxix–xcii, 1535–37 (hereafter cited as M by page number).

8. Étienne Gilson, "La Mystique de la grâce dans *La Queste del Saint Graal*," in *Les Idées et les lettres*, pp. 59–91.

the grace of God can be, and his perfection challenges the other knights. If we were reduced to allowing only one hero in the *Queste*, that hero would be Galahad; but not a few readers of the *Queste* find fault with Galahad because he is too perfect. To see that Perceval and Bors complement and shadow him does not entirely remove this objection to Galahad because Perceval and Bors share his qualities of saintliness. I doubt that the author of the *Queste* would have found these expressions of discomfort misplaced, though he probably expected his original audience to respond more sympathetically to saints: high medieval Christianity had a well-developed taste for the incomprehensibleness and outrageousness of saints that later ages have not often shared. The *Queste* author, however, offers these disgruntled readers a different sort of hero, a character in whom they might see themselves and their own most fruitful possibilities, and that character is Lancelot, an Everyman hero. His culminating adventures, sailing with Perceval's dead sister and Galahad and then visiting the Grail castle, foreshadow his fulfillment of the quest, understood, as it must be, as a quest for ultimate spiritual reward. In the Grail quest Lancelot sees and knows as much as he is capable of seeing and knowing, and his capacity is not negligible.

Behind the hierarchy of heroes in the *Queste* lies the biblical text, "In my Father's house there are many mansions" (John 14:2), interpreted in the Middle Ages to mean that there are degrees of celestial bliss, that every man is filled according to his capacity for happiness. Dante's *Paradiso*, on this principle, offers us ten degrees of Christian heroes. The three heroes of the *Queste*, Galahad, Perceval, and Bors, are analogues to the souls in the *Paradiso*. In addition, the souls in the *Purgatorio* must be accounted heroes, since they, too, are destined for paradise, and in Dante's imaginative world they cannot fail to reach their goal. Lancelot's place in the *Queste* is analogous to that of the souls in the *Purgatorio*. At the Resurrection of the Bodies, there are two states—damned and saved—rather than three; and those who have undertaken to participate in the conversion of penance will be among the saved. At the end of time, Dante's purgatory will disappear, its population absorbed into paradise. Like the souls in purgatory, Lancelot-as-exemplar occupies a middle position that will eventually disappear into the higher category of the saved; but since the *Queste*, unlike the *Commedia*, tells a story this side of death and since in life change for good or evil remains a possibility, Lancelot's achievement in the *Queste* is only provisional, while the end of the souls in the *Purgatorio* is assured.[9]

Malory, in giving Lancelot a more prominent role at the end of the quest than did his French source, places him among the successful questers:

> And whan they had etyn the kynge made grete clerkes to com before hym, for cause they shulde cronycle of the hyghe adventures of the good knyghtes. So whan sir Bors had tolde hym of the hyghe aventures of the Sankgreall such as had befalle hym and his three felowes, which were sir Launcelot, Percivale and sir Galahad and hymselff, than sir Launcelot tolde the adventures of the Sangreall that he had sene. And all thys was made in grete bookes and put up in almeryes at Salysbury. (M, 1036)

Malory's strategy at the end of the quest does not substantially alter the story he is translating, although Vinaver, for example, argues to the contrary, and his criticism has become the point of reference in the ongoing debate over Lancelot in Malory studies.

The author of the *Queste* attributes the stories of the Grail adventures to the records collected by King Arthur from the knights themselves, in order to enhance the value of his romance as witness.[10] The French text implies that the knights have told their stories as they returned to court, so that when Bors returns last, his is the only story that remains to be told and he is the only

9. There is no major recent attempt to study the analogies between the *Queste* and the *Commedia*; Lizette Andrews Fisher, in *The Mystic Vision in the Grail Legend and in the Divine Comedy* (1917), emphasizes the Eucharist as a vehicle to the mystic vision.

10. On autobiography as witness, see Dante Alighieri, *Il Convivio*, 1.2.12–17, pp. 5–6. On the concluding narrative device and the related question of authorship, see Gaston Paris, *La Littérature française au moyen âge (XIe–XIVe siècle)*, pp. 101–2; Lot, *Étude sur le Lancelot en prose*, pp. 126–29; and James Douglas Bruce, *The Evolution of Arthurian Romance from the Beginnings down to the Year 1300*, pp. 368–73, 419–25. For a convenient summary of theories of authorship in the last three books of the Vulgate cycle, see Fanni Bogdanow, *The Romance of the Grail*, p. 7, n. 3. I do not find Jean Frappier's "architect" theory of multiple authorship persuasive (see his *Étude sur la Mort le Roi Artu*, pp. 122–46, 440–55, and Roger Sherman Loomis, ed., *Arthurian Literature in the Middle Ages*, pp. 315–17); I find sympathetic Alexandre Micha's position in "L'Esprit du *Lancelot-Graal*."

witness specifically named. By naming Lancelot as well, Malory emphasizes the exemplary importance of his story of penance.[11] Both texts use this episode to insist on the autobiographical nature of the old chronicles and on their value as true histories, to be read, like any other history in the Middle Ages, for its examples of good and evil.

In contrast to Vinaver, who believes that Malory secularizes the *Queste* through his treatment of Lancelot, I suggest that by naming Lancelot along with Bors in the final scene of the *Sankgreal*, Malory calls the attention of his audience to the value of penance and makes explicit a message that is implicit in the *Queste*. Vinaver and I agree, however, that Malory's *Sankgreal* "still preserves the essential characteristics of its source. The hermits are fewer in number and less explicit in their utterances; but there are still quite enough of them, and they are far from having abandoned the habit of expounding each adventure in the bitterest detail" (M, 1538).[12] My disagreement with Vinaver on the *Sankgreal* is based on my interpretation of the *Queste*, which gives Lancelot a more positive role in that text than Vinaver allows him.

That readers find Malory's text different from the *Queste* in a qualitative as well as a quantitative sense is, nevertheless, beyond dispute. Since in the rest of this chapter I will primarily be discussing the two romances as one, I take this opportunity to recognize and account for their differences. What, if not the indulgent treatment of Lancelot or the secularization of the quest, makes them different?

In his translation, Malory drastically cuts the internal commen-

11. But see R. M. Lumiansky, "*The Tale of Lancelot and Guenevere*: Suspense," in *Malory's Originality*, pp. 209–10, who assumes that Malory implies that Lancelot confesses his adultery to Arthur and that Arthur forgives him. None of the writers, including Malory, who carry forward the Arthurian story to the death of Arthur, share this assumption.

12. Vinaver has always been an unsympathetic critic of the *Queste* and the *Sankgreal*; see Lewis, review of *Sir Thomas Wyatt and Some Collected Stories* by E. K. Chambers; and the exchange between C. S. Lewis, "The English Prose *Morte*," and Eugène Vinaver, "On Art and Nature: A Letter to C. S. Lewis," in J. A. W. Bennett, ed., *Essays on Malory*, esp. pp. 14–20, 31–34, in which Vinaver expresses greater regard for the *Queste* than for the *Sankgreal*; and, more recently, D. S. Brewer, "The Present Study of Malory," p. 85. For a different view from Vinaver's on the relationship between earthly and celestial chivalry, see Jean Frappier, "Le Graal et la chevalrie."

tary found in the *Queste*; as a result, in the *Sankgreal* events themselves carry a greater part of the burden of establishing their significance and shaping our attitude toward them.[13] The religious
who explain events and prophesy to the knights still appear, but
they do no more than hint at or sketch in the interpretations that
they offer in elaborate and pleasingly ordered detail in the *Queste*.
Malory usually retains enough of their comments to guide his readers to the conceptual framework within which an event is to be
understood. For example, he omits the parable of the talents from
the hermit's discourse to Lancelot,[14] although Malory's hermit lists
Lancelot's gifts and tells him how thankful he should be to God
for them (M, 897). Sometimes Malory provides brief explicit references to biblical passages that the French text explains in detail.
In the process of cutting, Malory seems to have assumed that one
or comparatively few references to a concept or interpretation
would suffice to convey a point. In fact, the nature of his cuts does
make us attend sharply to the interpretive hints and statements
that he makes. When Vinaver accuses Malory of not respecting the
difference between earthly and celestial knighthood (M, 1535-37),
he ignores Malory's explicit comments on the difference between
the Grail quest and ordinary quests. Vinaver assumes that Malory
found the spiritual quest an anomaly among his Arthurian romances, so he lends great significance to those places in the text
where Malory changes or omits references to the celestial quest;
makes the knights refer to King Arthur in addition to Christ or,
more rarely, instead of Christ; or sets virtuous living—rather than
chastity—as the prerequisite for success in the quest. But, that
Malory preserves references to the celestial quest and to Christ
argues that he does not change the nature of the quest. In omitting
the commentary, he tends to vary his own interpretations in a way
that preserves the resonance the *Queste* establishes through associated concepts: for example, the *Queste* treats chastity, cleanness, and sinlessness as synonymous conditions on which virtuous
living depends; because these concepts are interrelated (as the
*Cleanness* poet also acknowledges), Malory is not in fact changing

---

13. Note, however, that some of the differences between the *Sankgreal*
and the Pauphilet *Queste* may be attributable to the particular (unidentified) manuscript that Malory used. See M, 1534-35, 1542-84.

14. *La Queste del Saint Graal*, pp. 63-64 (hereafter cited as *Q* by page
number).

his idea of the quest when at any given point in the *Sankgreal* he allows one of them to stand for all.

Malory develops the larger historical context in which the Grail quest occurs less carefully than the *Queste* author does and shows more interest than the earlier author in the psychology of his characters, especially Lancelot: this shift in the balance of interests is one of the most significant differences between the two romances. It reflects the different dominant interests of the early thirteenth and the late fifteenth centuries. Malory's presentation of Lancelot's preparatory adventures deepens our sense of Lancelot's individuality, allowing us to see more clearly than in the *Queste* Lancelot's interior struggle to "forsake synne." Malory's omission of a passage in the *Queste* that explicitly connects the three successive Christian fellowships—Christ's Table, Joseph of Arimathea's Table of the Holy Grail, and the Round Table—indicates Malory's relative lack of interest in history: he preserves enough of the *Queste*'s allusions to the past to maintain the general structure of history articulated there, but his allusions to the past are less precise and less detailed.

Through the explicit connection of the three fellowships, the *Queste* implies that the Grail mass at Corbenic, celebrated at first by Josephes, Joseph of Arimathea's son (Table of the Holy Grail) and then by Christ (Last Supper), is a movement from the Round Table (fellowship of the world) back to the table of Joseph and Josephes and finally back to Christ's Table, to the fullness of time that is both the middle and the end of history.[15] Malory seems less concerned with the witty perceptions of the structure of history that delight the author of the *Queste*; but like him, Malory perceives the fulfillment of the Grail quest as an adventure reserved for the knights of the Round Table. In both texts the quest has a special relationship to Arthur's fellowship: its fulfillment brings honor to the fellowship as well as a challenge to the fellows to cleanse and perfect themselves.

Placed in the context of fifteenth-century English literature, the *Sankgreal* stands out as a text that comprehends its source remarkably well, even as it shares with other fifteenth-century literary texts a diminished interest in abstract philosophical and religious questions. If we compare to the *Sankgreal* texts like *Kingis Quhair*,

15. Alexandre Micha, "La Table ronde chez Robert de Boron et dans la *Queste del Saint Graal*," p. 130.

which uses and perverts the Boethian philosophical tradition of poetry, or like Dunbar's poems, which use Boethian and religious traditions accurately enough but with more care for the verse than for the content, we must conclude that Malory has kept faith with the *Queste* to a degree unusual in his time. There is an intellectual flaccidity in this fifteenth-century literature: the old concepts and arguments are there, often in a gracefully disguised yet horrible muddle; but the energy has gone out of them and the interest in penitential aspects of the older spirituality has to some degree evaporated. Three centuries separate Malory from the beginning of the twelfth-century penitential movement, and we should not be surprised that Malory seems to have understood and accepted the ideas implicit in penance without finding them as urgently in need of explanation as did his thirteenth-century predecessor.

In the end, I agree with Vinaver that Malory achieves something different from the French *Queste*, even if I disagree with his explanations of the difference. Through the use of dialogue, through the looser sentence structure behind the rhythms of his prose, through more sharply perceived images, and through his emphasis on events, Malory makes a different sort of imaginative world.[16] The resonance of his text comes not so much from the explanations of spiritual mysteries that give meaning and connection to events in the *Queste* as from the mystery of the events themselves. In the *Queste* the religious rationalize events through a transcendently directed Christian hermeneutics that clarifies the meaning of every incident; this hermeneutics is itself so full of mystery that it reintroduces a sense of mystery into the events it explains. The mystery of the *Queste* is thus the mystery of coherence. The *Sankgreal*, by refusing to give a fully rational interpretation of events, leaves the mystery in the events so that they seem always to be more significant than any explicit interpretation offered for them. The result is a fictional world more inexplicable than one in which every event can be read in a satisfyingly significant way. The result, in other words, is a more modern fictional world.

Any adequate assessment of Malory's *Sankgreal* depends on a reading of the *Queste*, but none of the available readings seems to

16. See Eugène Vinaver's introduction and commentaries in M, lvii–lxiv, lxviii, 1534–84; see also P. J. C. Field, *Romance and Chronicle*, pp. 67, 129.

me to have clearly grasped the narrative structure together with the significance of events and interpretations in the *Queste*. There are, however, several important and helpful studies: Albert Pauphilet's *Études sur la Queste del Saint Graal*, Gilson's essay on grace and Galahad, Frederick Locke's primarily typological study, Rosemond Tuve's analysis of the romance as allegory, Tzvetan Todorov's essay discussion of structural principles in the narrative of the *Queste*, and Esther Casier Quinn's essay on the Tree of Life and Solomon's ship.[17] The discussion that follows offers a reading of the *Queste* that is also applicable to the *Sankgreal*: the differences in the two texts are not great enough to require separate interpretations. Wherever possible in the rest of the chapter, I will refer to the parallel text in Malory, and whenever his changes or omissions are significant, I will remark on them.

## Call to the Quest for the Grail: A Search for Meaning

In the view of the author of the *Queste*, who is extending and fulfilling the vision of Robert de Boron, to understand the quest for the Grail requires nothing less than understanding universal history. As the quest itself educates the Grail knights, so the account of their adventures educates us to see significant patterns in universal history. Christianity begins with the Pentecost, and the quest begins on Pentecost and represents a renewed call to spiritual life. The *Queste* gradually unfolds the significance of history through the use of typologies, most of which are biblical. The legend of the Tree of Life contains the stories of the first sinners, Adam and Eve and Cain, whose sins are partially redressed through the Exodus and Solomon's Temple and finally redeemed by Christ, whom David prefigures and Galahad refigures. Each of the three tables in the *Queste*, the table of Joseph of Arimathea, Arthur's Round Table, and the table of the Grail companions, bears a typological relationship to the eucharistic table, itself an analogue of the table of the wedding feast. The author of the *Queste* models his narrative on the parable of the wedding feast, which he interprets as an eschatological event; he allows Arthur and Guine-

17. See above, nn. 1, 8: both Pauphilet and Gilson emphasize Cistercian influence on the *Queste*; Frederick Locke, *The Quest for the Holy Grail*; Tzvetan Todorov, "La Quête du récit"; and Esther Casier Quinn, "The Quest of Seth, Solomon's Ship and the Grail."

vere to understand intuitively the eschatological thrust of the quest for the Grail, for they lament in the beginning the knights who will not come back.

Pentecost, a conventional feast day for the beginning of Arthurian adventures, has no special significance in ordinary romances; in contrast, the *Queste* author makes the choice of this date an important element in his patterning of history.[18] Pentecostal signs accompany the appearances of Galahad and the Grail at the beginning of the *Queste*, and these signs and events give definition to the situation in the romance by reissuing the challenge to faith and penance instituted in the first Pentecost. Gawain recognizes the implications of these events as a call to the Grail quest, but he never understands the quest's spiritual nature, as Lancelot eventually does. First in a prophetic dream, then in event, Lancelot learns that the parable of the wedding feast, which sets as a goal for man the vision of God, is the model by which the quest must be understood. The *Queste* and the *Sankgreal* define the difficulties in achieving this quest by using Old Testament events: the Fall, the Exodus, and Solomon's Temple. These events serve as analogies to the temptations and achievements of the Grail knights, analogies that govern the interpretation of events given in the *Queste* and the *Sankgreal*. In short, the *Queste* author develops a meaningful pattern of history, which provides a context for the Grail adventures.

The mysterious appearances of Galahad and the Grail at Arthur's court during the celebration of Pentecost imply a connection between the Grail and Galahad that is made explicit in the visions of the Grail at the end of the quest, but in the beginning the Grail stands as a challenge that by right Galahad must and will perfectly meet. Just after the first dish of the midday meal has been served, the doors and windows of Arthur's palace shut by themselves, and an old man leads Galahad into the closed chamber —no one knows how—and says to the court: "Pes soit o vos" (Pees be with you, fayre lordys!), *Q*, 7; M, 859. These words, spoken on Galahad's behalf, echo the words of Christ to his disciples—"Peace be to you"—when he mysteriously appears to them after the Crucifixion (see John 20:19, 21–22); the marvel of the closed doors and windows suggests the Incarnation, imagined by medieval theo-

18. See Locke, *Quest*, pp. 40–64, who emphasizes liturgical patterns in the *Queste*.

logians and poets as the descent of Christ into the Virgin (a figure for the Church) whose womb is like a closed hall. These allusions point to the significance of Galahad's entrance, that it is an intrusion of grace into the Round Table fellowship. Later (*Q*, 78) Perceval's aunt interprets Galahad's appearance as a type of the Pentecost: Galahad, she explains, wears red because on the first Pentecost God appeared in the likeness of flames. That same day Galahad, who has been introduced as "le Chevalier Desirré," a title that echoes a prophecy of the Messiah (Aggeus 2:8), completes the adventure of the sword in the stone by drawing it out, a sign that he has begun his saintly mission as exemplar to his companions and minister of justice.

At the evening meal on the same day, the Grail appears, introduced by the Pentecostal signs of thunder and a brilliant shaft of sunlight (cf. Acts 2:2–4a), which signal an intrusion of the Holy Ghost (grace) into Arthur's court. Struck dumb by these wonders, the knights are fed by the Grail, which is fragrant but concealed; each one gets the food he desires. When it disappears, Arthur and his knights regain their speech and praise God, and Gawain vows to undertake a quest to see the Grail openly in its "vraie semblance." Neither he nor most of those who take up the quest understand that its requirements are virtually the same as those Peter sets out in answer to the Jews who want to know how to respond to the first Pentecost:

> But Peter said to them: Do penance; and be baptized every
> one of you in the name of Jesus Christ, for the remission
> of your sins. And you shall receive the gift of the Holy Ghost.
> For the promise is to you and to your children and to all
> that are far off, whomsoever the Lord our God shall call.
> (Acts 2:38–39)

As the first Pentecost called the Jews to purity and faith, so the Pentecostal signs accompanying Galahad and the Grail call the Round Table knights to penance: they are baptized but sinful Christians, a condition indicated by their speechlessness before the Grail, which contrasts with the gift of tongues given to the apostles at the first Pentecost. The grace signified by the appearances of Galahad and the Grail to the Round Table fellowship is sufficient, rather than efficacious; it represents a call but not, in itself, an election.

The knights do not at first understand why they must be pure to achieve the quest; they do not understand that they need faith to be made pure. A hermit warns them at the beginning that no knight may take his lady on this quest, which is a quest for spiritual reward, "qu'il ne chiee en pechié mortel" (Q, 19; cf. M, 868–69); sexual purity is a sign of ritual purity, required in its most intense form—abstinence—of those who would succeed in the Grail quest. Without it, as Gawain discovers, the questing knights find no adventures at all because, as the Queste implies, the unclean cannot do good works. An extraordinary adventure requires an extraordinary ascesis.

These requirements of faith and purity and the nature of the goal of the quest become clear to Lancelot and the Grail companions, Bors, Perceval, and Galahad, through the histories they hear and discover in their quest. As Todorov has demonstrated in his analysis of the Queste's narrative, the Grail quest is a search for sens (direction); to be more precise, it is a quest for the meaning of history. The last three books in the Vulgate cycle loosely recount the history of Lancelot and of Arthur's court, but the Queste alone provides the theoretical structure that establishes the significance of history for the rest of the cycle. The popularity of the last three books of the cycle—the Prose Lancelot (or the Prose Tristan), the Queste, and the Mort Artu, which are usually connected in the manuscript tradition and were apparently read as connected works in the Middle Ages[19]—must have depended on the taste of medieval audiences for history, especially fictional and universal history. The Queste recounts the story of the beginning of history in paradise and, in the advent of Galahad and the judgments on Carcelois and the leprous lady, foreshadows its ending. Through the interrelationships among these passages, several other biblical events, and several episodes from Christian history, the Queste provides a universal context for the Arthurian cycle by placing the Round Table fellowship into the pattern of sacred history. As we might expect, the Queste values history, that is, each man's time in the world, as an opportunity for every man to address himself to the problems of living in the world; and it finds the significance of each man's life, and hence of history, in the divine judgment made

19. For a catalogue of manuscripts of the Vulgate cycle and its parts, with references to further studies, see Brian Woledge, Bibliographie des romans et nouvelles en prose française antérieurs à 1500, pp. 71–97.

upon that life as it ends. The fulfillment of the Grail quest and the subsequent dissolution of the Round Table fellowship in the *Mort Artu* (prophesied to Gawain in the *Queste* through a dream [*Q*, 149, 155–57; M, 942, 946–47]) punctuates an age within Christian history and becomes a type of the ending of Christian history.

The *Queste* author uses the first of four concluding events, the adventure of Solomon's ship, to bring his Grail knights, Bors, Perceval, and Galahad, and their lady, Perceval's sister, into relationship with the past. This adventure gives coherence, retrospectively, to the fragmented histories the knights have heard earlier in the quest and reveals the significance of their own adventures. Traveling by sea, they find Solomon's ship, a marvelous vessel constructed by Solomon and his wife as a message to Galahad, the last of Solomon's lineage. Identified as the direct heir of Solomon, Galahad takes his place in Christian history, and through their companionship with him the other knights become also heirs of biblical history.

The message hidden in a purse that the Grail companions find on Solomon's ship relates to the *Queste* author's patterning of history. The stories of the Fall and of the construction of Solomon's ship, contained in the message of the purse, describe two of the three Old Testament events that the *Queste* author uses to shape his theory of history (the third is the Exodus). When Perceval reads the message enclosed in the purse, the four learn not only about the origin of the ship but also about its relics, chief of which is the three-colored frame built over the bed from the wood of the Tree of Life. To explain the colors, the message recounts the beginning of history from Adam's and Eve's fall, expulsion from paradise, and mating, to the fratricide of Cain.[20]

The changing colors of the Tree of Life, white to green to red, express in symbolic terms the mutability of the fallen world. The Tree of Life grows in the fallen world from a twig of the Tree of Knowledge that Eve has carried with her from paradise, to signify that the inheritance lost through a woman will be regained through a woman. First the Tree of Life springs up white, in sign of Adam's and Eve's virginity; in response to their mating it turns

20. In *The Quest of Seth for the Oil of Life*, Esther Casier Quinn concludes that the *Queste-Sankgreal* legend of the Tree of Life is probably a self-conscious alteration of the legend; see also Quinn, "The Quest of Seth."

green to symbolize fertility. The slips taken from the parent tree take root and flourish like their parent, white or green, until Cain kills Abel and the Tree of Life turns red. Slips taken from the red Tree of Life wither and die, at once a symbol of the blood-pollution of murder and a prefiguration of the unique sacrifice of Christ. The succession of events associated with the colors ends with Cain's fratricide, bringing the paradigm of history to a conclusion with the first fulfillment of God's curse of mortality. By ending there, the *Queste* author places a burden of significance on the crime of murder, more particularly on that of fratricide. He implies that if the problem of the individual in the fallen world is to overcome the concupiscence of Eve, represented in the *Queste* narrative as sexual sin, the problem of society and history is to overcome the urge to murder. The *Queste* story of the Fall authorizes the typology of Eve and the typology of Cain and reveals the great problem of history, in whatever time, to be the achievement of social order, of a life of justice and harmony. This order can be realized only when the sins of Eve and Cain are overcome, as they are by the good knights. In short, to overcome the effects of the Fall, which is to succeed in the Grail quest and achieve the goal of restoring harmony between man and man and God and man, requires faith and purity.

The *Queste* author gives special prominence in his Old Testament allusions to two events, the Exodus and the building of Solomon's Temple, because he regards them as major attempts to resolve the problems initiated by the Fall. Both of these events are related to the adventure of Solomon's ship, as I will show, although the link with the Exodus is not explicit.

By concentrating his allusions to the Exodus in the preparatory adventures of Perceval, whose chief temptation corresponds to Eve's sin, the *Queste* author implies that the Exodus represents to him the first major historical attempt to resolve the problem of Eve's sin. The Exodus was actually a complex event, often described in three stages and usually interpreted as an allegory of Christian conversion. The departure from Egypt, a land of fornications and idolatry, and the crossing of the Red Sea represent the first stage of conversion, the turning away from sin that foreshadows baptism and penance. The wilderness journey, during which God fed the Israelites with manna, prefigures Christian life in the world, during which God sustains his own with bread from heaven, with the Word that is Christ (see John 6:31–35, 47–58). Finally, crossing over the Jordan and into the land of milk and honey points toward the last stage of Christian conversion, the passage into the eschatological kingdom of heaven.[21] The first stage of the Exodus, which Perceval repeats when he rejects his temptress, establishes the Exodus as a partial resolution to the problem of Eve's sin. The second demonstrates that God sustains those who reject Eve's sin, as he does Perceval. More generally, the bread and wine of the Eucharist and the words of Scripture fulfill the promise implicit in God's provision of manna to the Israelites, that God will feed his people. The basic pattern of the Exodus story—of penitential exile and divine food—is repeated several times during Perceval's preparatory adventures in the stories he hears of early Christian history.

Joseph of Arimathea's people cannot find any food when they land in England, except for twelve loaves, which Joseph sets on a table by the Grail: miraculously, there is enough for all to eat (*Q*, 75). When the pagan British throw Josephes and other Christians into prison for forty days (analogous to the Israelites' forty years in the desert), they are fed by the Grail (*Q*, 84). In his exile on the rocky island, Perceval finds both material and spiritual sustenance in the words of his angelic visitor (*Q*, 105–6, 115; M, 916). These analogues of Exodus, set in the context of Perceval's temptation to sexual sin, reflect the association in Christian thought of eating and sex: rejecting the pleasure of sexual sin, the Christian finds sustenance and delight in eating the Word.

The building of Solomon's Temple is the second Old Testament event through which the *Queste* author establishes his vision of history. As Quinn has argued in her essay on the *Queste-Sankgreal* legend of the Tree of Life, Solomon's ship is Solomon's Temple allegorically transformed to suit the needs of the Grail romance.[22] Here, we find the *Queste* author manipulating vessel imagery in

21. On the typology of Exodus, see Jean Daniélou, *From Shadows to Reality*, pp. 153–226. For medieval literary use of the Exodus typology and further information on the patristic tradition, see Charles Singleton, "In Exitu Israel de Aegypto," *78th Annual Report of the Dante Society* (1960), reprint, in John Freccero, ed., *Dante*, pp. 102–21; John Freccero, "Dante's Prologue Scene," and idem, "The River of Death: *Inferno* II, 108."

22. Quinn, "The Quest of Seth," pp. 193, 216; see also Pauphilet, *Études*, pp. 144–54; and Locke, *Quest*, pp. 82–85.

order to make the historical connections in his story clear: thinking of the Temple as a reincarnation of the Garden of Eden and the arks of Noah and Moses and as a foreshadowing of the Church that is the vessel of salvation, the *Queste* author transforms Solomon's great feat of construction into a shipbuilding. Solomon and his treacherous wife cooperate to build the ship—which signifies the social harmony it will contain—so that it may be found by Galahad, who will then know not only his lineage but also his special role in history: as Solomon built the Temple, heir to the arks of Noah and Moses, so Galahad will fulfill the mission of the Church instituted by Christ and carried forward by Joseph of Arimathea and his son, the bishop Josephes. The cooperation of Solomon and his wife foreshadows the companionship of the Grail knights and thus demonstrates why the building of Solomon's ship (Temple) expresses a social harmony that resolves the problem of Cain's sin. The ship (Temple) is an image of community.

Solomon's ship presents itself to Galahad, Bors, Perceval, and his sister as a test of faith and purity: through words emblazoned on its side, it promises safety to the perfect and danger to the imperfect. The ship, then, is an image of the Church of the elect. To enter her is to enter the Promised Land. Although the *Queste* author makes no explicit reference to the Exodus in the adventure of Solomon's ship, its relationship to the Exodus is unmistakable: cleansing by a passage through water (Red Sea; baptism; penance, with its tears of contrition) and faith tested by exile (forty years in the wilderness, years in the wasteland) are the prerequisites for entrance into the Promised Land and into the ship. The *Queste* author implies through his choice and presentation of Old Testament events that to avoid the sin of Cain a man must overcome his tendency to Eve's sin, because sexual sin leaves a man corrupted and inevitably leads him to commit such aggressively corrupt acts as murder. Before a man can hope to participate in a harmonious and just community, to be part of a resolution of the problem of Cain's sin, he must overcome his lust: he must pass through an Exodus experience before he can enter the kingdom of the chosen people where a just social order becomes a reality.

A just social order must include both men and women to show that sexuality does not threaten it; hence, the presence of Perceval's sister on Solomon's ship. Contrary to the hermit's command at the beginning of the *Queste* that to keep themselves from mortal sin the knights must not take their ladies with them, the presence of Perceval's sister neither injures nor seduces the three companions because both they and she, through a type of Exodus experience, have purged themselves of the tendency to sexual sin before they board the ship.

The difference between the imperfect resolutions of the Fall in Old Testament history and the perfect resolutions achieved by Galahad and his companions is due to Christ. What was a shadow becomes in Christ a reality; what was a promise contained in the Old Testament events is fulfilled in him. Christ responds perfectly to the demands of God, thus revealing, as no previous encounter between God and man had, what that relationship can be and ought to be. By instituting the sacraments of baptism, penance, and the Eucharist, Christ makes available to man grace sufficient to overcome the impulse to sin and to join with him in a fellowship of love and justice. He gives meaning, retrospectively and prospectively, to history, on the one hand revealing that the significance of the Exodus and the Temple is spiritual, on the other hand making a perfect realization of this spiritual significance possible by becoming the source of grace and the exemplar of righteousness.

Henri de Lubac discusses Christ as the fulfillment of history in terms of Christ as the "Verbum Abbreviatum," the Word Incarnate who contains all meaning, while all other things have meaning only by virtue of their relationship to the Word. Lubac's presentation of Christ as the principle of history summarizes medieval biblical commentary, but such a summary accounts only by implication for the structure of history presented in the *Queste*.[23] A. C. Charity, whose interest in Dante's *Commedia* led him into the study of biblical typology, explains more clearly the relation of Christian history to Christ and the Old Testament. Charity argues that types contain both an indicative and an imperative: they simultaneously reveal an encounter between man and God and challenge men to conform themselves spiritually and ethically to the types of righteousness. As Christ fulfills all types, so he becomes the revelation and the challenge to all men living under the new dispensation. These men, like the men of the Old Testa-

---

23. Henri de Lubac, *Exégèse médiévale*, vol. 1, pt. 2, pp. 181–97.

ment, may be related to Christ as subfulfillment is to fulfillment.[24] I take Charity's discussion of typology to be as essential an introduction to the study of the *Queste* as it is to the *Commedia*.

The *Queste* author represents the centrality of Christ to history in what may seem a curious way: he rarely speaks directly of Christ until Christ has manifested himself to the knights in their visions of the Grail at the end of the quest. Up to that point, Christ is indirectly present in the text through Galahad, whom the religious explicitly compare to Christ ("de semblance ne mie de hautece" [*Q*, 38]), and through the Grail, which is implicitly associated with him.

Galahad is the subfulfillment of Christ. The *Queste* author explicitly develops the typology of Christ and Galahad, not only in a comparison of Galahad and David to Christ, but also through the similarly corrupt condition of society before the advents of Christ and of Galahad, both of whom God sends to deliver his people (*Q*, 38). The *Queste* author assumes, then, a retrospective as well as a prospective typology that is fulfilled in Christ: Galahad and David meet in Christ.

Galahad challenges the other knights of the Round Table to conform themselves to him, conformity to him being conformity to Christ. Bors, Perceval, and Lancelot respond to Galahad, the living witness of Christ, demonstrating the value of his witness and becoming in turn witnesses to the rest of the Round Table. Galahad's companionship with the other knights is necessary to the full realization of his role: he must participate in the realization of social harmony in Christian history. The stories of earlier Christian history, which the companions also discover on Solomon's ship and which I will discuss in detail later, recount earlier attempts to enter the promised society of Solomon's ship. But just as the Exodus and Solomon's Temple must wait upon Christ for their implications to be fulfilled, so these events in Christian history must wait upon Galahad for their intentions to be realized.

Perceval's aunt explains Christian history to him as a succession of fellowships (Malory omits this passage). The first fellowship is that of Christ and his disciples. Perceval's aunt's description of the Lord's table is a rare instance of a religious alluding directly to Christ, but it is comparatively brief. Like the monk (*Q*, 38) who

24. A. C. Charity, *Events and Their Afterlife*, pp. 1–164.

interprets Galahad as a type of Christ, she uses a Davidic prophecy to describe the Lord's table, which reduces the direct focus on Christ and establishes his centrality largely by prospective and retrospective references.

Of the second table Perceval's aunt has much more to say. She introduces it as a subfulfillment of the first Christian fellowship: "Aprés cele table [la Table Jhesucrist] fu une autre table en semblance et en remembrance de lui. Ce fu la Table dou Saint Graal, dont si grant miracle furent jadis veu en cest païs au tens Joseph d'Arimacie, au comencement que crestientez fu aportee en ceste terre" (*Q*, 74–75). She tells Perceval about the miracle of the twelve loaves that fed Joseph's company of four thousand in the wilderness of Logres and about the Sieges Redoutez reserved for Joseph's son, Josephes, and dangerous to all others (cf. the Siege Perilleus of the Round Table). Implicitly, the Table of the Holy Grail in Christian history corresponds to the Exodus in Old Testament history, but the direction of the journey is reversed in Christian history: instead of going from west to east, it goes from east to west. In the Exodus the chosen people, in order to become a pure people, separated themselves from the pagans and moved from Egypt to Israel; now, in Christian time, Joseph takes the Grail to the pagans to convert them, carrying it from Israel to Sarras and Logres. All the stories told in the *Queste* about Joseph of Arimathea and his company emphasize the work of conversion, and the fruit of this work becomes manifest in the third Christian fellowship, that of the Round Table.

The Round Table, Perceval's aunt tells Perceval, was designed by Merlin to signify, through its roundness, the whole world. It attracts knights from all over the earth, both Christians and pagans. Those who become its companions consider that they have gained the whole world and no longer need their natural families, as Perceval's own case illustrates. "Car puis que vos partistes de vostre mere et len vos ot fet compaignon de la Table Reonde, n'eustes vos talent de revenir ça, ainz fustes maintenant sorpris de la douçor et de la fraternité qui doit estre entre cels qui en sont compaignon" (*Q*, 77). Here Perceval's aunt echoes Christ's rejection of his natural family and his definition of his spiritual family, "whosoever shall do the will of my Father that is in heaven, he is my brother, and sister, and mother" (Matt. 12:50; see also Luke 8:19–21). The Round Table is characterized chiefly by the fra-

ternity it establishes,[25] which Merlin implies will be perfected by
those of its companions who achieve the quest of the Grail; it is
an analogue of the Church.

Augustine's observation that the Church contains both good
and bad Christians[26] applies to the Round Table fellowship as
well. Perfect fellowship is only possible among the elect, that is,
only among those who can achieve the adventure of Solomon's
ship, which represents the Church of the elect. The Round Table,
then, is to the companions of Solomon's ship as the earthly Church
is to the Church of the elect. Since Galahad is a type of Christ,
Galahad's witness is not complete until he has established a companionship worthy of comparison to the fellowship of Christ and
his disciples.

Malory omits Perceval's aunt's account of the Lord's table and
the Table of the Holy Grail, which makes the pattern of Christian history in the Sankgreal less explicit than it is in the Queste.
Nevertheless, the pattern—Exodus (Joseph of Arimathea in the
wilderness), Solomon's Temple (Galahad on Solomon's ship), and
the reference of all these events to Christ—is apparent in the Sankgreal. When Malory says that the fulfillment of the Grail quest
brings honor upon Arthur's Round Table, he is making a point
that is implicit in the Queste, but the Queste does not risk stating
the case in that way: the achievement of the Grail quest perfectly
realizes the intentions of the Round Table fellowship, and our
attention ought to focus on the achievement, on the Grail Table
at Corbenic and Sarras rather than on the intention represented
in the Round Table. Malory implies that fulfillment of the Grail
quest realizes the intentions of the Round Table, but his emphasis
on the Round Table opens a way to misread the Sankgreal by
overstressing the earthly perspective.

25. Alfred C. Kellogg argues that douçor suggests God's grace and is
to be distinguished from the concept of fraternité; while this interpretation seems correct, fraternité as it is here conceived is only possible
with grace and is the outward manifestation of grace. Kellogg claims that
Malory's failure to translate douçor is evidence of his failure to understand and respect the spiritual ideas of the Queste; see "Malory and
Color Symbolism: Two Notes on His Translation of the Queste del
Saint Graal," in Chaucer, Langland, Arthur, pp. 14–16.

26. Augustine, De civitate Dei (The City of God), 1.35, 18.49 (hereafter
cited as De civ. Dei).

The pattern of history proposed by the *Queste* stands revealed by the end of the adventure of Solomon's ship, which is the first narrative climax in the *Queste* and the *Sankgreal*; but its principle, Christ, is not manifest until the knights see him in their visions of the Grail. Until then, Christ is manifest to the knights only in shadows or types, both in their adventures and in the histories the religious tell them. In the last and culminating adventures, the three successive visions of the Grail, Christ miraculously appears before the knights in his incarnate form. In these episodes the knights experience the *visio Dei*, which biblical commentary understood to be the subject of the parable of the wedding feast.

The *Queste* author models his narrative on the parable of the wedding feast: the appearance of the Grail at the beginning of the romance signifies an invitation to come to the feast; the preparatory adventures define the nature of the spiritual garments (clean or unclean, good or bad) worn by the knights as they approach the feast; and the final visions of the Grail, which are visions of God, mystically celebrate the feast itself. That the parable, associated in biblical commentary with the sixth beatitude ("Blessed are the clean in heart"), is the model for the plot of the Grail quest is made explicit three times in the *Queste* and twice in the *Sankgreal*. First, a hermit instructs Lancelot by analogizing the Grail quest to the parable and explaining that the wedding garment is a sign of grace, of the purity that comes from true confession and good works (*Q*, 128). Then, Lancelot's brother Hector in a disturbing prophetic dream foresees the conclusion of the quest; his vision implies that the Grail feast is an analogue of the wedding feast:

> Et Hestors, qui nule foiz ne se remuoit, erroit tant forvoiant ça et la qu'il venoit en la meson a un riche home qui tenoit noces et feste grant. Il huichoit a l'uis et disoit: "Ouvrez, ouvrez!" et li sires venoit avant, si li disoit: "Sires chevaliers, autre ostel querez que cestui: car ceenz n'entre nus qui si haut soit montez com vos estes." (And in the meanewhyle he trowed that hymself, sir Ector, rode tylle that he com to a ryche mannes house where there was a weddynge. And there he saw a kynge whych seyd, "Sir knyght, here ys no place for you.") *Q*, 150; *M*, 942

This prophecy, that Hector will be excluded from the wedding feast, is fulfilled when Lancelot is sharing a meal provided by the Holy Grail with the company of the Grail castle: the doors of the palace swing shut by themselves to close out Hector who stands outside the castle, crying to no avail, "Ovrez, ovrez!" (Undo! . . . Undo!), Q, 260; M, 1019. Hector is not, like the ill-clothed guest of the wedding feast parable, thrown out; but as in the parables of the closed door (Luke 13:25–28) and of the wise and the foolish virgins (Matt. 25:10–12), the door closes against him who is not spiritually prepared to celebrate the feast.

In granting the knights direct knowledge of Christ only in the concluding visions, the *Queste* author respects the reality of their historical condition; for them, living in the time of the "already" of Christ and the "not yet" of the eschatological kingdom, actually keeping company with Christ and actually being able to see him is possible only through a vision or in death. What was possible for Christ's disciples is not possible for the knights, even though what they seek and what they find have analogues in the disciples' experience: the wedding feast, which once was celebrated on earth, has now removed to heaven, as Christ suggested that it must when he answered those who accused him of gluttony: "Can you make the children of the bridegroom fast whilst the bridegroom is with them? But the days will come when the bridegroom shall be taken away from them; then they shall fast" (Luke 5:34–35; see also Mark 2:19–20, Matt. 9:15). The knights' visions of Christ are a gift of grace, one not often merited by men in their earthly journey toward death, that allows them to come early, if briefly, to the wedding feast and grants them a foretaste of heavenly bliss.

By using the image of the wedding feast—a metaphor for the kingdom of heaven—as an analogue to the end of the Grail quest, the *Queste* author clarifies the eschatological overtones of the quest. In seeking the Grail, the knights are seeking the fellowship of the kingdom of heaven; and insofar as they realize perfect fellowship during their earthly lives, they are making the kingdom of heaven known on earth. What the knights seek can be found as a sustained experience only after death, and death is Galahad's reward at the end of the quest.

Because the Grail quest is actually a quest for death, for the death that is paradoxically life (Matt. 10:39; Luke 17:33), those

who must stay behind, like Arthur and Guinevere, become mourn-
ers. The laments of Arthur and Guinevere over the imminent departure of the knights express grief for the loss to the Round Table
fellowship that will result when the knights seek a higher fellowship.

The strategy of placing these laments at the beginning of the
Grail quest is subtle in its implications. On the one hand, it helps
to account for the relationship of the Round Table fellowship to
the fellowship Bors, Perceval, and Galahad find in the Table of
the Holy Grail by showing that the Round Table is the shadow
of the reality represented by the Grail table; at the end of the
*Queste* this reality becomes an eschatological one, when God
gathers the Holy Grail as well as Galahad's soul into heaven. On
the other hand, this strategy foreshadows the grief the audience
must feel in response to the last tales in the cycle, the tales of Arthur's death. At the beginning of the Grail quest, Arthur alone
seems to understand its difficulty and its implications for the
Round Table. Poignantly, the king reminds Gawain of the effort
of creating this fellowship of knights, which is now to become
only a memory:

> "Je les ai escreuz et alevez de tout mon pooir et les ai toz jors
> amez et encore les aim ausi com s'il fussent mi fil ou mi
> frere, et por ce me sera mult griez lor departie; car je avoie
> apris a veoir les sovent et a avoir lor compaignie; car je ne
> puis pas en moi veoir coment je m'en puisses offrir." ("I have
> loved them as well as my lyff. Wherefore hit shall greve me
> ryght sore, the departicion of thys felyship, for I have
> had an olde custom to have hem in my felyship.")
> *Q*, 17; M, 867

Later, talking to Lancelot, Arthur resigns himself to the departure
of his knights, whose oaths make it necessary that they go. The
queen, whose grief centers on her loss of Lancelot, also mourns
the departure of the whole company, "ausint come se ele veist
devant lui morz toz ses amis" (*Q*, 24; cf. M, 868). The poignancy
of these laments foreshadows the sense of loss that hangs over the
tale of Arthur's death and the formal dissolution of the Round
Table fellowship. Then, the audience finds itself in a position
analogous to that of the king and queen as the Grail quest begins,

caught in the midst of earthly life after all the heroes are dead. Arthur has done all that an earthly king can do to establish a great fellowship, but his effort is necessarily flawed and he must let his knights seek the fellowship of the Grail table. He must live on with loss and grief, as must we when later we hear the tale of Arthur's own death.

The Grail quest, which the knights themselves are eager to follow, introduces a heavenly perspective into the Vulgate cycle's loose history of Lancelot's career and Arthur's reign, which is otherwise told from an earthly perspective. From an earthly perspective, death means sadness and loss to those who survive: the Christian tradition of consolation, from Jerome and Ambrose to Bernard of Clairvaux and Aelred of Rievaulx does not deny the legitimacy of this response.[27] Arthur and Guinevere speak from our own earthly perspective when they see the knights' departure as a loss; but the knights who succeed in the quest show us the joy that results from a heavenly perspective, as their visions bring them fellowship with the resurrected Christ. The Grail quest, then, provides the antidote to the loss we feel at the death of Arthur and his remaining knights because the expectations of the Round Table fellowship are gloriously fulfilled. In the largest structural sense, the demise of the Round Table is all that can follow the Grail quest and, to make the history complete, the one must follow the other.

Those who enter the Grail quest leave behind the mourning king and queen and subject themselves to the tests that they hope will bring them to a vision of the Grail in its "vraie semblance." The vision of the Grail completes the celestial quest, defined by a monk at the outset as a search "des grans secrez et des privetez Nostre Seignor et des grans repostailles" (Q, 19) that will reveal to the blessed knight what mortal heart cannot conceive nor

---

27. See Jerome, *Lettres*, 60 (3:90–110), 75 (4:32–37), 108 (5:159–201); Ambrose, *De excessu fratis*, pp. 207–325, *De obitu Valentiniani*, pp. 327–67, and *De obitu Theodosii*, pp. 369–401; Bernard of Clairvaux, *Sermones super Cantica canticorum* (*On the Song of Songs*), 26 (hereafter cited as *Serm. Cant. cant.*); and Aelred of Rievaulx, *Speculum caritatis*, 3.34. See also Charles Favez, *La Consolation latine chrétienne*; Jean Leclercq, *Recueil d'études sur Saint-Bernard et ses écrits*, pp. 90–94; and Peter von Moos, *Consolatio* (vol. 4 has comprehensive bibliographies of texts and critical studies).

tongue of man devise. In the concluding adventures of the quest, Galahad experiences fully the vision that the monk describes in the language of 1 Cor. 2:9, in phrases that are echoed throughout the literature of Christian vision. We and the knights discover then the principle that binds Galahad and the Grail: they both contain the vision of God.

The earlier, longer part of the quest narrative gives Galahad a personal history—in which he completes all the adventures reserved for him—that individualizes him; but because he does not sin during the quest (although he could, see *Q*, 116), he conforms so closely to Christ that he seems to some a dull character. In contrast to Galahad's history, the particular histories of the other questing knights, all of whom are sinners or at least subject to temptation, satisfy an audience's desire for tension and possibility in fiction, even though the good knights, as we will see, imitate Galahad's cleanness and charity.

## The Typology of Eve: Lancelot and Perceval

The preparatory adventures in the *Queste* and the *Sankgreal* illustrate how individuals in the age of knighthood meet the problems introduced into history by the Fall. Lancelot and Perceval resolve the sin of Eve in their adventures; while Bors resolves the sin of Cain, as Gawain should but does not.

The first episode in the story of Lancelot's adventures suggests an analogy between him and Perceval: riding together, they both attack Galahad, whom they do not recognize. That we meet Perceval and Lancelot at the same time sets up the later revelation of the similarity between Perceval's proneness to sexual sin and Lancelot's actual adultery. That both of them attack Galahad shows the inability of the sinner or of the unredeemed naif to direct his aggressive acts to proper ends; characteristically, the *Queste* author perceives aimless or misdirected aggression to be a consequence of personal impurity, impurity that is actual for Lancelot and potential in Perceval. This episode also allows Galahad to fulfill part of the prophecy connected with his sword, and applicable to Perceval and Gawain as a result of their lack of self-knowledge, that whoever has failed in attempting to draw the sword from the stone will receive a wound. Galahad lands a harsh blow on Perceval and, having defeated both him and Lancelot, rides away, a gesture that expresses Perceval's and Lancelot's spiritual distance from Galahad in physical terms.

## Lancelot: Everyman Hero

After the encounter with Galahad, Perceval and Lancelot separate, and Lancelot finds the adventure of the sick knight that makes his own sinfulness manifest. As he lies at night unarmed near a cross with an inscription that he cannot read and an abandoned chapel that he cannot enter, a sick knight borne on a litter between two horses arrives, laments his ailment suffered on account of wrongdoing, and asks God for relief brought by the Holy Grail, "li Sainz Vessiaus" (Q, 58; M, 894). A procession, led by a candlestick, from the chapel and an appearance of the Holy Grail on a silver table answer his prayer. He rolls out of his litter and drags himself to the Grail; in the Queste he kisses the silver table, in the Sankgreal he kisses the Grail itself; in both he is healed (Malory's version makes the connection of man as a vessel analogous to the holy vessel explicit).[28] In contrast to the knight, Lancelot, half asleep and half awake (that is, in a trance), sees and hears everything but is paralyzed and dumb: the knight and his squire recognize that Lancelot's immobility is a consequence of a grave and unconfessed sin. They take his sword, his helmet, and his horse to put them to a worthy use, a theft that demonstrates Lancelot's lack of spiritual armor. After they depart Lancelot wakes up as if from deep sleep and tries to decide whether he has merely been dreaming or the Grail has actually appeared. A voice curses him, he discovers the loss of his horse and his armor, and he knows then that "il a veu verité" (Q, 61) and that his sin has made him incapable of response to the Grail.

As Lancelot acknowledges in his laments, sin has blurred his vision. Through the device of the trance, the Queste author grants Lancelot a corporeal vision of the Grail: that is, he allows Lance-

---

28. Vinaver and Moorman have argued over the implications of Malory's changes in this incident; see Thomas Malory, *The Works of Sir Thomas Malory*, ed. Eugène Vinaver, 3 vols., 1st ed. (Oxford: Clarendon, 1947), p. 1539; M, 1552–53; and Moorman, "*The Tale of the Sankgreall*" p. 190, who thinks that Malory changes his source in order to emphasize the doctrine of transubstantiation (Malory says that God is "within the holy vessell").

lot to register the physical image but not to use the higher powers of his mind to understand and respond.[29] His sin has made him dead to spiritual realities. Although Lancelot has not earned the right to see the Grail himself, God allows him to see the sick knight responding to the Grail so that Lancelot may move toward an understanding of his unworthiness: the vision, in effect, invites and challenges Lancelot to reform. Earlier, soon after Galahad's arrival at Camelot, a messenger had ridden in and disclaimed Lancelot as "the best knyght of the worlde" since "one bettir than ye be" had arrived (M, 863). Lancelot granted the truth of her statement, but he does not fully understand its implications until he sees the sick knight and the Grail. Lancelot reacts to the demonstration of his unworthiness by grieving for his sins and by seeking a priest to whom he can confess.

The hermit-priest whom Lancelot finds the next day reproves him for wasting the talents God gave him, but tells him that he may yet put himself back on the way to God. Their dialogue—Lancelot's hesitation and the hermit's kindly encouragement—reveals a sinner's reluctance to break with his past and exemplifies the patience, skill, and charity a confessor ought to show to a penitent. In the *Queste* the hermit interprets the shape of the cross to Lancelot as Christ's invitation to mercy (the arms are stretched wide as if to receive the sinner, as if Christ were saying "Venez, venez!"), and he explains that Christ refuses no one who offers himself through "veraie confession de bouche et de repentance de cuer et en amendement de vie" (Q, 65). Both the *Queste* and the *Sankgreal* present Lancelot's confession as the climax of his first adventure.

Fully conscious of the magnitude of the hidden sin he must now reveal if he is to continue in the Grail quest, Lancelot admits his adultery with the queen as if it were idolatry:

> "Sire, fet Lancelot, il est einsi que je sui morz de pechié d'une moie dame que je ai amee toute ma vie, et ce est la reine Guenievre, la fame le roi Artus. Ce est cele qui a plenté m'a doné l'or et l'argent et les riches dons que je ai aucune foiz donez as povres chevaliers. Ce est cele qui m'a mis ou grant boban et en la grant hautece ou je sui. Ce est cele por qui amor j'ai faites les granz proeces dont toz li mondes parole. Ce est cele qui m'a fet venir de povreté en richece

29. See below, pp. 127–28 and n. 48.

et de mesaise a toutes les terriannes beneurtez. Mes je
sai bien que par cest pechié de li s'est Nostre Sires si durement
corociez a moi qu'il le m'a bien mostré puis ersoir."
   (And than he tolde there the good man all hys lyff, and
how he had loved a quene unmesurabely and oute of mesure
longe.
   "And all my grete dedis of armys that I have done for
the moste party was for the quenys sake, and for hir sake
wolde I do batayle were hit ryght other wronge. And never
dud I batayle all only for Goddis sake, but for to wynne
worship and to cause me the bettir to be beloved, and litill or
nought I thanked never God of hit.") Q, 66; M, 897

Although Malory shortens Lancelot's confession and prefaces it
with the recognition that concludes it in the French text ("for . . . I
never discoverde [disclosed] one thynge that I have used, and that
may I now wyghte my shame and my disadventure"), the substance
of the two confessions is the same.
   Lancelot confesses to having made the queen his god, acknowledging in the French text that he sees her as the source of his
wealth, his dignity, and his pleasure and that he does his deeds
of prowess for her. Malory abbreviates the rewards Lancelot has
received from the queen and restructures the syntax so that his
valiant deeds seem to have been offerings to his goddess, given in
order to receive honor and love. Malory's changes make Lancelot
seem more crudely selfish than he does in the French text. The
noun *worship* had two meanings in Middle English: it was used
in the modern sense, to refer to a religious act praising and honor-
ing God or some other object of devotion; and it was used in a
more general sense, to indicate reputation or fame. Malory uses
the word *worship* here with ironic propriety to suggest that Lancelot has seen himself rather than God as the person worthy to be
honored and that he has sought honor, not before God, but before
the queen.
   The rhetoric of the confession in both texts is heightened by the
repetition of phrases, which gives these passages, which simultaneously express triumph and horror, a ritual and poetic quality.
As Lancelot repeats the phase, "Ce est cele qui," we hear paren-
thetically "et non dieu"; and as Lancelot repeats "Ce est cele qui"
at the beginning of each elaboration of what he has understood
his love to mean, we catch a sense of the delicious horror of that

love. "Ce est cele qui" is spoken by a man whose growing consciousness of God's wrath at his love mutes the triumphant claim of love's benefits. He speaks now with a certain irony and yet with a lingering sense of the glory of his love for Guinevere.

Malory's Lancelot equivocates, and in that equivocation he expresses a sardonic attitude toward the love he once thought noble. As he acknowledges the grounds for God's objection to his sin, that he acts with reference to his lady and not to God, he tries to minimize the objection by suggesting that perhaps occasionally he remembered God. Malory shifts the repeating phrase to suggest that Lancelot's attempt to save his love is futile: "For the quenys sake, and for hir sake. . . . never . . . for Goddis sake." That he would do battle for the queen "were it ryght other wronge" condemns the love that leads him to ignore the ethical status of his acts. The psychological verisimilitude of Malory's Lancelot as he damns himself and yet tries to excuse himself is convincing.

The hermit accepts Lancelot's confession and counsels him explicitly in the *Queste* never to commit mortal sin with Guinevere; in the *Sankgreal* the hermit urges Lancelot to avoid the queen's company, which is practical advice that intends the same thing. In neither text does the hermit regard Lancelot's reform as an easy thing, but in both he promises a great reward to Lancelot if he perseveres in his commitment to God and to virtue.

In a later section of the *Queste* devoted to Lancelot, another hermit explicitly interprets Lancelot's sin as idolatry by showing him that the Devil used Queen Guinevere as his instrument of seduction: when Lancelot committed himself to the queen above all others, the Devil took possession of Lancelot's soul and drove Christ out. In the hermit's interpretation, Lancelot's sin becomes an episode in the cosmic struggle between God and the Devil for men's souls.[30] Malory omits this history of Lancelot's sin, having already established that it is both adultery and idolatry. His omission makes Lancelot and Guinevere seem less like counters in a cosmic struggle and leaves his audience to assume that temptation to sin rises out of human nature itself. In effect, Malory implies a more complex view of human nature that insists on personal responsibility in a new way: Lancelot's battle is with himself, not with a supernatural force such as the Devil. Malory felt less need

---

30. Pauphilet, in *Études*, pp. 115–16, sees this struggle as a central motif of the *Queste*.

than did the author of the *Queste* to use the allegory of psycho-machy to analyze and rationalize human psychology.

Using the imagery of temple and lodging, both vessel images that imply a link with the Grail, the *Queste* hermit explains that by confession Lancelot can cleanse himself and become again a faithful servant: "Or ne t'esmaier donc, fet li preudons. Car se Nostre Sires voit que tu li requieres pardon de bon cuer, il t'en-voiera tant de grace que tu li seras temples et ostel et qu'il se her-bergera dedenz toi" (*Q*, 128). Although Malory preserves rather fully the aspects of penance that the *Queste* introduces in this epi-sode (the hermit requires Lancelot to mortify his flesh by wearing a hair shirt and by abstaining from meat and wine and tells him to hear mass daily if he can), all that remains in Malory's version of the conversation on sin is a reference to confession.

To return to the episode of the sick knight, Lancelot asks the first hermit to explain the curse that the voice at the abandoned chapel pronounced on him, defining him as harder than stone, bitterer than wood, and barer than the fig, and demanding that he leave, in the *Queste* because his presence stinks, in the *Sank-greal* because he is not fit to be in such a holy place: Malory here interprets the *Queste* correctly. The hermit glosses the metaphors of the curse, showing how each comparison implies what Lancelot has and what he lacks. The allegorical explanations for the meta-phors are substantially the same, but they are worked out in de-tails appropriate to stone, wood, or fig tree. One example from these glosses suffices to illustrate the hermit's method of interpre-tation, and I have chosen the first since it has implications for the reading of the *Queste* as a whole. Having asserted that stones are naturally hard, the hermit allegorically interprets the stone as the sinner's heart, which neither fire nor rain can penetrate; in other words, the Holy Spirit can find no entrance there, "por le vessel qui est orz et les desviez pechiez que cil a acreuz et amon-celez de jor en jor. . . . Car Nostre Sires ne se herbergera ja en leu ou ses anemis soit, ainz veut que li ostiex ou il descendra soit nez et espurgiez de toz vices et de toutes ordures" (*Q*, 68; cf. M, 898). The hermit's allegory distinguishes fire and rain from filth by using the former to symbolize spiritual energy and the latter to symbolize material inertness. Sin corresponds to filth because it results from an overvaluation of material good and deadens the spirit. The *Queste* hermit reads the stone as a heart and the heart as a lodging and a vessel, into which fire and rain (the energizing spirit and the cleansing nourishing power of the Holy Ghost) ought to be able to come. Filth, crusted and hardened ordure (or sin), can, however, block the entry of fire or rain into a vessel or lodging.

Lancelot, the habitual sinner, contains filth rather than fire or water: he is not a vessel analogous to the Holy Grail and therefore he has not been able to move toward identification with the Grail. In this allegorization of the stone, the hermit understands an analogy between Lancelot and the Grail to be a possibility but distinguishes them from one another by the differences in what the two vessels contain, adultery (filth of sin) and purity (fire and water). The hermit goes on to contrast Lancelot to the rock Moses struck in the desert to cause water to flow: Lancelot is harder than that rock because no water (healing nourishment or good works) flows from him. The Holy Grail has, however, just healed the sick knight. Through this allegory, the hermit clarifies the nature of the relationship between Lancelot and the Grail: they are two vessels with radically opposite contents; and the difference in their contents was objectified earlier in Lancelot's adventure by the physical distance that separated Lancelot and the Grail, which Lancelot had no power to lessen. Other adventures in the *Queste* make it clear that the distance between the Grail and another vessel, such as a man, is a function of the likeness or unlikeness of that other vessel to the Grail.

Lancelot's further adventures in the *Queste* test his capacity to amend his life through penance, which becomes for him an almost permanent way of life. When we pick up his story again, after Perceval's adventure on the rocky island, Lancelot is completing his visit with the hermit and setting off again on his wandering journey. As he rides through the forest, he meets a squire who berates him for his inability to respond to the Grail and insults him for his love of the queen. The squire condemns Lancelot more harshly than does anyone else in the *Queste*: "Certes, mauvés failliz, mout poez avoir grant duel, qui soliez estre tenuz au meillor chevalier dou monde, or estes tenuz au plus mauvés et au plus desloial!" (*Q*, 118). These insults are spoken by one who lacks the authority conferred by high rank or holiness, by one who has no right to criticize Lancelot. His words would be true only if Lancelot were to die in sin. Here, they test Lancelot's new commitment to humility and self-restraint, and he passes the test. He does not dispute, even to himself, the squire's accusations, but takes them as a reminder of his former sinfulness and rides off begging God to show him mercy and the path of righteousness.

Lancelot's further adventures illustrate his struggle to find that path and reveal to him the consequences of losing it; he is Everyman on trial. His encounter with the hermit who lies dead in a comfortable shirt, which is apparently a sign of broken vows, warns Lancelot of the unceasing nature of the demands of Christian faith. As Lancelot and a living hermit discover by conjuring the Devil, who refuses to claim the dead hermit, apparent signs do not necessarily reveal the truth: the dead hermit did not choose the fine shirt but had it forced upon him. Intentionality means more than physical signs, and the dead hermit is saved. Lancelot then finds an opportunity for action, though not of the kind knights-errant expect; he helps the living hermit bury the dead, a corporeal act of mercy. In penance for his own sins, Lancelot dons the dead hermit's hair shirt.

From this living hermit, who is a white monk, and from a hermit he visits after having a dream, Lancelot learns about the eschatological nature of the Grail quest and about his role as a penitent. This first hermit interprets the quest as a fulfillment of the wedding feast parable. For Lancelot to accept the invitation to the wedding feast and be accepted in return, he must return to God's service through true confession. The second hermit understands the quest as the proving ground for Lancelot's faithfulness, Lancelot's reward in it as dependent on his own choice, and his choice as an event in the cosmic drama in which God and the Devil compete, however unequally, for men's souls (again, Malory omits explicit reference to the Devil and reduces emphasis on the cosmic nature of the struggle).

The second hermit also interprets Lancelot's prophetic dream of his genealogy. This dream is a pageant of salvation in three parts: first, a procession consisting of a man surrounded by stars and crowned with a gold crown, who is attended by seven kings and two knights (images of Christ, Lancelot's own ancestors, Lancelot himself, and his son, Galahad), who ask for judgment; second, the descent of a man through the clouds who blesses and curses; and third, the ascent of the last knight, in the shape of a winged lion,

into the clouds (*Q*, 130–31; M, 928–29). The hermit analogizes the
first part of the dream to another prophetic dream, that of Lancelot's ancestor King Mordrain, who sees his nine descendants as
rivers. A man in the semblance of Christ comes and washes his
hands and feet in each river and in the ninth washes his body as
well *(Q*, 135–38). The procession in Lancelot's dream figures the
companionship of Christ and men, while Mordrain's vision of
the rivers reveals Christ's power to cleanse those in whom, paradoxically, he washes himself: Christ is king, companion, servant,
and lover. In Lancelot's dream the nine men ask for judgment:
"Swete Fadir of Hevyn, com and visite us, and yelde unto everych
of us as we have deserved" (M, 928; cf. *Q*, 131). Christ comes, blessing and cursing, promising to the "serjanz bons et loiax" (serv-
auntes and . . . good and trew knyghtes) that "Mes ostiex est
apareilliez a vos toz" (*Q*, 131), and dooming the eighth figure
(Lancelot) to flight from him because the treasure set in the eighth
figure is lost. Grief stricken, the accursed one flees, asking for mercy; and a voice tells him that the gift of mercy depends on his own
choice, that the curse is conditional: "Se tu velz je t'amerai, se tu
velz je te harrai" (*Q*, 131). The final part of the pageant, the vision
of the winged lion, images salvation, the triumphant ascent of
Galahad's soul into heaven.

Lancelot's dream and his conversations with the hermits make
his conditional status clear enough: he is a vessel whose content is
now grace; but, since he yet has time to sin, he may again pollute
himself and again become a filthy vessel, doomed to the destruction of sin. The curse pronounced on him in his dream is a provisional prophecy, a prophecy of what will happen to him if he
does not permanently amend his life.

Lancelot at first responds to his dream with an erroneously easy
optimism. This is the last of his interpretive mistakes in the preparatory adventures, as his participation on the wrong side in a
tournament will be the last of his actual mistakes; and both mistakes, once understood, lead him to submit himself humbly to
Christ. Upon learning that the ninth figure of his dream is his
son, Lancelot assumes that his fatherhood will bring him reward;
but the hermit quickly corrects him, telling him that every man,
father or son, bears his own burden of guilt that only God can re-
lieve. Then, since he is already confessed, Lancelot prays to Christ

for sustenance in the quest. By quoting in his prayer Christ's promises of heavenly joy or eternal fire, Lancelot seems at last to have
recognized the God who is greater than his lady.

The tournament is Lancelot's final preparatory adventure, and
it becomes a reproof to him because he fails to use proper judgment, a sign that an active amendment of life is not easy for a
habitual sinner like Lancelot. This episode both summarizes
Lancelot's past mistakes and foretells the nature of the mistakes
he will make in the future. Without thinking, he joins the wrong
and losing side, the black rather than the white knights. He fights
until he is exhausted; and as soon as he is taken captive, the black
knights are defeated. His captors take him into the woods and let
him go, leaving him to realize that his defeat results from his sin.
The next day he discovers an anchoress who explains the tournament as an analogue of the Grail quest. The white knights whose
goal is heaven are pitted against the black knights whose sin commits them to earth: Lancelot had taken the sinners' side, as he and
Perceval had in attacking Galahad. The tournament experience,
which the anchoress asserts to be real, stands as a further reproof
to Lancelot's pride and as a reminder of the ultimate defeat awaiting him if he should fail in his faith and trust in God.

All Lancelot's adventures, then, demonstrate both to him and
to us his conditional status in the quest, whose goal he now knows
to be spiritual and eschatological. When he leaves the recluse, he
rides on to the edge of a perilous river, the Marcoise, or the Mor-
tays, that divides the forest in two and that he must cross. As he
is considering his situation a black knight on a black horse comes
out of the river, kills Lancelot's horse, and gallops away, leaving
Lancelot hemmed in by forest, rock cliffs, and river. Recognizing
that he can do nothing to help himself, Lancelot puts his trust in
God and waits on his help. His resignation to God's will signals
that he has arrived at a new stage in the quest, he has achieved a
humble confidence in God that replaces the humiliation before
God and the grief for his own sins that his earlier adventures
brought him.

Perceval: Temptation of Innocence

The story of Perceval's temptation, an analogue of Lancelot's
sin, separates the two parts of Lancelot's adventures. Through
Perceval's adventures on the rocky island, we see more clearly the

relationship of gluttony and sexual sin to idolatry, and we see the alternative to these sins. Because he is not a habitual sinner, but one whose fall is intended rather than actual, Perceval's reform is easier and more effective than Lancelot's, whose confession and reform frame Perceval's preparatory adventures.

Early in his adventures, Perceval's horse is killed; from then on he has such difficulty with his mounts that he carelessly swears loyalty to a woman who offers him a horse: he is heedless of the implications of her gift, even when the horse turns out to be "inky black." The moonlit ride that follows is supernaturally swift and thoroughly strange. At length the horse carries him to the edge of a river so dangerous looking (described by Malory as "a rowghe watir whych rored" [M, 912]) that Perceval is afraid and crosses himself. At that sign, the horse shakes him off and disappears crying and shrieking into the water, which seems to burn. Perceval recognizes that grace has saved him and spends the night in prayer. The next morning he discovers that he has been left on a rocky island. Here he meets beasts and has visions; here he has visitors, a man from a white ship and a woman from a black ship.

The lady from the black ship, subsequently revealed to be the Devil in disguise, intends to subvert Perceval's innocence and virtue. She woos Perceval with great cunning. First she plays on his fear of starving to death, unable to escape from the mountain wilderness. When he argues that his previous visitor, the holy man from the white ship, has brought him comfort, if not earthly meat, the lady derides Perceval's sense of security, telling him that the man is an enchanter and that his apparent concern is deceitful. At this point she offers to rescue Perceval from the island and tells him she needs strong champions to win back her heritage. Her distress draws Perceval into a sympathetic offer of assistance, which he thinks is in accord with his oath as a knight of the Round Table to help maidens in need. This lady, however, wants Perceval to be loyal to her only; so, having won his sympathy, she patiently lulls him into trust and desire. As a foretaste of the comfort she promises, she brings a tent to protect him from the sun; and there, in the shadow of the tent, unarmed, unprotected by the armor of faith (see Eph. 6:11–17), he naps. Then he and she share an enormous meal, drinking freely, until Perceval, enamored by her beauty and encouraged by her friendliness, lusts after her and finally begs her to take him. As when Lancelot falls in love with Guinevere, Perce-

val's vision narrows until he can see and think only of the lady
before him. She realizes her advantage and wins from the heedless
Perceval a pledge of total loyalty. To seal his pledge, she plans to
take him into her luxurious bed, into her arms, to receive into
herself the offering of his seed as signal of his adoration and loyalty;
but at the last moment, just as he is pulling the coverlet over them,
Perceval glimpses the cross inlaid in his sword hilt and makes the
sign of the cross. That sign cancels the seal between them. The
tent disappears in stench and smoke, and the black ship departs
with the lady in a sea of flame.

Perceval, realizing that he had almost lost the virginity that is
the sign of his purity, deliberately stabs himself through the left
thigh in an attempt to follow the advice of the New Testament in
repenting his sin: "And, if thy hand or thy foot scandalize thee, cut
it off and cast it from thee. It is better for thee to go into life
maimed or lamed than, having two hands or two feet, to be cast
into everlasting fire" (Matt. 18:8; cf. 18:9, 5:29–30; Mark 9:42–44).
Perceval's thigh wound causes blood to spurt in every direction and
makes impotent the part of his body that has offended God, the
part that since the Fall has been the visible index of man's concupiscence.[31] Prudentius, for example, interprets the thigh wound
Jacob receives wrestling with the angel as a sexual wound and as a
punishment for his concupiscence:

> sub nocte Iacob caerula,
> luctator audax angeli,
> eo usque dum lux surgeret,
> sudavit inpar proelium;
>     sed cum iubar claresceret,
> lapsante claudus poplite
> femurque victus debile,
> culpae vigorem perdidit.
>     nutabat inguen saucium,
> quae corporis pars vilior
> longeque sub cordis loco
> diram fovet libidinem.

31. C. Brunel, in "Les Hanches du roi pêcheur," argues on the basis
of medieval medical vocabulary that "les hanches," "les quisses," and
"les jambes" (the latter two expressions are variants in the manuscripts
of Chrêtien's Conte du Graal) refer to the genitals, which is a widely accepted interpretation.

(It was under the dusk of night that Jacob, wrestling boldly
with the angel, toiled hard in unequal fight until the light
arose. But when the beam shone forth his ham gave way
and he was lamed, and being overcome in the infirmity of his
thigh he lost the strength to sin. His loins were wounded
and enfeebled, that baser part of the body, far below the
heart, which nurtures fearful lust.)[32]

Perceval's aunt warned Perceval at the beginning of his adventures that he would jeopardize his achievement of the Grail quest
if he stained his virgin body with sexual sin. Eating and drinking
with the lady of the black ship, Perceval almost repeats the sin of
Eve, which was to enter into communion with the Devil; but he
stops short of the act—fornication—that would have completed a
union with the Devil and signaled his total commitment to sin.

On Perceval's third day in the wilderness, the light of the sun
floods the rock and the white ship returns from the east bearing
the holy man back; the sun and the return of the man in white are
both signs that Perceval's repentance will bring him absolution.
The man in white identifies Perceval's temptress to him as the
fallen angel who by playing on Eve's concupiscence lured her and
Adam into sin and infected all mankind with mortality. Perceval,
to whom the holy man initially exclaims, "Ha! Perceval . . . toz
jorz seras tu nices!" (*Q*, 112), at last understands the nature of his
experience. From the time his mentor arrives, Perceval's wound
ceases to pain him; and he attributes his healing to the holy man's
words and looks: "ainz me vient de vostre parole et de vostre regart
une si grant douçor et un si grant asouagement de mes membres
que je ne croi pas que vos soiez hons terriens, mes esperitiex. . . .
et se je l'osoie dire, je diroie que vos estes li Pains vis qui descent
des ciex" (*Q*, 115). When Perceval recognizes his visitor, the visitor
vanishes and a voice tells Perceval that he is healed, a message of
spiritual as well as physical significance.

The words that are Living Bread contrast with the food of the
lady from the black ship, and this contrast offers us another way
to the conclusion that Perceval almost falls into idolatry or heresy.
The Word that is Christ, the words of Scripture, and the words of
religious writing had long been regarded as spiritual food. Medieval heretics were accused of misinterpreting the Scriptures and

32. Prudentius, "Hymnus matutinis," lines 73–92, in *Prudentius*, 1:
16–18.

hence making them no more nourishing and far more dangerous
than ordinary material food; to indulge a taste for such interpretation was regarded as a form of gluttony. The night before Perceval's encounters with the man in white and the lady from the black
ship, who test his taste in food, he had seen a vision of two ladies,
one astride a lion and the other riding a serpent; the man in white
identifies the first as the New Law and the other as the Synagogue,
or first law. In explicating the latter, the man in white refers to
misinterpretations of the Scriptures by the Jews, who were considered, like heretics, as *lapsi*:

> Et li serpenz qui la porte, ce est l'Escriture mauvesement
> entendue et mauvesement esponse, ce est ypocrisie et
> heresie et iniquitez et pechié mortel, ce est li anemis meismes;
> ce est li serpenz qui par son orgueil fu gitez de paradis; ce
> est li serpenz qui dist a Adam et a sa moillier: "Se vos mengiez
> de cest fruit vos seroiz ausi come Dieu," et par ceste parole
> entra en aus covoitise. (*Q*, 103)

The words of the serpent, like the fruit in the Garden, are not
nourishment, but deadly poison. So, too, the words and the food
of the lady in black, who is an incarnation of the enemy, are poi-
sonous. To believe her or to eat her food, analogous acts, is to fall
into heresy and idolatry, which is a spiritual form of adultery.[33]
By contrast, to "eat" the Living Bread is to unite oneself with
Christ and to become his bride. Perceval, then, has almost committed himself to adultery and idolatry by joining the Devil, but
by wounding himself through the thigh he effectively purges his
proneness to sin and enables himself to find the sustenance of
grace in the words of the man in white, which are his initial foretaste of the delights of the heavenly wedding feast.

33. See de Lubac, *Exégèse médiévale*, vol. 1, pt. 2, pp. 99–181; there he
discusses the *sens propre* and the perverse interpretation of Scripture
associated especially with Jewish interpretation in the early Christian
centuries but also with heretics (pp. 99–113); the *bovinus intellectus*, a
term for those who reject the spiritual or allegorical sense (as the Jews
and other "literalists" do [pp. 113–28]); and the *perfidi*, a term for Jewish
infidels (pp. 153–81); (note the association of venom with perfidy, p. 158,
and the tendency for this word to accommodate itself to secular concepts:
"L'esclave ou l'amant trompeur, l'épouse ou l'amie secrètement infidèle,
sont des 'perfidi,' " p. 179; Perceval's lady in black is just such an "épouse
. . . infidèle").

## The Typology of Cain and Abel: Gawain and Bors

Gawain, whose name Arthur connects with Lancelot's in the laments at the beginning of the quest, fares worse than Lancelot does in the search for the Grail mysteries. Unlike Lancelot, Gawain never sees the Grail again. He complains of his lack of adventures and, indeed, his story is comparatively brief, even though it is told in two segments to contrast with the stories that follow: Lancelot's adventure with the sick knight and Bors's preparatory adventures. Gawain never grasps the principle of the quest as Lancelot implicitly does, that adventures come to those who are spiritually prepared for them through confession and penance. Bors, the antitype of Gawain, has the most varied adventures of all.

### Gawain and Hector, Anti-heroes

In Gawain's first adventure, the *Queste* contrasts him to Galahad and to Lancelot. Desperate for the kinds of adventures he understands, Gawain takes every opportunity he finds to fight, often murdering his opponents. After Galahad has chased seven corrupt brothers from the Castle of Maidens, they meet Gawain, who, with the help of Gaheriet and Owein, kills them. Gawain assumes that, since the brothers attacked him, he is justified in killing them; but the hermit he visits that night criticizes him for killing the brothers without giving them time to repent, which Galahad had done. The hermit urges Gawain to repent: repentance would bring Gawain into a state of justice in which, at least by the conventions that govern the world of the *Queste*, he would be able to distinguish those who deserve death from those who do not. The hermit promises Gawain that he can yet be reconciled to God if he will forsake his life of sin, but Gawain says that he could not bear to suffer the hardships of penance and so departs. His indifference to the hermit's accusation and counsel contrasts sharply to Lancelot's contrition in response to the adventure of the Grail and the sick knight.

Later, in the second segment of his history, Gawain murders a fellow knight of the Round Table, which is spiritual fratricide, a crime that Bors subsequently avoids. Gawain and Hector are riding together, frustrated because they have found no adventures in many days of wandering, when a knight, whom they cannot see clearly, challenges them to joust. Relieved and eager to find some kind of adventurous action, they argue over who will respond to the challenge. Gawain takes it up and hits the other knight so hard that he falls onto the ground, mortally wounded. Gawain then learns that the fallen knight is Owein, a knight of the Round Table, a fact that Malory explicitly interprets when he has Owein say to Gawain: "And now forgyff the God, for hit shall be ever rehersed that the tone sworne brother hath slayne the other" (M, 945). As Perceval's aunt has explained to Perceval, when knights join the Round Table they become members of a spiritual family; to kill a fellow companion is, then, a form of fratricide and a repetition of Cain's crime. Committing such acts is Gawain's constant fate in the quest because he refuses to prepare himself, through penance, to realize the quest's high goals, one of which is the establishment of a fully realized spiritual fraternity. At the beginning of the *Mort Artu*, King Arthur commands Gawain to tell him how many knights he has killed in the Grail quest, and sadly Gawain confesses that he has killed eighteen, not through his chivalry, but through his sin.

Just before they meet Owein, during a night that they spend in an old chapel, Gawain and Hector dream dreams and see a vision that, through Nascien's interpretation, reveal to them their spiritual conditions and imply contrasts between them and Lancelot and Bors. Hector's dream of the wedding feast forecasts that he and his brother, Lancelot, who has confessed and undertaken the life of a penitent as Hector has not, will find that the quest ends differently for them: while Lancelot is inside the Grail castle, the host refuses entry to Hector and tells him that it will never be granted him because of his sin. Gawain's dream is a prophecy that the Round Table will end in an orgy of spiritual fratricide. This dream, in which the knights are figured under the image of one hundred and fifty bulls, corresponds to the plot of the *Queste* and the *Mort Artu*, as Nascien's interpretation clearly suggests. Gawain sees the bulls, all but three of them dappled (*black* in Malory), feeding at a hayrack. To seek better pasture, they wander off across the moor. Of the three white bulls, only one returns; the dappled bulls who eventually return come back thin and weak. Together again, they fight so much that they destroy their fodder and are forced to separate. Nascien explains this dream as an analogue of the quest: the hayrack is an analogue of the Round Table; the search for good pasture is the quest for the heavenly food of the

Holy Grail; the final, forced separation is the end of the Round
Table. The spots (of blackness) on the bulls are outward and visible signs of sinfulness (*Q*, 156; M, 946). Clearly Gawain is one of
the spotted bulls who will murder their fellows in the quest, as the
white bulls, representing Galahad, Perceval, and Bors, will not.[34]
Of these latter three, Bors is the most like Gawain: he has sinned
but has repented and taken up a life of chastity, patience, and
humility; he murders no one in his preparatory adventures in the
quest. Since the dream reveals Gawain's sinfulness, Nascien urges
him to repent; but again he refuses—as does Hector—and his refusal to repent results in the failure of his quest.

The vision that Gawain and Hector see in the chapel, after their
disturbing dreams wake them up, further manifests their sinful
condition. In this vision, which is an analogue of Lancelot's vision
of the Grail and the sick knight, the *Queste* author manipulates
a set of vessel images to suggest the lack of correspondence between
the holy vessel—the Grail—and these two knights. At the end of
their vision, a voice accuses them of lacking the things that have
passed before them like a pageant: a hand draped in red samite, a
bridle, and a burning candle. Nascien the hermit allegorizes the
hand as charity, the red of the samite as grace, the bridle as abstinence, and the light of the candle as the truth of the Gospel. He
also explains the significance of the chapel: Gawain and Hector,
whose bodies are potentially hostels for Christ, are so polluted
with the filth of sin that they pollute the chapel where they lie;
their presence drives Christ out (*Q*, 160; M, 948). Just as in the
explanation of the spots on the bulls, an inner reality leads to an
outward condition. Gawain and Hector are unlike the vessel—the
old chapel—that is an analogue of the Grail, until Christ departs
from the chapel as he has from the two knights. Then the analogy
holds, then both the chapel and the knights are abandoned.

The contrast between Lancelot and the unrepentant Gawain
and Hector, which is illustrated through vessel imagery, develops
after the quest begins. All three knights enter the quest as habitual
sinners; during their adventures the *Queste* author demonstrates
the spiritual condition of the sinful knights by contrasting them
to other pure vessels. The curse on Lancelot for defiling a holy
place during his adventure with the Grail and the sick knight

34. For a view critical of Malory's translation of this passage, see
Kellogg, *Chaucer, Langland, Arthur,* pp. 12–14.

pushes him to contrition and confession; but Gawain and Hector
continue to reject the remedy of penance—Gawain excuses himself
because he is in a hurry. After telling Gawain that the Grail does
not appear to sinners and murderers, Malory's Nascien makes the
contrast between the two sinful knights and Lancelot explicit:

> "For I dare sey, as synfull as ever sir Launcelot hath byn,
> sith that he wente into the queste of the Sankgreal he slew
> never man nother nought shall, tylle that he com to Camelot
> agayne; for he hath takyn upon hym to forsake synne. And
> nere were that he ys nat stable, but by hys thoughte he
> ys lyckly to turne agayne, he sholde be nexte to encheve
> hit sauff sir Galahad, hys sonne; but God knowith hys
> thought and hys unstablenesse. And yett shall he dye ryght
> an holy man, and no doute he hath no felow of none erthly
> synfull man lyvyng." (M, 948)

Although Vinaver judges this passage to be a sign of Malory's indulgent treatment of Lancelot, its point is to contrast Lancelot
to Gawain and Hector, a contrast also explicit in the *Queste* (158),
and to condemn murder.

In retelling the Cain and Abel story during the adventure of
Solomon's ship, the *Queste* author invokes the authority of this
story and of its interpretative tradition to support the division he
makes among the knights on the basis of murder: Galahad, Perceval, Bors, and Lancelot correspond to Abel; Gawain, Hector, and
the rest correspond to Cain. Augustine uses the Cain and Abel
story in his influential interpretation of history, *De civitate Dei*.
He makes Cain and Abel the patrons of the cities of man and God
respectively (*De civ. Dei*, 15.1) and interprets Cain's murder of
Abel as the prototype of crimes against the social order, an interpretation the *Queste* and the *Sankgreal* follow. The generations
of the earthly city descend from Cain, and those of the heavenly
city from Seth, whom Adam begat in the place of Abel (*De civ.
Dei*, 15.15). That Cain built a city on earth while Abel did not
leads Augustine to conclude that: "Superna est . . . sanctorum civi-
tas, quamvis hic pariat cives, in quibus peregrinatur, donec regni
eius tempus adveniat, cum congregatura est omnes in suis corpori-
bus resurgentes" (The city of the saints is above, although here below it begets citizens, in whom it sojourns till the time of its reign
arrives, when it shall gather together all in the day of the resurrection), *De civ. Dei*, 15.1. The destiny of the Grail companions, whose

adventures are a kind of pilgrimage, is the heavenly city, as Galahad's apotheosis at the end of the quest illustrates. For Augustine,
the meaning of history can be summarized in the story of Cain and
Abel, since every individual at the end of his life is judged to belong either in the company of Cain or in the company of Abel.
The *Queste* and the *Sankgreal* predict the ultimate significance of
the lives of the Round Table knights by dividing them into those
who see the Grail revealed and hence belong, provided that they
sin no more, to Abel's company and those who cannot find the
Grail—the *visio Dei*—and hence belong, unless they repent, to
the company of Cain.

In the particular event that makes manifest in time the distinction between Cain and Abel, that is, in the fratricide, Augustine
sees the course of history predicted: Abel's suffering foreshadows
the persecution that the sojourning city of God will endure at the
hands of the wicked whose concern is the earthly happiness of the
earthly city (*De civ. Dei*, 15.15). Since he is writing to the Roman
Empire, whose capital city was also founded by a fratricide, Augustine acknowledges a correspondence but distinguishes the two
fratricides: Cain and Abel represent the enmity of the heavenly
city and the earthly city, while Romulus and Remus demonstrate
how the wicked war against the wicked (*De civ. Dei*, 15.5).

In fact, only perfectly good men are able not to war against each
other; while "concupiscentiae carnales inter se duorum bonorum,
nondum utique perfectorum, sicut inter se pugnant mali et mali,
donec eorum, qui curantur, ad ultimam victoriam sanitas per-
ducatur" (the carnal lusts of two men, good but not yet perfect,
contend together, just as the wicked contend with the wicked,
until the health of those who are under the treatment of grace
attains final victory), *De civ. Dei*, 15.5. This last point explains
some of the otherwise mysterious conflicts recounted by the *Queste*
author, such as Perceval's and Lancelot's attack on Galahad and
the war of Varlan and Lambar.

Augustine's purpose in contrasting the two fratricides was to
depreciate the glory of Roman history by showing it to be inferior,
on a moral and hence eschatological level, to Christian history. By
showing that biblical history provides the archetype by which
Roman history can be measured, Augustine establishes the precedence of biblical history and demonstrates its universality. When
the *Queste* author sets the Cain and Abel story in a context that

makes it one of two archetypal historical events, he is, like Augustine, universalizing the story.

### Bors: The Testing of Charity

Bors's adventures in the *Queste* explore the implications of what it means to be, like Abel, a citizen of the city of God while still in the journey of this life.[35] His adventures complicate the concept of Cain's sin and offer resolutions to it. Bors, like the habitual sinners in the quest and unlike Perceval and Galahad, has had sexual experience. Already a penitent, Bors confesses at the beginning of the Grail quest. Personal purity is a prerequisite to his adventures, which involve him in choices of social, rather than personal, consequences. Perceval's and Lancelot's adventures illustrate responses to the personal problem of sexual temptation; Bors's adventures illustrate responses to death, a social problem that enters history as a consequence of Eve's concupiscence and threatens the order of justice.

To be a citizen of the city of God is to enjoy immortal life, but to distinguish precisely what actions in this world are life supporting is often difficult. For example, the fruits of sexual union offer one kind of triumph over death. In the trials of Bors the *Queste* author explores two conflicting avenues to immortality: the pagan way of sex, death, and fame (mortal immortality) and the Christian way of chastity, death, and spiritual immortality. Bors is tempted to condone or engage in sexual sin that prevents the literal death of mortal life; but he twice blocks unsanctioned sexual activity, each time placing spiritual being above the demands of simple physical existence. Because his previous sexual experience allows him to recognize the manipulative strategies of a seductress, Bors cannot be led unaware into sensual indulgence as Perceval and Lancelot are; and since Bors has intellectually committed himself to chastity, he will not engage in sexual play to gratify himself. The seduction direct is not the only way in which man's chastity can be assailed, however. Called upon to act rather than simply to react, Bors discovers that his commitment to chastity and spiritual life can be tested by the choices he makes with respect to others. That each of the episodes ties sex and death together reveals that for the *Queste* author the fundamental issue in life

35. On Malory's characterization of Bors, see R. M. Lumiansky, "Malory's Steadfast Bors."

choices is whether a choice reflects or cancels a commitment to spiritual life. In the most abstract, the most generalized form, Bors's choices are always between sex and death, on the one hand, and chastity and eternal life on the other.

In the first of his adventures, foreshadowed in his vision of birds reenacting the pelican myth, Bors puts his life in jeopardy in the defense of a young woman about to be wrongfully disinherited by her older sister. The holy abbot whom Bors at length finds to comment on his adventures tells him that in risking his life for the young woman, an embodiment of Holy Church, Bors has fought Christ's battle. By implication, he has followed the example of the pelican (a symbol of Christ) who sacrifices himself to preserve the lives of his young. This first adventure illustrates Bors's selflessness, but to champion the cause of distressed maidens hardly represents an unusual undertaking for a knight of the Round Table: this battle reveals Bors's loyalty to the Arthurian code of knighthood and shows him to be careless of death and pain himself.

In the next adventures the *Queste* author increases the difficulty of the test: simple response in terms of the knightly code no longer suffices. Riding up to a crossroads, Bors looks in one direction and sees his beloved brother Lionel being dragged off and beaten; in the other direction he sees an armed knight kidnapping a maiden who cries for help in the name of Jesus. Although Bors assumes that his brother will be killed, he elects to save the maiden from rape. The *Queste* author confronts no other knight with such startling alternatives, alternatives foreshadowed in Bors's dream of the rotten tree about to fall and the two lilies bent toward each other, about to be blighted by contact. In rejecting the appeal of natural love (that is, of familial concern for his brother) in order to save the maiden, Bors grants priority to sexual purity over the instinct to preserve mortal life. He upholds the claims of spiritual over natural kinship. Subsequent events justify his action. Had not Bors intervened, the lust of the knight for his own cousin would have defiled both their virgin bodies, imperiled their souls, and, as an abbot later assures Bors, brought the judgment of the wrath of God upon them in the form of sudden death to their bodies and souls. While leaving his own kinsman in jeopardy, Bors preserves the life of another family who will, the abbot says, in the legitimate descendants of both the knight and the maiden, produce many true knights and men of honor. This adventure represents sexual defilement as murder, as both spiritual and literal death. The death of the body, which threatens Lionel, need not imply the second death, the destruction of the soul; hence, Lionel's plight is less grave than that of the maiden.

Having saved the maiden's life and that of her attacker, Bors sets off to rescue Lionel but instead finds an adventure that calls the value of Bors's chastity into question by showing that it can also be a cause of death. A monk riding a black horse confirms Bors's fear that Lionel is dead and questions Bors's decision to let his brother die to save a virgin's maidenhood; he charges that Bors's chastity is merely a way of gaining earthly renown and encourages him to abandon it. He offers Bors lodging in a tower where a beautiful lady, foreshadowed in Bors's dream by a white swan, claims to love Bors more than anyone in the world and urges her love as a reason for him to reciprocate her passion. Her strategy for winning Bors, if illogical, is not an uncommon one in the literary tradition of *fin amour*: she tells him that she loves him so much that he must love her. She heightens the pressure on him by threatening to die for love, to kill herself if rejected. Bors, however, keeps his wits: though he does not want her to die, he need not endanger his own soul to save another; so he refuses her.

Bors has good authority for his decision. Gregory the Great comments in the *Moralia* on just such a problem as Bors faces:

> Genimina . . . sunt animae operationes bonae. . . . Nulla quippe ante omnipotentis Dei oculos justitiae pietatisque sunt opera, quae corruptionis contagio monstrantur immunda. Quid enim prodest si pie quisquam necessitati compatitur proximi, quando impie semetipsum destruit habitationem Dei? Si ergo per cordis munditiam libidinis flamma non exstinguitur, incassum quaelibet virtutes oriuntur. ("The offsprings" of the soul are good practices. . . . For before the eyes of almighty God there are no works of justice and piety, which are shown to be unclean by the infection of corruption. For what does it profit, if a man piously has compassion for the need of his neighbor, when he impiously destroys himself, the habitation of God? So then if by purity of heart the flame of lust is not quenched, any virtues whatever spring up in vain.)[36]

36. Gregory the Great, *Moralia in Job*, 21.12.19, in *Patrologia latina* (hereafter cited as *PL*) 76:201; my translation.

However correct Bors thinks his decision to be, the adventure tests his conviction, for the lady carries out her threat. She and her maidens hurl themselves to their deaths. In pity Bors crosses himself, and at the sign of the cross the tower and maidens vanish in a tumult of noise, like fiends.

That the *Queste* author associates the white swan, rather than the black, with this evil lady indicates the deceptiveness of appearances in earthly adventures. This reversal of black and white symbolism is, in fact, appropriately attached to the swan, whose white feathers, according to bestiary tradition, hide its black skin, a sign of the deceitful habit of veiling sins of the flesh.[37]

When Bors again meets Lionel, who, after all, is not physically dead, Bors greets Lionel saying: "Biau frere, quant venistes vos ci?" (Fayre swete brothir, whan cam ye hydir?), *Q*, 188; M, 969. This is similar to the way Abel greets Cain when Cain is about to murder him: "Bien viegniez, biau frere!" (*Q*, 217). Because of Lionel's fratricidal intentions, natural brotherhood again proves to be insufficient to guarantee the social harmony that is a primary goal in the quest. God's miraculous intervention to prevent Bors's death demonstrates divine approval of Bors's disregard for natural relationships, sexual or familial, in favor of spiritual ones. Because this adventure happens to one of the chief knights on the quest, and because it is a conflict between natural brothers patterned in some detail on the Cain and Abel story, it stands out from the *Queste*'s other Cain and Abel typologies. Considered together with the hermit's gloss on Bors's decision to rescue the maiden instead of Lionel, this episode illustrates that spiritual brotherhood is the only ground for social harmony on earth as well as in heaven, and it provides a gloss for other and earlier adventures in the *Queste*. The maiden whom Bors saves from rape, whom he has seen in a dream under the image of a lily, is a loyal and pure Christian. A hermit commends Bors for aiding her, Bors's spiritual sister: "Ele vos pria si doucement que vos fustes par pitié conquis, et meistes arriere dos toute naturel amor por amor de Jhesucrist: si alastes la pucele secorre et lessastes vostre frere mener en peril" (*Q*, 187; cf. M, 968). In contrast to the maiden, Lional has become through his sins like the rotten and withered tree of Bors's dream. He is like those who cause Holy Church to appear to Bors as a

---

37. See *De bestiis et aliis rebus*, 1.53, wrongly attributed to Hugh of St. Victor or to Hugh of Folieto, in *PL* 177:51.

woman weeping for sons who betray her: "Ele vos aparut triste et noire por le corroz meismes que si fil li font, ce sont li crestien pecheor, qui li deussent estre fil, et il li sont fillastre" (Q, 185). By becoming a false son to Holy Church, Lionel denies his spiritual brotherhood in Christ with Bors. The hermit clearly implies that the claims of spiritual brotherhood take precedence over those of the natural brother, but because ideal spiritual fraternity draws its affective power from natural brotherhood, a conflict between natural brothers is felt in the *Queste* to be especially terrible.

## The Adventure of Solomon's Ship: Return to Eden and Fulfillment of History

The adventure of Solomon's ship and the two episodes that follow it complete the pattern of history in the *Queste*. The last adventures, the visions of the holy Grail, are primarily eschatological and pass beyond history.

My earlier discussion of the *Queste*'s patterning of history, which is centered in the adventure of Solomon's ship, postponed a consideration of the stories of Christian history that Perceval's sister relates. These stories link the Christian past to the present, and we see that past fulfilled in the Grail companions' adventures with Solomon's ship, the Castle of Carcelois, and the leprous lady. To understand why it is appropriate to see these adventures as the completion of the pattern of history, we must first consider their structural significance in the lives of Galahad, Perceval, Bors, and Perceval's sister.

The adventure of Solomon's ship in the *Queste* and the *Sankgreal* is an analogue of the last cantos of Dante's *Purgatorio*. As I suggested earlier, when the four companions board Solomon's ship, they in effect enter the Promised Land; in other words, they recover Eden, just as Dante does when he enters the garden on the top of Mount Purgatory.[38] Conventionally, the Church is called a garden or a paradise in biblical commentary; and Solomon's ship, a symbol of the Church of the elect, is an analogue of paradise. The canopy or frame over Solomon's bed, made from the Tree of Life, is the principal sign that the ship is a garden; the white, green, and red beams of the canopy are, as it were, flowers. Entry

38. See Charles Singleton, "Return to Eden," in *Dante Studies*, vol. 2, *Journey to Beatrice*, pp. 139–287.

into the garden, closed to man since Adam's sin and opened now only by Christ's grace, signifies the recovery of the state of original justice.

The preparatory adventures of the Grail knights correspond to Dante's purgatorial journey. Each one of them, like Dante, is tried; each one of them, as the discussion of the preparatory adventures of Bors and Perceval shows, has undergone confession before he boards Solomon's ship. Galahad confesses before he is knighted, and he does not sin after that. Although Galahad's adventures do not really seem to test him, he completes those reserved for him (taking up Mordrain's shield with the red cross made by Joseph of Arimathea's blood, delivering the Castle of Maidens), just as Christ, of whom Galahad is a type, fulfilled the roles and the tasks prophesied for him. Yet Galahad is less than Christ; so he must, like any other man, recover Edenic innocence through penance, which he undergoes before he is knighted; and he must do what is expected of him without falling into error before he can reach Solomon's ship.[39]

Structurally, in the *Queste*, the adventure of Solomon's ship forms the climax of the preparatory adventures, just as, theologically, this adventure is the culmination of the preparatory tests and trials of Galahad, Perceval, and Bors: this episode gives narrative expression to the knights' justification by grace. Theologically, to be justified is to have received sanctifying grace, to be conformed to the likeness of God. It signifies right order in the soul and can only come when sin and its consequences have been purged from the soul.

The *Queste* author expresses the justification of Galahad and his companions simply: they board Solomon's ship without incurring any of the injuries the ship promises to those unworthy to enter her. On the ship they find a golden crown lying on Solomon's bed, Solomon's own crown of justice. Although none of the knights places it upon his head, the crown is not forbidden to them (early

---

39. Myrrha Lot-Borodine takes the hermit's reference to Mordrain's dream of the ninth river, muddy at its source, clear in the middle, and doubly clear and sweet at the end (*Q*, 135) to be an allegory of the progress of Galahad's life; see "Les Deux conquerants du Graal," in *Trois Essais sur le roman de Lancelot du Lac et la Quête du Saint Graal*, p. 112; see also her related essay, "Christ-chevalier: Galaad," in *De l'Amour profane à l'amour sacré*, pp. 158–85, esp. 177.

in the quest, a crown is forbidden to Melias, who suffers a great injury for stealing it before he has proven his right to it by submitting himself to trials [Q, 41–46; M, 883–86]). Galahad does not wear a crown until he is made king of Sarras, after his Grail vision at Corbenic, his journey to Sarras, his bearing of the Grail table into that city, and his year of imprisonment there; his last experiences are the subfulfillment of Christ's entry into Jerusalem, Christ's Passion, his descent into hell, his Resurrection, and his Ascension. When Galahad wears the crown in Sarras, he becomes an analogue of the figure of Christ that appeared in Lancelot's eschatological dream, of the man crowned with a golden crown and attended by nine companions (Q, 130; M, 928).

Galahad and his companions also discover a sword lying on Solomon's bed, and this sword is the primary instrument through which the *Queste* author illustrates Galahad's justification. In the adventure of Carcelois, after the knights leave Solomon's ship, this sword becomes an instrument of divine vengeance; Galahad's battle there prefigures the Second Advent of Christ, when Christ will judge the world. Galahad's new sword gives him, while he carries it, special gifts that make him wise and absolutely impervious to temptation. The pommel, made of a single stone of all colors, contains Solomon's wisdom; but the principal active power of the sword comes from its hilt, fashioned for Galahad by Solomon out of the ribs of a papalust, a snake from Caledonia, and an ortenax, a fish from the Euphrates. The origin of the ribs suggests that whoever holds them has authority over the world, from one end to the other, from Scotland to the East. More precisely, whoever holds the sword hilt becomes insensible to heat through the power of the papalust and forgetful of joy, sorrow, and everything except his immediate purpose through the power of the ortenax. Literally, the ribs give battle strength to whoever grips them. If the battle is an allegorical or spiritual one, then the power of the ribs makes a man incapable of feeling desire to sin (insensible to heat) and forgetful of the joys and sorrows of sin (intent only upon God's justice). When Galahad draws the sword, its blade—originally from King David's sword—is so bright that he can see his face mirrored in it. This image suggests that Galahad, whose soul is now conformed to the likeness of God (Galahad's entry into the ship and his ability to grip the sword make manifest his just condition), mirrors God's justice and is mirrored in the emblem of

God's justice, the sword blade. The sword and Galahad are reciprocal images, each reflecting the justice of the other, each an image
of divine justice.

A remark earlier in the *Queste* corroborates this interpretation
of the sword. One of the hermits explains Lancelot's sinfulness to
him by suggesting that his vision is so blurred that he would no
more see the Holy Grail than a blind man would see a sword before
him (Malory says "bryght swerde" [M, 927]). The hermit then compares the darkness of sin to the true light to which Christ calls men.
This discourse connects the sword to the true light, suggesting
that to come to the true light is to be prepared for judgment—for
God's sword—and implies that a properly ordered soul must precede a vision of the Holy Grail. That the *Queste* links the sword,
the true light, and the state of justice through penance in this
earlier passage (*Q*, 123) helps to explain this scene, where Galahad
sees himself in the sword blade.

What it means to hold this sword becomes evident through Galahad's adventure at Carcelois, which can be compared to an earlier
adventure at the Castle of Maidens.[40] In the later, Carcelois episode, Galahad kills for the first time, becoming an instrument of
God's judgment. The parallel between the two adventures derives
from the nature of the crimes that make Galahad's intervention de-
sirable to restore order. In both castles, the conditions of injustice
prevailing when Galahad arrives were initiated by sexual sins that
led to murder and a reign of injustice: these particular histories
belong to the typologies of Eve and Cain. After Galahad frees the
Castle of Maidens from the seven brothers who have been holding
it, he learns the history of the brothers' custom of imprisoning
every maiden who comes to the castle: the seven brothers came to
the castle, sought and received hospitality from Duke Lynor, then
quarreled with him over one of his daughters whom they wanted
to defile, killing the duke and one of his sons. From their lust came
murder. The daughter prophesies to them that the castle won on
account of a maid will be lost through a maid. To prevent this,
the brothers imprison the maidens who come there until the maid-
en (that is, virgin) Galahad comes and restores justice (clearly,
Galahad is not the kind of maiden the brothers expected). Here,

40. Luc Cornet, in "Trois Épisodes de la *Queste del Graal*," argues
that these two episodes and the episode of the leprous lady are variations
on the same anecdote.

as in the principal narrative of Gawain's and Bors's adventures, the conflict repeats the typology of Cain and Abel: in accepting the hospitality of Duke Lynor's table, the brothers have entered his fellowship; in destroying the fellowship they commit spiritual fratricide and institute a reign of cruel injustice. Galahad restores order to the Castle of Maidens by defeating the seven brothers and driving them out. He does not kill them; and Gawain, who does, is severely reprimanded for his murder.

In the principal narrative line the early conflicts such as that between Gawain and Owein involve spiritual fratricide; but as the narrative moves toward its conclusion, the conflicts grow more terrible, pitting natural brothers against each other and destroying both natural and spiritual kinship, as in the conflict between Bors and Lionel. The same development can be seen in the histories of the two castles: at the Castle of Maidens disorder results from spiritual fratricide, but at Carcelois it comes from incest and a fratricide that is natural as well as spiritual. God's judgment on Carcelois is correspondingly harsher. For the first time in the *Queste*, Galahad actually kills his enemies. He is so powerful that they do not think he is mortal, but the fact that Galahad is troubled by the deaths he has caused signals his humanity even at the moment when he has become the instrument of Christ's judgment. Only when Galahad hears the history of the castle does he recognize the justice in his destruction. At Carcelois, Count Ernol's castle, the disorder began when the count's three sons raped his daughter. She complained, and fratricidal war broke out. The brothers killed their sister, imprisoned their father, and murdered men of religion; therefore, death is justice to the traitorous brothers because they are already spiritually dead. The adventure of Carcelois demonstrates that, with his new sword, Galahad's justice accords perfectly with God's: after the adventure of Solomon's ship, Galahad can act definitively without his action being sinful. His reason and will are ordered to God's justice.

In the state of justification, sex offers no temptation, and human love is purged of its sinful tendencies; that is why the *Queste* author introduces a woman into the company of the three knights in the adventure of Solomon's ship. Analogously, in the *Commedia*, Dante and Beatrice meet again in the garden of *Purgatorio*. The *Queste* author does not make us respond to Perceval's sister as strongly as we react to Beatrice, but he does give her a moving scene that is a celebration of spiritual marriage. Solomon's sword must have a new belt made by a woman; Solomon's wife supplied it only with a mean hempen belt, a sign that the conflict between the sexes engendered by Eve's sin cannot be overcome until Mary has borne Christ, who resolves sexual conflict because male and female are equal members in Christ (see Gal. 3:28). The knights do not know where to find a woman to make the belt until Perceval's sister tells them that she has already made it:

> "Bel seignor, . . . veez ci les renges qui i doivent estre. Sachiez, . . . que je les fis de la chose de sus moi que je avoie plus chiere, ce fu de mes cheveux. Et se je les avoie chiers ce ne fu mie de merveille, car le jor de Pentecoste que vos fustes chevaliers, sire, dit ele a Galaad, avoie je le plus bel chief que fame dou monde eust. Mes si tost come je soi que ceste aventure m'estoit apareilliee et qu'il le me covenoit fere, si me fis tondre erramment et en fis ces treces teles com vos les poez veoir." ("Lo lordys," she seyde, "here ys a gurdill that ought to be sette aboute the swerde. And wete you well the grettist parte of thys gurdyll was made of my hayre, whych somme tyme I loved well, whyle that I was woman of the worlde. But as sone as I wyste that thys adventure was ordayned me, I clipped off my heyre and made thys gurdyll.") Q, 227; M, 995

The mission Perceval's sister takes on is the feminine counterpart of the knights' Grail quest; by cutting off her hair, she, too, renounces the values of the world for a higher and more spiritual set of values.

She removes the rope girdle supplied by Solomon's wife for Solomon's sword, takes off Galahad's old sword—the one that he drew from the rock on the day of Pentecost when he arrived at Arthur's court (that Galahad gets a new sword suggests that he has now surpassed Arthur, who also drew his sword from a rock)—then she girds the new sword on Galahad with her new girdle. They exchange the following words:

> "Certes, sire, or ne me chaut il mes quant je muire; car je me tiegn orendroit a la plus beneuree pucele dou monde, qui ai fet le plus preudome dou siecle chevalier. . . ."
> "Damoisele, fet Galaad, vos en avez tant fet que je en seré vostre chevaliers a toz jorz mes. Et moutes merciz de tant com vos en dites."

("Now recke I nat though I dye, for now I holde me one
of the beste blyssed maydyns of the worlde, whych hath
made the worthyest knyght of the worlde."

"Damesell," seyde sir Galahad, "ye have done so muche
that I shall be your knyght all the dayes of my lyff.") Q, 228;
M, 995

Perceval's sister is saying, I think, that Galahad has now actually
become what he potentially was before, the knight who is the subfulfillment of Christ. Galahad promises to be her knight in a cere-
mony reminiscent of initiations into knighthood; but in pledging
loyalty to a lady rather than to a feudal lord, Galahad implies that
they have entered into a kind of spiritual marriage. Because spiritual marriage is not a sexual union but a fellowship, it does not
exclude others; and Perceval's sister continues to be the companion
of Bors and Perceval as well as of Galahad. A vision they experience on the path from Carcelois to the leprous lady makes manifest
the nature of their companionship. They follow a white hart
guarded by four lions into a chapel, where the hart becomes a man
and the lions become the symbols of the four Evangelists. A hermit
implies to the four companions of Solomon's ship that they are
types of the Evangelists, and, like them, the close companions of
Christ. Christ, then, is the principle of their companionship, a
fellowship that is a spiritual marriage.

The peacefulness and joy of this companionship, this spiritual
marriage, foreshadow the repose of the saints bound to Christ in
the eschatological marriage prophesied in the parable of the wedding feast. The *Queste* author associates the idea of repose with
the spiritual union of Galahad and Perceval's sister on Solomon's
ship through the bed beside which their promises are exchanged.
As Locke explains, this bed is also a figure of the cross and of the
Christian altar.[41] To lie in it is to foreshadow, more exactly than
does the spiritual union of two souls through Christ, the final
consummation of the divine marriage of Christ and the soul. Galahad does not consummate physically his union with Perceval's
sister, just as Dante does not express his love for Beatrice through
physical union. When, at last, Galahad lies in the bed, while the
three companions are sailing to Sarras, he lies alone with Christ,
joined to Christ in mystic contemplation as he lies on the bed of
contemplation that Solomon praised in the Song of Songs. At this

41. Locke, *Quest*, p. 91.

point, Galahad, who already bears the red of charity and the white of purity, finds the green of fruition, of spiritual fertility, for as the Bride says in the Song of Songs, "Our bed is flourishing" (1:15).[42] He then possesses all three of the colors of the beams from the Tree of Life that make a canopy over the bed.

History, however, rather than contemplative vision, dominates the adventure of Solomon's ship. In the narrative structure of the *Queste*, the Grail visions and Galahad's sleep on the bed of contemplation come after the pattern of history is complete; so, in human life, death and resurrection come after the time of trial. Justification, the state into which the companions enter through this adventure, must precede entrance into the heavenly wedding feast, which is Galahad's destiny in the *Queste*. Since justification became necessary to man as a result of the Fall, which is the beginning of human history, and since the purpose of justification is to restore man to his original relationship with God, a proper perspective on human history is a function of justification. Both Dante and the *Queste* author grant their characters a vision of history in order to demonstrate what justification means. The resemblances in the details and structure of the presentation of history in the *Queste* and the *Commedia* do not necessarily imply that one is a source of the other, since both draw from the same Christion tradition; they do, however, suggest that these texts can be read as analogues of one another. Dante, the pilgrim, sees two pageants: one shows him a paradigm of history, the other shows him the history of the Church. The *Queste* author similarly separates the paradigm of history, which is contained in the legend of the Tree of Life, from the stories of Christian history recounted by Perceval's sister.

Dante sees the first pageant before he crosses Lethe; this pageant is a procession of the books of the Bible and contains all history from Eden to the Apocalypse. The Old Testament authors wear white lilies to signify their faith; the Evangelists are wreathed in green leaves to signify the fruitfulness of Christ's marriage to

42. On the bed of mystical repose, see William of Saint-Thierry, *Exposé sur le Cantique des cantiques*, 95–106, 139–42; *Serm. Cant. cant.*, 46. Both gloss Cant. 1:15–16 ("Our bed is flourishing. The beams of our houses are of cedar, our rafters of cypress-trees") as an allegory of the Church. William's comment on the bed and the beams of faith and hope illuminates the nature of Solomon's ship in the *Queste*.

the Church; the other New Testament authors wear the red roses of martyrdom. On Solomon's ship, the three posts from the Tree of Life, colored white, green, and red, symbolize virginity, marriage, and martyrdom. These three colors are also the emblems of the theological virtues: faith, hope, and charity. As I suggested earlier, the progression of these colors, interpreted in the *Queste* by the events that occurred under the tree, is also a paradigm of history: from Adam's and Eve's innocence, through their mating, to Cain's fratricide. Implicitly, we can read these colors in reverse order to find the conclusion of history, which they foreshadow: the red becomes, then, Christ's martyrdom (the *Queste* legend of the tree makes the typological relationship of Abel to Christ explicit [*Q*, 218–19]); the green becomes natural Christian marriage; the white becomes virginity or chastity and represents the spiritual condition of paradise restored. The significance of red and white in this context is clear. The legend of the Tree of Life, which turned green when Adam and Eve mated, associates green with marriage. A hermit's remark to Bors corroborates this interpretation: the hermit associates ordinary trees (green) with Christian marriage; and his remark also shows that the *Queste* author, though he considers virginity or chastity (white) a higher spiritual state, is not opposed to marriage:

> "Car, si com Nostre Sires dit: 'Li bons arbres fet le bon fruit,' vos devez estre bons par droiture, car vos estes le fruit del tres bon arbre. Car vostre peres, li rois Boors, fu uns des meillors homes que je onques veisse, rois piteus et humbles; et vostre mere, la reine Eveine, fu une des meillors dames que je veisse pieça. Cil dui furent un sol arbre et une meisme char par conjonction de mariage. Et puis que vos en estes fruit vos devriez estre bons quant li arbre furent bon."
> (*Q*, 164–65)

The end of history, if we read the three colors in reverse order, is associated with the color white, which frequently symbolizes Galahad, Perceval, and Bors (as in Gawain's dream of the bulls). When, at Carcelois, the Grail knights effect God's judgment, they foreshadow the completion of history in the Last Judgment.

Christian history is also represented to Dante, the pilgrim, in the form of a pageant. The cart, which represents Ecclesia and is an imperfect analogue of Solomon's ship and of the Garden itself

—imperfect because it is not exclusively the Church of the elect and hence is compared to a "nave in fortuna" (see *Purgatorio*, 32. 115–17)—suffers enormous outrages. R. E. Kaske interprets these outrages to be a history of the main stages of Church history, and he has found glosses to explain the imagery of the poem's account of the pageant.[43] Dante identifies the tree to which the cart is tied by Christ—in the shape of a griffin—as the Tree of Life, which is now flowering reddish purple to symbolize Christ's sacrifice. In the *Queste*, after Abel's death, the type of Christ's martyrdom, the tree turns red and remains red forever.

Like the stories of Christian history represented in Dante's pageant, the three stories Perceval's sister tells to explain prophecies written on the sword and on its scabbard also recount disasters, but the paradigm to which they conform, that of sexual sin and murder, is simpler than Dante's: the three stories recount the crimes into which those who follow the Grail quest without being confessed will fall, as the hermit tells Bors: "Seront ort et mauvés plus que jel ne porroie penser, et en charra li uns en avoutire, li autres en fornicacion et li autre en homicide" (*Q*, 163). They are also the crimes that lie behind the greatest of the two enchantments that will be dispelled in the quest of the Grail, but Perceval's sister's earliest story of Christian history, which fulfilled the sword's prophecy, "HE THAT SHALL PRAYSE ME MOSTE, MOSTE SHALL HE FYNDE ME TO BLAME AT A GRETE NEDE" (*M*, 988; cf. *Q*, 206), refers us back to the first generation of gentile Christians, to Nascien and Mordrain. Once the pagan rulers of Sarras, Nascien and Mordrain were converted by Joseph of Arimathea, whom they followed to Logres; they are the ancestors of Lancelot and Galahad. Their conversion is the initial stage in the Church's fulfillment of her history; according to the *Queste*, the Church's goal is to join all men, Jews and gentiles, in Christ, the principle of social harmony and justice. Nascien's and Mordrain's adventure, here recounted by Perceval's sister, reveals the principle by which the disasters of Christian history will occur.

The histories of Nascien and Mordrain, the former recalled here by Perceval's sister and the latter told elsewhere in the *Queste* (85–86; cf. *M*, 908), show that sin prevents them from accomplishing adventures reserved for Galahad. Nascien, who was once mirac-

43. Kaske, "Dante's *Purgatorio* XXXII and XXXIII: A Survey of Christian History."

ulously carried to an island in the west where he found Solomon's ship and its sword, discovers through his adventure that sin is the impediment to possession of that ship. He tries to use the sword, reserved for Galahad, to kill a giant; but the sword breaks. He kills the giant anyway and then sails until he meets his brother, Mordrain, who mends the sword with Christ's help and explains that it broke not from any intrinsic fault but "par aucune sene-fiance ou par aucun pechié de Nascien" (*Q*, 208). Malory is more decisive: "So whan Mordrayns saw the swerde he praysed hit muche, 'but the brekyng was do by wyckednesse of thyselffward, for thou arte in som synne' " (*M*, 989). Mordrain's explanation implies that sin is the basis for all three disasters in Christian history. As he and Nascien leave the ship, a flying lance wounds Nascien to signify his presumption in drawing the sword (though not a thigh wound, this wound is analogous to Perceval's and the maimed king's wounds). Mordrain also suffers for trying to fulfill an adventure reserved for Galahad: for going too near the Grail, Mordrain is blinded and robbed of his strength. He then asks to live to see Galahad. Healing him is one of Galahad's major adventures, to be completed before he goes to Corbenic, the Grail castle.

The *Queste* author separates the two enchantments, the maiming of the king and the wasting of the land, into separate histories (recounted by Perceval's sister) in order to clarify his own interpretation of the relationship between individual and society in the fallen world. The maimed king is Parlan, who one day found Solomon's ship and attempted to draw the sword, only to be struck through the thighs by a flying lance. The correspondence between this wound and the one Perceval inflicts upon himself earlier in the *Queste* as a penance for risking his chastity suggests that Parlan's sin is sexual, hence individual. His crime, then, is linked to Eve's sin and the sexual sins that precede murder in the histories of the Castle of Maidens and Carcelois. After the Grail mass at Corbenic, Galahad takes blood from the holy lance to annoint the maimed king and heals him with this medicine.

The story of the wasteland brings us to consider fraternity as a social ideal on a universal scale. In this history the converted pagan, King Varlan, fights the Grailkeeper, King Lambar, with the sword from Solomon's ship. (The Grailkeepers descend from Joseph of Arimathea, a Jewish Christian.) With the blow that kills

Lambar, the land is wasted. Varlan returns to the ship for the scabbard, sheathes the sword, and falls down dead. Perceval's sister gives us no reason for preferring one king over the other: they are equally good Christians and equally heinous in warring on each other. Their crime is to have violated the spiritual fraternity that their faith implies. The cosmic significance given to their battle derives from their identities as the representatives of the two great lineages united in Christianity, the Jews and the gentiles. The goal of Christian fraternity is to achieve the peace of Christ between Jew and gentile, the two branches of mankind (see Rom. 11:1–32). The wasting of the land results from the battle between the two branches of the Church, which are not yet joined in perfect faith and perfect justice.

Earlier in the *Queste* the author treats the problem of the Jews, characterized as pagans, who reject Christ. In adventures belonging to Perceval and Bors, the *Queste* author figures the enmity between Old Law and New Law under the image of two ladies or two sisters. In his adventure, Perceval dreams of two ladies, one bestride a serpent and the other upon a lion. The first lady accuses Perceval of betraying her, while the other warns him of the battle he must fight next day with Satan, who is disguised as a woman in black. Later Perceval learns that these two ladies signify the Old Law of the Synagogue and the New Law of the Holy Church. The reign of the younger has displaced that of the elder, but the two ladies are implicitly related as successive brides of the same lord. Paul uses a similar allegory in Rom. 7:1–5, where he imagines one bride with successive husbands, the Old Law and Christ; the *Queste* author transposes the sex roles to insist on the continuity of God and the changing definition of his people, who are his bride. In an adventure belonging to Bors, the *Queste* author explicitly connects the conflict between the two ladies with the Cain and Abel typology by representing the successive brides of King Amanz as natural sisters. By incarnating the Holy Church and the Synagogue as sisters, the *Queste* author suggests the kind of love and loyalty that should have existed between them. Instead, when Christ comes and displaces the elder sister for having instituted evil customs, putting the younger sister in her stead, the elder refuses to be reconciled and expresses her hatred of her younger sister by attacking her. Bors champions the younger sister's case by fighting the elder sister's knight and defeating him;

but he does not kill either the elder sister or her knight, and the
*Queste* predicts that the new peace will not last. We are invited
to perceive the conflict between the two sisters, the Synagogue and
the Church, as a fratricidal battle like that between Cain and Abel,
except that the battle between the sisters is inconclusive. The adventure of Bors, the vision of Perceval, and the contest between
Lambar and Varlan seem tragic when these events are measured
against the peace through faith achieved between the earliest Jewish Christians—Joseph of Arimathea and his company—and the
first converted pagans—Mordrain and Nascien.

Galahad, Perceval's sister, Bors, and Perceval complete the work
begun by Joseph, Nascien, and Mordrain. The companions of the
Grail quest, having purged sin from themselves, demonstrate the
disenchantment of the wasteland, cure King Mordrain, heal
the maimed King Parlan, and realize the celestial fellowship of the
Church of the elect in this life.

Although the fulfillment of history belongs chiefly to Galahad
and is focused in him, the adventure of the leprous lady, which
shows how the wasteland may be restored, belongs to Perceval's
sister. A lady of mercy, like the Blessed Virgin,[44] Perceval's sister
volunteers to die so that the leprous lady who requires the medicine of a noble virgin's blood may be cured. The knights come
upon her castle after they leave Carcelois and fight a hard battle
before yielding to the custom of the castle and allowing Perceval's
sister to complete the adventure that belongs to her. Leprosy was
usually considered a punishment for sin, sometimes, more specifically, for sexual sin; so it is fitting that it should be Perceval's sister,
a virgin in thought as well as deed, who sacrifices her blood to heal
the leprous lady and thus puts an end to her murders.[45] This adventure reiterates the pattern of conflict between elder sister and

44. See Myrrha Lot-Borodine, "L'Ève pecheresse et la rédemption de
la femme dans la *Quête du Graal*," in *Trois Essais*, pp. 54, 64.

45. Adam Scot, for example, associates leprosy and sexual sin in his
discussion of Naaman, 4 Kings 5, asking, "Nam quid est inhonestas
leprae, nisi peccatum luxuriae?," *Sermones*, 45, in *PL* 198:411. See also
Saul Nathaniel Brody, *The Disease of the Soul*, pp. 52–58, 124–27, 143–46,
151–52; and Paul Remy, "La Lèpre, thème littéraire au moyen âge: Commentaire d'un passage du roman provençal de Jaufré." For the connection of leprosy with heresy and the association of leprosy with sexual sin,
see R. I. Moore, "Heresy as Disease," in *The Concept of Heresy in the
Middle Ages (11th–13th C.)*, ed. W. Lourdaux and D. Verhelst, pp. 1–11.

younger sister, between the old life of sin and the new life of grace. Perceval's sister has no other name than sister, a detail now significant: she dies for the leprous lady who is potentially her spiritual sister in Christ.

Curiously, as a result of this cure, the three companions discover the only natural sign of fertility they ever see in the *Queste*. After they have set Perceval's now-dead sister aboard the ship that will bear her to Sarras, and after a storm has destroyed the leprous lady's castle, Galahad and Perceval return to the ruined castle and conclude from the terrible destruction that the storm was the vengeance of God, as a heavenly voice confirms. The voice reveals that the cure of the old lady's sickness and the change of her people from a life of war to one of peace does not represent a true inward change in her or her people. The absence of change in their inward being makes them unacceptable to God, who sends the storm to destroy them and to reveal the difference between them and the innocent maidens they have killed. When Perceval and Galahad see the graves of all the innocent maidens who died for the sake of the wicked leprous lady, they perceive a contrast to the ruin that has befallen the leprous lady's castle:

> Si troverent au chief d'une chapele un cimetiere tot plein
> d'arbrisiax fueilluz et d'erbe vert, et estoit toz pleins de beles
> tombes. . . . Si estoit si biax et si delitables qu'il ne sembloit
> mie que tempeste i eust esté. Et non avoit il, car laienz
> gisoient les cors des puceles.
>
> ("Also they founde at the ende of the chappel a chirche-
> yarde, and therein they myght se a sixti fayre tumbis. And
> that place was fayre and so delectable that hit semed hem
> there had bene no tempeste. And there lay the bodyes of all
> the good maydyns which were martirde for the syke lady.")
> *Q*, 245; *M*, 1005

By her death, Perceval's sister causes the graves of the martyrs to become a garden of delights, green and pleasant. God responds to Perceval's sister's sacrifice of herself to him by causing the land to be fertile in sign of her and her fellow martyrs' spiritual fertility. Perceval and Galahad understand then that when God judges, through an agent or a storm, there is a conclusion, there is death but also life, and the nature of God's justice stands revealed to them as a warning of the Last Judgment.

The land lies wasted on account of sin, and its restoration must be accomplished by spiritual means. The *Queste* author does not develop the concept of the wasteland literally, for at no point do any of his characters experience dire physical need. The wasteland lies within the characters, as a hermit tells Lancelot: "Ce fu en la voie de luxure, ce fu en la voie qui gaste cors et ame si merveilleusement que nus nel puet tres bien savoir qui essaié ne l'a" (*Q*, 125–26). Or, from another point of view, the world is the wasteland in which the citizens of the city of God must sojourn to prove themselves, for the world is never without sin, nor can it ever be wholly redeemed in history. To nullify the wasteland altogether would be to lift the stain of Original Sin from all men without qualification, and not even Christ did that.

Galahad, on whose coming history has focused since the time of Solomon, has special qualifications for curing the maimed King Parlan, whose wound is a thigh wound, which implies through analogy to Perceval's wound that Parlan's sin was a sexual sin, the root and cause of evil. Whoever cures sexual sin must be free of that sin himself, as Galahad is, and must also have resolved the sin that results from it, namely fratricide, as Galahad has. Galahad's sexual purity is never in question, and he is also the companion desired above all others by the questing knights; he is a type of Abel, the good brother. The *Queste* offers further grounds for seeing Galahad as the one on whom history has waited and the one who will complete the pattern of history: by the fact of his genealogy, he resolves in his own person the conflicts of history, the conflicts of elder sister and younger sister, of Jew and gentile. Descended on his mother's side from the Grailkeepers whose line extends back to Joseph of Arimathea and ultimately to David and Solomon, Galahad descends on his father's side from the prototypes of the converted gentiles, Mordrain and Nascien.[46] The lineage

46. See Henri de Briel and Manuel Herrmann, *King Arthur's Knights and the Myths of the Round Table*, pp. 245, 247. G. D. West, in "Grail Problems, II: The Grail Family in Old French Verse Romances," reviews genealogies of Perceval in the verse romances and notes a tendency for his connection to the Grail family to be through the maternal line (as is Galahad's in the *Queste*). Frappier, in "Le Graal et la chevalrie," p. 198, points out that Galahad is descended from David on both sides, through his mother and through Lancelot's mother (see *The Vulgate Version of the Arthurian Romances*, 3:13); this kinship, like Lancelot's other name, "Galahos" (var. Galaad [*The Vulgate Version*, 3: 3]), suggests that Galahad is a double of his father. The *Queste* does not remind its audience

of the Grailkeepers is clear enough without a detailed account; they are the remnant of Israel who accept Christ. Galahad's paternal line is another matter; and to establish it, the *Queste* author gives to Galahad's father, Lancelot, a dream of his lineage, the dream of the seven kings and the two knights who attend the man surrounded by stars and crowned with a golden crown. A hermit reveals to Lancelot the identity of the seven kings and two knights by referring to Mordrain's dream-vision of Mordrain's descendants, from his nephew, the son of Nascien, to Lancelot and Galahad. That Galahad represents the union of the two great lineages of Christianity (the remnant of Israel, which accepts Christ, and the gentiles) makes him the incarnate symbol of the Church, makes him, in the view of the author of the *Queste*, the perfect manifestation of one faithful to Christ. Like Christ in semblance but not in degree, Galahad joins two natures in one and unites in himself the two branches of the Church, Jew and gentile. Appropriately, then, Galahad is, like Christ, the desired one for whom the maimed king waits and for whom Mordrain, like Simeon, waits. All the knights on the quest have desired his companionship; but he grants it only to those who are, through penance, without sin and therefore capable of realizing true fellowship. The *Queste* resolves the conflicts of history in the only way a Christian author can resolve them, and that is by the conversion of Jew and gentile to Christ and to the discovery in Christ of spiritual brotherhood: converted Jew and converted gentile meet in Galahad, who manifests to the world the implications of his genealogy—his inner reality—through his companionship with Bors and Perceval.

### The Climax of the Quest: The Grail Visions and Eschatological Marriage

The first and most limited of the Grail visions belongs to Lancelot, whose spiritual progress is not sufficient to allow him to participate in the adventure of Solomon's ship, at the outset of which Bors laments Lancelot's absence to Galahad:

---

either of Lancelot's other name or of his maternal genealogy, but instead explicitly develops Lancelot's paternal line, which goes back to the converted pagans, Mordrain and Nascien. Galahad's mission fulfills the promise of his name and his maternal genealogy, just as Christ the Son fulfills the promise of Adam the father. See also Grace Armstrong Savage, "Father and Son in the *Queste del Saint Graal.*"

"Sire, se or fust ci messires Lancelot vostre peres, il me fust
avis que riens ne nos fausist." Et cil dist qu'il n'i puet estre,
puis qu'il ne plest a Nostre Seignor.

("A, sir Galahad," seyde sir Bors, "if sir Launcelot, your
fadir, were here, than were we well at ease, for than mesemed
we fayled nothynge."

"That may nat be," seyd sir Galahad, "but if hit pleased
our Lorde.") Q, 200; M, 984

Lancelot, then, is clearly distinguished from the other three
knights: when he sets out for Corbenic, he has not been justified
as they have been.

A ship adventure is, however, granted to Lancelot before he goes
to Corbenic, which allows him some of the joys of grace and companionship that the three companions on Solomon's ship experience more fully. While Lancelot is sitting by the shore described
at the end of his previous adventure, hemmed in by wild forest,
rock cliffs, and dangerous water, a voice directs him to enter the
first boat that appears. A ship without sail or oars arrives, and
Lancelot boards her, noticing at first only a fragrance. Later he
discovers the corpse of Perceval's sister, whose tale he learns from
a letter beneath her head. The ship carries him to an old hermit,
who joins him briefly and encourages him to persevere in God's
service, interpreting Perceval's sister to Lancelot as a blessing and
a warning:

"Lancelot, saches que molt t'a Nostre Sires mostree grant
debonereté, quant il en la compaignie de si haute pucele
et de si sainte t'a amené. Or gardes que tu soies chastes en
pensee et en oevre des or en avant, si que la chasteé de toi
s'acort a la virginité de lui. Et ainsi porra durer la compaignie
de vos deus." (Q, 248–49)

Because his sins were primarily sexual, and because Lancelot has
not yet entirely overcome their effect, he is not yet ready for companionship with a living woman; but in granting him companionship with the blessed corpse of a woman, the Queste author
foreshadows the living companionship Lancelot will eventually
enjoy, if only after death.

The food that fills Lancelot while he is aboard the ship, which
the Queste and the Sankgreal compare to the manna that fed the
Israelites in the desert, signals the state of grace into which Lance-

lot has come and yet suggests that he is not yet out of the wilderness of the journey of this life. He is, however, so overwhelmed by the sweetness of his experience that he wonders whether he is "en terre ou en paradis terrestre" (*Q*, 247). Here, as later in the visions, the *Queste* author uses Lancelot's responses to the grace granted to him to clarify the experiences of the Grail companions—Galahad, Perceval, and Bors—who do indeed find the "paradis terrestre," made new by Christ, on Solomon's ship.

Galahad joins Lancelot in his ship adventure for a little while, a sign that in Christ the conflict between fathers and sons is reconciled. A monk at the abbey where Galahad finds his shield and disenchants a tomb tells Galahad that Christ came to earth to resolve the conflict between fathers and sons, a conflict that is always a sign of sin. But the monk also explains to Galahad that the conflict has not been wholly overcome, as is demonstrated by the way Count Ernol of Carcelois is treated by his sons. Christ does, however, make resolution of that conflict available to those who accept him by erasing the significance of generations and making father and son brother in him. No jealousy or envy infects Lancelot's response to Galahad, nor does Galahad rebel against his father. Their half year's journey passes delightfully; and when, at Easter, Galahad is called away, father and son exchange kisses and weep as Lancelot commends Galahad to his adventures and Galahad commends Lancelot to Christ while acknowledging that they will not meet again until, as a heavenly voice confirms, the Day of Judgment (*Q*, 252; M, 1013). That knowledge renders their parting the more affecting. Lancelot asks Galahad to pray for him, but his wise son warns him that the most efficacious prayers will be Lancelot's own.

The boat at length puts Lancelot down at the Grail castle, where he sees his vision of the holy vessel. A voice tells Lancelot to enter the castle; but lions guarding its gate frighten him, and he draws his sword to fight them. A flaming hand plunges down from heaven and knocks the sword from Lancelot's hand, while a voice accuses him of lack of faith and trust. Although this incident illustrates again that Lancelot's judgment is not sure, he is granted entry into the castle. Once inside, he finds no one until he discovers a closed door and hears singing, more beautiful than mortal voice could utter. He cannot open the door, so he prays that Christ not spurn him. The door opens, light floods out (though it is mid-

night), and a voice warns Lancelot not to enter the room. As he
watches, he sees the Holy Grail, ministering angels intent upon
some service, and an old man in priestly vestments apparently
celebrating the Mass:

> Et quant il dut lever *corpus domini*, il fu avis a Lancelot
> que desus les mains au preudome en haut avoit trois homes,
> dont li dui metoient le plus juene entre les mains au
> provoire; et il le levoit en haut, si fesoit semblant qu'il le
> mostrast au pueple.
>
> Et Lancelot, qui resgarde ceste chose, ne s'en merveille
> pas petit: car il voit que li prestres est si chargiez de la figure
> qu'il tient, qu'il li est bien avis que il doie chaoir a terre.
> (And hit semed that he was at the sakerynge of the masse.
> And hit semed to sir Launcelot that above the prystis hondys
> were three men, whereof the two put the yongyste by
> lyknes betwene the prystes hondis; and so he lyffte hym up
> ryght hyghe, and hit semed to shew so to the peple.
>
> And than sir Launcelot mervayled nat a litill, for hym
> thought the pryste was so gretly charged of the vygoure that
> hym semed that he sholde falle to the erth.) *Q*, 255;
> M, 1015–16

Praying that his aid not be taken as a sin, Lancelot rushes forward
to help the priest, but before he reaches the priest a scorching
wind paralyzes him and he feels himself being seized and carried
away.

The visions at the end of the *Queste* are mysterious only by virtue of the truth they represent. Their significance is not obscure,
and they do not require interpretation by the religious figures
whose counsel the knights constantly seek in their preparatory adventures. These visions reward the knights for the degree of spiritual commitment and understanding they have achieved, granting
them a foretaste of the heavenly banquet in the form of the sacrament of the Mass, which is the banquet's celebration on earth.
For example, Lancelot sees the Host transformed into the image
of what it becomes through the words of consecration said in the
Mass; he sees it transformed into the Body of Christ, the perfect
sacrifice for man's sin, offered by Christ and the other two persons
of the Trinity. The generosity of God's gift to man places a burden
on man to respond if he will; to the habitual sinner that burden
may seem heavy, despite Christ's promise, "my yoke is sweet and

my burden light" (Matt. 11:30). In seeming to be weighed down by the Host, the priest represents Lancelot's condition to Lancelot, whose decision to serve Christ is still a weight to him and whose judgment is not yet perfected. In rushing forward, he mistakes a spiritual reality for a physical one; and to show him that he must still undergo penance, he lies as if dead for twenty-four days, one day for each year he has sinfully loved the queen.

Lancelot cannot be said to have fulfilled the quest because he is not granted full communication in the Grail mysteries, but the *Queste* author does not adopt a condescending attitude toward the reward Lancelot does achieve. The custom of elevating the Host during the Mass became common around the turn of the twelfth century; and this custom supported a theory of two kinds of communication, visual and actual.[47] All Christians were invited to visual communication in the sacraments at every celebration of the Mass; and, in an age when actual communication was rare, the elevation of the Host became for many the climax of the Mass. The laity tended to participate in actual communication, that is, in the eating of the elements of the Mass sacrifice, only on the great feast days, Easter, Christmas, and Pentecost.

The vision granted to Lancelot corresponds, then, to the lesser kind of communication, visual communion. When he wakes up after twenty-four days, he seems to have experienced nothing during them except the continual memory of his vision: "Ha! Diex, por quoi m'avez vos si tost esveillié? Tant je estoie ore plus aeise que je ne seré hui mes!" ('Why have ye awaked me? For I was more at ease than I am now'), *Q*, 257; *M*, 1017. Asked by those who have been watching over him what he has seen, Lancelot replies:

> "Je ai . . . veu si granz merveilles et si granz beneurtez que ma langue nel vos porroit mie descovrir, ne mes cuers meismes nel porroit mie penser, com grant chose ce est. Car ce n'a mie esté chose terriane, mes esperitel. Et se mes granz pechiez et ma grant maleurtez ne fust, j'eusse encor plus

47. See Édouard Dumoutet, *Le Désir de voir l'hostie et les origines de la dévotion au saint-sacrement*, pp. 16–36; V. L. Kennedy, "The Moment of Consecration and the Elevation of the Host"; idem, "The Date of the Parisian Decree on the Elevation of the Host"; Joseph A. Jungmann, *The Mass of the Roman Rite*, 1:116–22, 2:206–16, 364–65; and Camille Hontoir, "La Dévotion au Saint Sacrement chez les premiers Cisterciens (XIIe–XIIIe siècles)," pp. 132–56.

veu." ("I have sene . . . grete mervayles that no tunge may
telle, and more than ony herte can thynke. And had nat my
synne bene beforetyme, ellis I had sene muche more.")
Q, 258; M, 1017 (cf. I Cor. 2:9)

Lancelot, over whom the king rejoices, remains at Corbenic for
five days. On the fifth day, while the court sits at a table supplied
by the Holy Grail, the doors of the palace mysteriously close. Hector rides up, but cannot get in. When Lancelot realizes that the
petitioner was his brother, he says farewell, knowing that he has
accomplished all that he can, and rides after his brother toward
Camelot. Lancelot must submit himself again to the trial of history, until death comes and with it the hope of the heavenly banquet, the wedding feast to which he now knows he will gain
entrance if he dies a true penitent.

The narrative turns again to Galahad, whose healing miracles
frame the Grail vision granted to him and his companions, Perceval and Bors. King Mordrain, who compares himself to Simeon
awaiting the advent of Jesus, finds his sight restored as soon as
Galahad approaches him. As he petitions to die in Galahad's arms,
the king describes the good knight for us with his recovered
vision. White and red, Galahad's purity precedes his charity; and,
as his shield, a red cross on a white field, also suggests, charity is
grounded on purity:

> "Tu es ausi nez et virges sus toz chevaliers come est la flor
> de lys, en qui virginitez est senefiee, qui est plus blanche que
> totes les autres. Tu es lys en virginité, tu es droite rose,
> droite flors de bone vertu et en color de feu, car li feus dou
> Saint Esperit est en toi si espris et alumez que ma char,
> qui tote estoit morte et envieillie, est ja tote rajuenie et en
> bone vertu." ("For thou arte a clene virgyne above all
> knyghtes, as the floure of the lyly in whom virginité is
> signified. And thou arte the rose which ys the floure of all
> good vertu, and in colour of fyre. For the fyre of the Holy
> Goste ys takyn so in the that my fleyssh, whych was all dede of
> oldenes, ys becom agayne yonge.") Q, 263; M, 1025

The healing of Mordrain is more elaborately described than that
of the maimed king, which Galahad accomplishes with blood
from the holy lance (Q, 271–72). In Mordrain's case, the virtues of

Christ and the grace of the Holy Ghost, which are present in Galahad, overflow to effect a miracle of healing, an act of mercy.

Galahad's companions rejoin him, and they go to Corbenic, where the adventures that fulfill the quest begin. At vespers a hot wind blows through the hall where the three companions stand, and a voice directs everyone else to leave. After nine foreign knights and the maimed king arrive, the mystery of the Grail unfolds. The twelve knights receive a fully elaborated vision of the mystery of the Grail mass, of which Lancelot had seen only a static image.

The Grail mass again makes the Christ-event visible to the knights, and it reveals to us the spiritual reality hidden in every celebration of the Mass: its ritual suspends time in order to bring about a return to sacred time and reenact efficaciously the sacred event. When Josephes (the first Christian bishop and the son of Joseph of Arimathea) elevates the Host, his words of consecration make the knights see that God has become flesh. Angels bring first Josephes, his throne, the Grail, and its table into the presence of the knights, and then they bring the candles, the veil of red samite, and the bleeding lance, which is an emblematic reminder of the suffering Christ bore out of love for mankind. When the table of the Grail is set, Josephes celebrates Mass. At the elevation of the Host, the knights see a eucharistic miracle that demonstrates the doctrine of transubstantiation by recalling the Incarnation and the Advent: the figure of an infant descends from heaven, rosy and glowing like fire, and strikes itself into the bread to reveal that "li pains avoit forme d'ome charnel" (*Q,* 269; cf. M, 1029); the bread (flesh) and the child (God) become one. After giving the kiss of peace and inviting the knights to the Grail table, Josephes vanishes. After Josephes vanishes, Christ, crucified and still bleeding (a sign that his blood continues to flow for mankind) rises out of the Grail to offer his body, the food of the Grail, to the knights. Communication, then, is the eating of Christ's sacrifice, which was made efficacious for all time through the Passion and Resurrection of Christ. Christ offers his body to the servants who have already given their bodies to him, which results in a mutual sacrifice and a mutual exchange of bodies. The rite is simultaneously the celebration of a feast and of a marriage.

Christ creates a point of disjunction in the continuum of his-

tory but at the same time he is, like the Grail itself, the center
through which old things pass to be made new:

> "Ce est, fet il, l'escuele ou Jhesucriz menja l'aignel le jor de
> Pasques o ses deciples. Ce est l'escuele qui a servi a gré toz
> çax que j'ai trovez en mon servise; ce est l'escuele que onques
> hons mescreanz ne vit a qui ele ne grevast molt. Et por ce
> que ele a si servi a gré toutes genz doit ele estre apelee le
> Saint Graal." ("Thys ys," seyde He, "the holy dysshe
> wherein I ete the lambe on Estir Day.") Q, 270; M, 1030

The dish of the Passover lamb now holds that other lamb (Christ),
which is a disjunction with the past; but the dish has always contained the acceptable sacrifice, which is an assertion of continuity
with the past. The *Queste* shows Christ, the very one responsible
for the change in the content of the Grail, using the dish for its
ancient purpose before he turns it to his new purpose. Through
wordplay the *Queste* author explains the power of the Grail
(French *graal*): it gives pleasure (*servi a gré*) to those loyal to Christ
and hurts (*grevast*) any miscreants who so much as look upon it;
its dual power to please or to blight seems to proceed from one
source, the symbol of which is the syllable *gre*.

The opposition of *a gré* and *grevast* points to the biblical prophesies of judgment, primarily to Paul's on the unworthy communicant (1 Cor. 11:27–29), but also to the separation of the sheep from
the goats (Matt. 25:33), to the promise that "one shall be taken
and one shall be left" (Matt. 24:40–41; cf. Luke 17:34–35)—a promise especially appropriate to the brothers Lancelot and Hector,
Bors and Lionel—and to the prophecy of the wedding feast that
some shall be fed and one cast into the outer darkness. In Christ's
wordplay, as in all the concluding Grail visions, the *Queste* author shapes his story to project the end of history, the Last Judgment.

At the conclusion of the feast, Christ commands the twelve
knights, as he once directed his twelve apostles, to disperse. He
directs Galahad to heal the maimed king with holy blood and
then, with Perceval and Bors, to accompany the Grail to Sarras.
The three knights are to travel on Solomon's ship. Sarras is the
city where Jews and gentiles first joined together in the fellowship
of Christ; it is the holy city of Josephes and of Mordrain. In returning the Grail to Sarras, the three companions reassert and

fulfill that first fellowship. Their adventures in Sarras repeat the adventures of Josephes and Mordrain in Logres: they are thrown into prison and fed by the Grail, the old king dies, and Galahad becomes king until his death.

During the journey by sea to Sarras, Galahad tells Perceval that he has seen more deeply into the Grail during the Mass at Corbenic than have the other knights, an experience that explains his request to be allowed to die at the moment of his own choosing:

> "Fu mes cuers en si grant soatume et en si grant joie que
> se je fusse maintenant trespassez de cest siecle, je sai bien que
> onques hom en si grant beneurté ne morut come je feisse
> lors. Car il avoit devant moi si grant compaignie d'angleres
> et si grant plenté de choses esperitex que je fusse lors
> translatez de la terrienne vie en la celestiel, en la joie des
> glorieus martirs et des amis Nostre Seignor." (*Q*, 274;
> cf. M, 1032)

Galahad's death comes on the anniversary of his coronation as king of Sarras (his kingship completes the typology of David, to whom Galahad is compared early in the *Queste*). The three knights see, but do not recognize, Josephes beside the Grail table reciting the confiteor and then celebrating the Mass of the Blessed Virgin. When Josephes gets to the consecration, he calls Galahad forward to look into the Holy Grail. Trembling at the mysteries he sees, Galahad petitions God to grant him death. Josephes communicates Galahad, then identifies himself and associates himself with Galahad. Galahad kisses Perceval and Bors and gives Bors a greeting for Lancelot. Then Galahad dies, his soul borne to heaven by angels; and a hand descends from heaven and carries the Holy Grail and the lance into heaven. Galahad and the Grail, analogous vessels, have analogous fates. When Perceval dies a year later, Bors buries him beside Galahad and Perceval's own sister before returning to Camelot to report the fulfillment of the quest to Arthur's court.

The *Queste* author arranges the Grail visions seen by the knights according to the hierarchy of Augustinian vision.[48] When Lancelot

48. See Augustine, *De Genesi ad litteram*, 12, CSEL 28.1: 379–435; the twelfth-century pseudo-Augustine *De Spiritu et anima*, in *PL* 40:796–98; and F. X. Newman, "St. Augustine's Three Visions and the Structure of the *Commedia*." Gilson uses Bernard of Clairvaux's distinctions of three

sees the Grail appear before the sick knight, all he sees is its physical manifestation. That is, he sees with his corporeal vision. Both
of the visions at Corbenic are spiritual: the knights see bodily
images, and both the *Queste* and the *Sankgreal* use verbs and
phrases that respect the process of spiritual vision: *il fu avis a,
semblance, besemed, lyknesse.* Since these visions are of the highest form of Augustinian spiritual vision, they may appropriately
be called ecstasies. The spiritual understanding of the knights is
equally matched to their capacity for ecstatic spiritual vision: the
three companions see more than Lancelot sees. Intellectual vision,
the highest of all forms of vision and totally independent of bodies
or bodily images, is granted to Galahad alone. To describe the intellectual vision of God in words is utterly impossible: even Dante
does not try (*Paradiso*, 33.106–41). To have seen God by intellectual vision is to see him as he will be seen in heaven. When
Galahad prays to be allowed to die when he wishes, it is so that,
when the vision returns, he may be able to sustain it forever. Truly,
for him, death holds no sting. He passes from the shadow of the
heavenly banquet, the sacrament of the Mass, to the reality of its
eternal celebration, a passage from time to eternity without any
division between the two conditions.

---

kinds of mystic experience—dreams, visions, and "excessum purae mentis"
—to gloss the *Queste*, noting, however, the close connection between
Cistercian thought and the Augustinian tradition; see *Les Idées et les
lettres*, pp. 79–86, 88–91.

# 4

## Cleanness

The *Cleanness* poet makes a pattern of judgment by recounting a series of divine judgments drawn from biblical history. The poet uses the Flood, the destruction of Sodom, and the devastation of Jerusalem and Babylon to reveal the criteria by which God saves or destroys. He looks at history through the model provided by the parable of the wedding feast, which is a prophecy of the division that will take place, separating the chosen from those who are called. According to the poet's vision of history, from its beginning, after the Fall, to its end in the Apocalypse, the significance of events is determined by God, who accepts or rejects men on the basis of their attitudes toward him, as expressed through both their intentions and actions.

### The Structure of History in *Cleanness*

The poem is overtly didactic. In the opening lines the poet obliquely announces his intention of commending cleanness through examples:

> Clannesse who so kyndly cowþe comende,
> And rekken up alle þe resounz þat ho by riȝt askez,
> Fayre formez myȝt he fynde in forþering his speche,
> And in þe contrare, kark and combraunce huge.[1]

The poet is here speaking of his own function: he himself has found "fayre formez" to commend cleanness, as the rest of the poem shows. By "fayre formez" the poet means that he has found a tradition of examples to commend cleanness; line 4 then means that a search for good (beautiful?) examples in praise of uncleanness would be a toilsome and difficult undertaking. Already, then,

1. *Cleanness*, lines 1–4 (hereafter cited as *C* by line).

the poet has established his pattern of opposition between cleanness and uncleanness.

The rest of the poem develops this pattern of opposition. A
series of analogies to the parable of the wedding feast leads up to a
retelling and interpretation of the parable, which is the climax of
the introductory part of the poem: in the analogies, as in the parable, the poet distinguishes the clean among those who serve at the
feast and among those who come to it as guests from the unclean.
To elaborate his pattern of opposition, he then turns to clerical
tradition and the authority of his books. These authorities show,
the poet claims, that while God hates all sin, he especially hates
"fylþe of þe flesch." The poet uses stories from biblical history to
illustrate his claim. Although God judges Lucifer and Adam,
whose falls the poet recounts, he judges them not in an angry but
in a temperate mood. Divine judgments on the antediluvian world
and on Sodom, by contrast, proceed from divine anger at the filth
of the people. In these stories of the Flood and of Sodom, the poet
asserts again the pattern of opposition, illustrating by the examples of Noah, Abraham, and Lot what cleanness is and using the
behavior of antediluvian men and of the Sodomites to show what
uncleanness is. In the exhortation to cleanness that follows the
lively account of the destruction of Sodom, the poet introduces
Christ as the exemplar of cleanness and uses the story of Christ's
Incarnation and Advent to demonstrate his cleanness. The story
of his ministry invites men to imitate his good works; but more
than that, because Christ is God, it reveals the way for men to
purify themselves by seeking Christ's medicine through the sacraments. Christ, then, makes possible a conversion from filth to
cleanness. By the poet's analogy, men are to Christ as vessels are
to men, and as men can pollute clean vessels by touch, Christ can
cleanse impure men by his gracious touch. In the last story in the
poem, that of the Temple vessels and their Babylonian captivity,
the poet introduces the plot of penance into the poem through the
story of Nebuchadnezzar's madness; but like the earlier stories,
this one again emphasizes the pattern of opposition, contrasting
both the Jewish King Sedecias and the Babylonian King Belshazzar to Daniel and Nebuchadnezzar. After a gory account of Belshazzar's death, the poem closes with a brief prayer of petition
that God grant the poet and his audience grace to come to his
feast.

The *Cleanness* poet uses a different strategy from that of the *Queste* author in presenting the continuum of history, even though both authors depend on biblical typology to interpret history. The *Queste* author sets his primary narrative in the world of King Arthur's court, a world that is an idealized analogue of the author's contemporary, historical world. Even though Arthur was supposed to have lived in a golden age, sometime in the Christian past, Arthurian romances in fact reflect their authors' contemporary worlds and use the Arthurian world as a model of social or religious courtesy by which the audience may measure itself. The primary narrative of the *Queste* follows Arthur's knights on their adventures in search of the Grail and recounts the knights' conversations with monks and hermits who interpret the moral and spiritual significance of the knights' adventures to them. These same monks and hermits also tell the knights stories from history, more of which the knights discover in the messages of Solomon's ship. These stories are secondary narratives. Except for those in the legend of the Tree of Life, they are not explicitly connected to each other; but through that legend, which establishes a principle of chronology, and through the patterns of similarities in these stories, the *Queste* author implies not only a continuum of history but the significance of the stories in that continuum. In other words, he creates a history through patterns, or types, that the reader must see for himself. For all the allegorizing of the hermits and monks, they do not ever make explicit the typologies through which the *Queste* author works.

The kind of stories that in the *Queste* are secondary narratives are in *Cleanness* the only narratives, and they serve the same function as the secondary narratives in the *Queste*. In fact, only two of the poet's many exempla, both among the introductory analogues of the wedding feast parable, deliberately reflect the poet's contemporary world. The *Cleanness* poet begins with the end of history, with analogues to the wedding feast parable, which is a prophecy of the Last Judgment. In contrast to the *Queste* author, who puts monks and hermits in his romance to moralize the knights' adventures, the *Cleanness* poet supplies moral interpretations of his exempla in his own voice (*C*, 165–92, 545–56, 1049–1148, 1805–10). Having established through the parable of the wedding feast and its analogues the opposition between cleanness and filth, the poet then uses the Bible as the source of his examples

of cleanness and filth, choosing stories that mimetically differenti-
ate the elect from the lost. He respects the chronology of biblical
history, except in his placement of Christ's Incarnation, Advent,
and Ministry. This exception, as I will shortly argue, influences
the significance of the Old Testament story that follows it, the
story of the Babylonian exile. Before and after the example of
Christ the poet presents two stories of destruction (types of damnation) and one story of hope (a type of salvation). Expressed sche-
matically, the poet's disposition of biblical stories looks like this:

| JUDGMENT | SALVATION | JUDGMENT |
|---|---|---|
| | **1**<br>**Falls of Lucifer**<br>**and Adam**<br>Introduction to<br>History<br>(205–48) | |
| **2**<br>**Flood**<br>Noah saved<br>(249–540) | **3**<br>**Three Angels**<br>**Visit Abraham**<br>Banquet and Promise<br>Church<br>(557–780) | **4**<br>**Sodom Destroyed**<br>Lot saved<br>(781–1048) |
| | **5**<br>**Christ**<br>Fulfillment of History<br>(1065–1108) | |
| **6**<br>**Jerusalem destroyed**<br>Sedecias murdered<br>(1157–1303) | **7**<br>**Temple Vessels "visit"**<br>**Nebuchadnezzar**<br>Faith and Penance<br>Church<br>(1304–32, 1642–1708) | **8**<br>**Babylon Destroyed**<br>Belshazzar murdered<br>(1333–1640, 1709–<br>1804) |

Generally, the patterns of the analogies are clear; and, in fact, the poet has extensive biblical authority for linking the Flood, Sodom, and Babylon to judgment and for linking Noah, Abraham, Lot, and Daniel (a kind of Temple vessel, as we shall see) to salvation.[2] The poet does not explain his analogies as types, any more than the *Queste* author explains the interrelationships among his secondary narratives.

The reason for the poet's placement of the Christ story, a reason that will show how the histories in *Cleanness* represent the whole continuum of history, derives from Christian theories of history. That the *Cleanness* poet composed his poem with such theories in mind is an inference—he does not talk about them explicitly—but it seems to me a necessary inference if we are to understand the poem as anything more than a disjunctive collection of exempla. The poem can be read as such, but the result is not particularly satisfying. Such a reading explains not at all why the poet's example of Christ occurs where it does. Medieval Christian historiography, however, does provide a rationale for this placement through its two conventional methods of dividing history into periods. One method marks three ages of history, each characterized by a different law: the Age of Nature, when natural law prevails (the category under which the stories of the Flood and Sodom take place); the Age of the Written Law, when the law given to Moses prevails (the category under which the stories of Jerusalem and Babylon occur); and the Age of Grace, when the

2. For biblical typologies of Judgment, see Job 22:16 (Flood); Ecclus. 44:17–23 (Flood and Sodom); Sodom and Babylon, separately or linked, occur frequently, e.g., Deut. 29:22–23; Jer. 49:18, 50:38–40; Isa. 13:19; Amos 4:11; Soph. 2:9; Matt. 10:15, 11:23–24; Luke 10:12; Jude 1:7; and Apocalypse 11:8. Noah and the Flood are linked with Lot and Sodom as types of the Last Judgment in Luke 17:26–30 and 2 Pet. 2:4–9; Matt. 24:37 refers to Noah alone. The faithful who are saved are also arranged into typologies; in addition to Noah and Lot, see Ecclus. 44:17–23 and Heb. 11:7–8 (Noah and Abraham); and Ezek. 14:14 (Noah and Daniel). In *De civitate Dei* Augustine uses Babylon as the name of the city of man (the damned city), a practice authorized by Apocalypse 18 and general in Christian commentary. For the typology of Babylon as it relates to *Cleanness*, see David J. Williams, "A Literary Study of the Middle English Poems *Purity* and *Patience*"; and Joseph Benedict Zavadil, "A Study of Meaning in *Patience* and *Cleanness*." Edward Wilson discusses 2 Pet. 2:4–9 in *The Gawain-Poet*, p. 94.

law of love instituted by Christ prevails (the category that includes all of Christian history, from Christ to the end in Judgment).

The other method recognized seven or eight ages. It divided Old Testament history into six ages, marked by Adam, Noah, Abraham, David, a fifth figure chosen from the period of the Babylonian captivity, and Christ, who introduces the sixth age. The seventh age is doomsday and may be considered contemporaneous with all the rest. The eighth age, sometimes omitted from the scheme, is the age of the resurrected life after the Last Judgment, when time is subsumed into eternity.[3] Medieval historians sometimes used a similar scheme of six ages, analogous to those in the Old Testament, to mark divisions in Christian history.[4] Under this scheme, the Babylonian exile usually becomes the age analogous to the contemporary Christian period, that is, the time in which the historians lived. The significance of this for *Cleanness* is clear: the story of the Babylonian exile occurs after the poet introduces the example of Christ because the exile is, conventionally, a figure of the poet's own age.

Within the story of the exile, Daniel's account of Nebuchadnezzar's lapse from faith in God and his restoration to God through penitential madness (*C*, 1642–1708) has a special significance. Nebuchadnezzar is a figure of the converted gentile—the Christian—who sins, goes mad (repents), and regains his sanity (his spiritual health) through God's grace.[5] His is the only story in *Cleanness*

3. See M.-D. Chenu, *Nature, Man, and Society in the Twelfth Century*, pp. 179–82, and V. A. Kolve, *The Play Called Corpus Christi*, pp. 88–100. Augustine is the primary source in the Latin West for both the three and the seven/eight age divisions of history. For the latter, see Augustine, *De civitate Dei* (*The City of God*), 22.30 (hereafter cited as *De civ. Dei*), and G. Folliet, "La Typologie du sabbat chez St. Augustine"; for the former, see *Enchiridion*, 117, in *Patrologia latina* 40:287 (hereafter cited as *PL*). See also Hugh of St. Victor, *De Sacramentis christianae fidei*, 1.1.28, 1.8.11, in *PL* 176:203–4, 312–13.

4. See Martin of Léon, *Expositio libri Apocalypsis*, 16, in *PL* 209:379–84, who associates the seven seals of the Apocalypse with the conventional six ages from Adam through Christ and the Church and parallels the primitive history of the Church to the first five ages; and comment by Henri de Lubac, *Exégèse médiévale*, vol. 1, pt. 2, pp. 505–9, 526–27. On the "translatio imperii," based on Daniel's vision (Dan. 2:31–45), see Chenu, *Nature, Man, and Society*, pp. 179, 184–96; and de Lubac, *Exégèse médiévale*, vol. 1, pt. 2, pp. 504–27.

5. See Penelope B. R. Doob, *Nebuchadnezzar's Children*, pp. 54–74, 81–87.

that uses the plot of penance. Like Lancelot in the *Queste*, he is a type whose example is particularly applicable to the author's general Christian audience.

The evidence for this medieval convention of periodizing Christian history and interpreting the period of the Babylonian exile as the present (that is, as the twelfth, thirteenth, or fourteenth century) is associated with the historiography of Joachim of Fiore. Marjorie Reeves has studied this and other aspects of Joachim's effect on late medieval thinking in *The Influence of Prophecy in the Later Middle Ages: A Study in Joachimism*. The spread of Joachimism in the thirteenth and fourteenth centuries encouraged this habit of dividing Christian history into ages, although Joachim was not the first to make such divisions. Joachim's theory of history, as it was propounded by his followers among the Spiritual Franciscans, was condemned as heretical; but the influence of Joachimism affected orthodox writers who adapted some of the ideas, chief among them the notion that there are divisions in the history of the Church that parallel the divisions of Old Testament history into ages. Reeves shows that the association of Nebuchadnezzar with thirteenth- and fourteenth-century figures and the association of the period of the Babylonian captivity with the contemporary age by medieval writers was common. For example, she cites the story of Joachim's visit to Emperor Henry VI when he came to south Italy to claim the kingdom: Joachim compared the emperor to Nebuchadnezzar, visiting doom on Tyre by God's will; and Henry VI "accepted the role of Nebuchadnezzar."[6] She also cites Ralph of Coggeshall's "exposition of Joachim's method of concords between the Old and New Testaments, with his pattern of seven seals and their parallel openings," which sets "the contemporary moment in the persecution of the fifth seal"—that is, Joachim typologically relates the persecution of Saladin in his own age to that of the Old Testament "in quo muri Hierusalem eversi sunt . . . et populus in Babylonem a Nebuchodonosor captivus addictus fuit."[7] Ralph goes on to point out that, according to Joachim, in 1199 the sixth seal will be opened, introducing the

6. Marjorie Reeves, *The Influence of Prophecy in the Later Middle Ages*, p. 11; see pp. 16–27 for a brief account of Joachim's view of history. See also de Lubac, *Exégèse médiévale*, vol. 1, pt. 2, pp. 437–558.

7. Reeves, *The Influnce of Prophecy*, p. 12; for Ralph of Coggeshall's text, see *Chronicon Anglicanum*, p. 68.

time when the persecution and death and damnation of Antichrist
will be fulfilled. Reeves concludes from Ralph's date of 1199 that
Joachim's fame and method spread very early to England.

  Robert of Auxerre, writing before 1215, also follows Joachim in
paralleling the Augustinian six ages from Adam to Christ with
six "little ages" from the history of the Church. These "little ages"
correspond to the pattern of seals and openings in the Apocalypse;
they all occur within Augustine's sixth age (which lasts from
Christ's Advent until his return as judge at the end of time). Robert thought that the time of Antichrist would come within two
generations, which is to say, he believed that he was living in the
fifth "little age," which corresponds to the Old Testament period
of the Babylonian captivity.[8] Thus, Reeves's study supports the
assumption that the *Cleanness* poet's choice and placement of the
story of the Babylonian exile, with its histories of Sedecias, Nebuchadnezzar, Daniel, and Belshazzar, was a result of the poet's
having discovered in the exile a figure for his own age.

  The Joachist way of reading Babylon as a figure for the contemporary age reinforces an older convention of interpreting the
destruction of Babylon as a type of divine justice (as is done by
the Old Testament prophets) and as a figure for the damned in the
Last Judgment (as is done in the New Testament Apocalypse).
Just as Hosea and Ezekiel treat unfaithful Israel and unfaithful
Jerusalem as adulteresses, so Jeremiah and Isaiah treat Babylon
under the figure of a woman (Isa. 47; Jer. 50–51) who has made
the nations drunk with her idols, that is, with her worldly self-
sufficient wisdom and power (Jer. 51:7; cf. Apocalypse 14:8, 17–18).
The period of exile ends in Babylon's destruction, according to the
prophets; and Babylon becomes par excellence the figure of the
people judged and destroyed by God. The Apocalypse makes her,
rather than Sodom (a frequent choice of the prophets), the chief

---

  8. Morton W. Bloomfield and Marjorie Reeves, in "The Penetration
of Joachism into Northern Europe," show that Joachim's ideas were
initially spread from a Calabrian group of Florensian and Cistercian disciples and only later in the thirteenth century by Franciscans, to whom
Joachim was an important if not always acknowledged source of ideas,
particularly in commentaries on the Apocalypse (p. 792). See also Morton
W. Bloomfield, *Piers Plowman as a Fourteenth-Century Apocalypse*, pp.
95, 157–60; Marjorie Reeves, "The 'Liber Figurarum' of Joachim of
Fiore"; idem, *Joachim of Fiore and the Prophetic Future*, pp. 1–28, 36–
38, 73, 79–80; and idem, *The Influence of Prophecy*, pp. 179–86.

figure for those sinners who will be destroyed when Christ comes again in judgment: this time the end will be definitive, and Babylon will be broken forever. Christian exegesis and homiletics insure Babylon's image as the whore who maddens those who fornicate with her (that is, indulge in her worldly philosophies and pleasures to their own destruction).

The *Cleanness* poet, by placing the story of Babylon the historical city after he introduces Christ, implies that this story has a special application to Christian history, to himself and his audience, an application that lends apocalyptic urgency to the poem. If the history of ancient Babylon, the last major story in Christian historiography before the first Advent of Christ, is parallel to the present age, then the Last Judgment—the Second Coming of Christ— is imminent. According to medieval thinking, judgment is always imminent for an individual, since no one knows the time of his death (the contemporaneous seventh age) and repentance is always a matter of urgency. By also implying, through typology, that the end of history (the eighth age) may be here, the poet intensifies the sense of urgency.

A sense that the pattern of history may be almost complete seems to have permeated the thinking of the later Middle Ages.[9] Several recent studies, both literary and historical, have investigated this phenomenon, this fascination of medieval audiences and religious groups with the idea of an ending. In addition to Reeves's study of Joachimism, I think, for example, of Morton W. Bloomfield's *Piers Plowman as a Fourteenth-Century Apocalypse* and Norman Cohn's *The Pursuit of the Millennium*. This medieval interest in history and its ending bore fruit in narrative art, as *Piers Plowman*, Dante's *Commedia*, the *Queste*, and *Cleanness* show. Works of fiction that embody in their narratives a theory of the structure of history and that contain in their endings a type of the end of history, both on an individual and a social level, as the *Queste*, *Sankgreal*, and *Cleanness* do, offer us an intensified experience of what

9. See n. 4 above. Another theory of history, derived from comparing the six ages of history to the stages of the life of man, used, e.g., by Otto of Freising, suggests that the world is old and about to die; see Chenu, *Nature, Man, and Society*, pp. 181, 183. The theory of the "translatio imperii," considered as a movement from East to West, suggests that with Rome and the Western empires history must end; see Chenu, *Nature, Man, and Society*, pp. 170, 179, 186–87.

every object of art promises us, the experience of a completed design. Perhaps that desire for order, for a completed design, explains the medieval fascination with the sense of an ending. Both the *Queste* and *Cleanness* use types of the end (the *visio Dei* of Galahad's last Grail mass and the destruction of Babylon) to foreshadow the End, which is not yet a historical fact. Both conclude with responses to their own theoretical designs of history that implicitly or explicitly call upon their audiences to repent: at the end of the *Queste* Bors's testimony about the final Grail adventures, which he, Perceval, and Galahad complete by virtue of their cleanness (a condition achieved through penance), implies that penance is the avenue to success in the Grail quest, which is more clearly than ever a heavenly quest, since the Grail has removed to heaven; the *Sankgreal* includes in its ending the testimony of Lancelot, the chief example of a penitent who achieves conditional success in his search for the Grail, and it thus makes the implicit call to penance stronger; and *Cleanness* closes with an exhortation to cleanness and a prayer for the *visio Dei*.

## The Wedding Feast in *Cleanness*: Prologue to the Poem and Epilogue to History

The analogues to the wedding feast lead up to the poet's retelling of the parable in the opening part of *Cleanness*: this design clearly invites us to read the analogues as types of the wedding feast. By extending this way of reading to the rest of the poem, each of the stories that follow the parable should also be read as a type of the parable, a process that I shall take up later in this chapter.

The first of the analogues, which contrasts bad priests to good ones, implicitly introduces vessel imagery into the poem. The poet uses the specific example of the priests to illustrate his general point: "For wonder wroth is þe Wyȝ þat wroȝt alle þinges / Wyth þe freke þat in fylþe folȝes hym after" (*C*, 5–6). Priests are the servants of God on earth who celebrate his banquet, the sacrament of the Mass. They are, the poet insists, attached in fealty to God: "Thay teen unto his temmple and temen to hymselven" (*C*, 9). As they approach the altar, God's banquet table, they move into the presence of God and, as celebrants, "þay hondel þer his aune body and usen hit boþe" (*C*, 11); that is, they both touch and eat the body of God. The poet's description of the priests alludes to their roles as brides of Christ, to whom they have granted their bodies in the vows of the priesthood. Commonly, in the medieval Mass only the priests actually communicate. Their action expresses on behalf of the congregation (who communicate visually by gazing upon the consecrated species) the spiritual marriage of Christ and his faithful.[10] The priest in the celebration of the Eucharist also fills Christ's role by speaking Christ's words to consecrate the species. These words alone suffice to change the bread and wine into the Body and Blood, but the priest who says them without imitating Christ's cleanness and courtesy is disjoined from Christ, as the poet says in commenting on the priests' office as celebrants:

> If þay in clannes be clos, þay cleche gret mede;
> Bot if þay conterfete crafte, and cortaysye wont,
> As be honest utwyth, and inwith alle fylþez,
> Þen ar þay synful hemself, and sulped altogeder,
> Loþe God and his gere, and hym to greme cachen. (C, 12–16)

"Crafte," the proper exercise of the office of priesthood (intention and action must coincide: the priest must be like Christ in his heart as well as in his act, but his act in any case is efficacious for others by virtue of Christ's words), and "cortaysye," the manner of graciousness and the deeds that proceed from it, depend on a state of cleanness. Without "honesty" (meaning fairness, chastity, righteousness), no one can have "crafte" or "cortaysye." Polluted and defiled, the filthy priests express hatred and contempt for God and his "gere" (the vessels and furniture of God's altar); and in return the priests get, not the joys of siritual marriage to God, but God's wrath.[11] The reality of these priests' condition corresponds neither

10. For theories of spiritual communication—frequent gazing on the Eucharist—and of the priest communicating as the representative of the entire community, see Joseph A. Jungmann, *The Mass of the Roman Rite,* 2:364–65. The latter theory may account for the poet's choice of the exemplum of priests with which the poem opens.

11. Editors of *Cleanness* have treated lines 15b–16a variously; Robert J. Menner emends *Boþe* to *Loþe* ("Then are they sinful themselves, and defiled altogether;/ They hate God and his gear, and drive him to wrath"). Although recent editors have not generally followed Menner, his emendation recommends itself on both substantive and stylistic grounds. To accept the reading *Boþe* makes lines 15b–16a heretical, because whether *sulped* is emended or not, the lines then mean that God can be defiled and they imply that the sacrament celebrated by an unclean priest is

to God nor to his vessels, and the priests' unlikeness to God calls
for their separation from him. The wrath of God tolerates no irony,
no failed analogies, no hypocrisies; these priests, like all unworthy
communicants, eat damnation. Now filthy vessels, they will be in
the end broken vessels. The poet returns to the vessel image in the
story of Christ and in the story of the Temple vessels to make explicit what the relationship between God, vessel, and man ought
to be.

The second analogue of the wedding feast—the story of the court
of heaven—contrasts with that of the bad priests. In God's heavenly
household, his servants are angels "enorled in alle þat is clene,/
Boþe wythinne and wythouten, in wedez ful bryȝt" (C, 19–20). To
imagine that heaven's court might be filled with any other kind of
servants would be ridiculous, because, as the poet reminds his audience, Christ himself promised heaven only to the clean of heart
(Matt. 5:8). God banishes anyone who "any unclannesse hatz on,
auwhere abowte" (C, 30).

In this analogue to the wedding feast, the poet introduces clothing imagery—the bright weeds of the angels and the spotted clothes
of the sinner—as a correlative to the imagery of clean and dirty
vessels. In the first analogue, the poet does not describe the clothing of the unworthy priests, whose hypocrisy, in the world of every-
day reality, is concealed by their vestments. He reserves clothing
imagery to describe exact correspondences between appearance
and reality. When he uses this imagery, he sees as if with God's
eyes that men wear clothes expressive of their internal spiritual
condition.

Urging his audience to avoid God's anger by wearing clean
clothes, the poet justifies God's requirements to his audience by

---

inefficacious, but see Chap. 2, pp. 36–37, above, and, e.g., *The Book of
Vices and Virtues*, p. 263. I do not see any other signs of unorthodoxy in
the poem. Equally persuasive is the argument on stylistic grounds. Following Menner, line 16 exemplifies what Marie Borroff calls "reciprocality": "First the action is stated, then the response to the action." She
finds this a pervasive tendency, not only in *Sir Gawain and the Green
Knight*, but also in *Patience* and *Cleanness*, in which lines 2, 72, 559,
1796, and 1811, for example, also show reciprocality, all in instances
where the two reciprocal units are half lines. Borroff has discussed these
lines with me, and she has kindly corroborated this conversation in a
letter dated 6 November 1977. See also her discussion of reciprocality in
her stylistic study, *Sir Gawain and the Green Knight*, p. 121.

asking them to imagine how a contemporary nobleman would respond to a tattered guest. The description of this earthly and secular banquet is the third analogue to the wedding feast of the parable. The narrative description of this feast exactly corresponds, on a secular level, to God's actions in the parable. The poet describes the ill-clothed interloper with gusto:

> Þen þe harlot wyth haste helded to þe table
> Wyth rent cokrez at þe kne, and his clutte traschez,
> And his tabarde totorne, and his totez oute. (*C*, 39–41)

The nobleman, the poet suggests, would take this fellow and, with harsh words and maybe a buffet, hurl him through the hall door and banish him forever. The poet connects the banquet of the worldly prince to God's feast through the concept of courtesy: "And if unwelcum he were to a wordlych prynce,/ Ʒet hym is þe hyʒe Kyng harder in heven" (*C*, 49–50). The courtesy that men pay to the king of an earthly kingdom cannot be less than that they grant to God. Christ, as we will see in his story, is the "courteous one": we must finally learn from him what true courtesy is. Courtesy, the poet insists, is basically a religious ideal; it expresses how men ought to act toward God, in imitation of Christ's courtesy toward man. Courtesy as a social concept, defining the proper relationships of men among themselves, finds its sanction in the religious ideal of courtesy.

Having implied that the rich man of the parable of the wedding feast is a figure for God, the poet moves into his paraphrase of the parable, combining elements from both Matthew and Luke to illustrate the nature of the courtesy owed to God and the penalty for failing to observe the proper courtesy. God issues his invitation to the feast twice: his first guests refuse, so he seeks out others. The parable, then, falls into two distinct parts. The first guests are not discourteous in their refusal but are rather self-defeating; however, in the group who accept, one is discourteous, appearing in ragged clothes, "fyled with werkkez" (*C*, 136). The rest of the poem, as we shall see, focuses not on those who refuse God's invitation, but rather on those who, like the ragged guest, accept the invitation without considering whether they are worthy to be God's guests. *Cleanness* implies that Lucifer, Adam, and Nebuchadnezzar are types of the guests who refuse: God judges them all, but they do not make him as angry as do the hypocrites who unworthily accept the invitation. Those who deliberately refuse God are clearly his enemies, and he treats them as they ask to be treated. He allows men but not the angel to repent if they will. His wrath, however, is reserved for the lukewarm, for those who pretend to belong to God's order and to merit its benefits when, in fact, their lives express contempt for that order.

The contrast between the ragged guest and the other members of the second group in their wedding garments gives the poet an opportunity to develop the pattern of opposition between the rewards of the clean and the punishment of the unclean. In the allegorical interpretation of the parable that follows his paraphrase, the poet deals only with the second invited group, identifying them with those baptized into the promise of the kingdom (*C*, 163–64)—these are the guests who correspond to the poet's audience. The rich man's messengers go out twice to invite the second group of guests, gathering them up from the streets and the shores, bringing them in from the fields and the gorse bushes, paying no attention to rank or station or physical health. The openness of this invitation corresponds in the allegorical interpretation to Christ's unlimited offer to mankind. Matthew and Luke make no attempt to describe the joy of the feast, but the poet invents an account of the feast that emphasizes what the filthily clothed guest loses through his discourtesy:

> Wheþer þay wern worþy oþer wers, wel wern þay stowed,
> Ay þe best byfore and bryȝtest atyred,
> Þe derrest at þe hyȝe dese þat dubbed wer fayrest;
> And syþen on lenþe bilooghe ledez inogh,
> And ay a segge soerly semed by her wedez.
> So with marschal at her mete mensked þay were;
> Clene men in compaynye forknowen wern lyte,
> And ȝet þe symplest in þat sale watz served to þe fulle,
> Boþe with menske and wyth mete and mynstrasy noble,
> And alle þe laykez þat a lorde aȝt in londe schewe.
> And þay bigonne to be glad þat god drink haden,
> And uch mon wyth his mach made hym at ese. (*C*, 113–24)

The host then circulates among his guests, bidding them welcome and talking mirthfully, until he comes to the man without a festival frock, "bot fyled with werkkez" (*C*, 136), a fault in his clothing that has moral implications corresponding to the social implications of the tattered clothes worn by the worldly prince's bad guest.

The punishment of the discourteously ragged and dirty guest, who has no answer for the host's accusations, is worse than the exile that befalls the worldly prince's tattered guest:

> Þen þe lorde wonder loude laled and cryed,
> And talkez to his tormenttorez: "Takez hym," he biddez,
> "Byndez byhynde, at his bak, boþe two his handez,
> Stik hym stifly in stokez, and stekez hym þerafter
> And felle fetterez to his fete festenez bylyve;
> Depe in my doungoun þer doel ever dwellez,
> Greving and gretyng and gryspyng harde
> Of teþe tenfully togeder, to teche hym be quoynt." (*C*, 153–60)

The poet has essentially followed Matt. 22:13 but has substituted *tormentors* for the blander term *waiters (ministris)* and replaced the rather vague *outer darkness (tenebras exteriores)* by *a dungeon*.

The *Cleanness* poet imagines the parable banquet in a medieval context: he supplies nonbiblical details that had the effect, we must suppose, of making the feast seem more real to its medieval audience. For example, he extends the catalogue of foods prepared for the feast from the "beeves and fatlings" in Matthew's version and describes the cooking methods; God announces his feast:

> "For my boles and my borez arn bayted and slayne,
> And my fedde foulez fatted wyth sclaȝt,
> My polyle þat is penne-fed and partrykez boþe,
> Wyth scheldez of wylde swyn, swanez and cronez—
> Al is roþeled and rosted ryȝt to þe sete;
> Comez cof to my corte, er hit colde worþe." (*C*, 55–60)

The menu is appropriate to a medieval banquet. The call to come before the food grows cold adds a familiar touch that contributes in the allegorical reading of the parable to the apocalyptic urgency of God's invitation. The second group of guests includes wayfaring men, on foot and on horseback; bachelors and squires; freemen and bondmen. The attendants at the feast hold special designations—steward, marshal, and sergeants. No small part of an audience's delight in *Cleanness* derives from the poet's skill in making lively paraphrases of biblical stories. As twentieth-century writers have made us realize, anachronisms in the retelling of old stories lend both charm and immediacy to the tale and tend to force a contemporary audience to recognize the application of the story to its own condition. A few examples suffice: W. H. Auden's "Horae Canonicae," Jean Giradoux's *Electra*, and Jean Anouilh's

*Antigone.* Medieval writers were generally unaware of the anachronisms to which they customarily resorted in telling old stories, but the effect created by the anachronisms is the same in the medieval fiction as it is in the self-consciously anachronistic modern fiction.

The poet's allegorical interpretation of the parable stresses the necessity of coming in clean clothes to the feast—the kingdom of heaven—and identifies clothing with works. He suggests in line 172 that a man's intention, that is, the desire in his heart, affects whether or not he will be noble and spotless, fair of form, and "lapped" (clothed) cleanly. Without the intention or the desire to be faithful to God, which a man signifies through the sacraments of baptism (and confirmation), penance, and the Eucharist, his works cannot, according to orthodox Christian interpretations, redeem him. Although the possibility that a sinner might perform some good acts was admitted, these acts were not usually considered to be fruitful for the sinner, though some theologians allowed that these "accidental" good works might mitigate the sinner's punishment. This point is clearly expressed in the *Queste*, when a hermit admits that the residue of grace in Lancelot, the talents God gave him, has permitted him to perform some good works; but the hermit insists that these works, without confession and amendment, will bring Lancelot no reward in the Grail quest.[12] Only after Lancelot repents and makes himself the loyal servant of God can he begin to perform the acts of mercy, such as burying the dead, that are the fruit of grace in a man.

A return to sin undoes the purification effected through baptism or penance; as the *Cleanness* poet says, "for fele fautez may a freke forfete his blysse" (*C*, 177). Whenever the *Cleanness* poet uses clothing imagery, he stresses that good works are a prerequisite for admission to the kingdom; whenever he uses vessel imagery, he stresses the state of faith and purity that is a precondition for doing good works. Through the concept of cleanness, these images are, I admit, closely related; no one, however, can wear clean clothes (do good works) unless first the vessel of the body (and the soul in the vessel) is clean by virtue of faith and penance. Except in the case of sincere deathbed penance, the Church ordinarily

12. *La Queste del Saint Graal*, pp. 126–27 (hereafter cited as *Q* by page number).

assumed that the elect were clean inside and out; that is, they were free from sin (pure and holy vessels) and doers of good works.

## Lucifer, Adam, and Nebuchadnezzar: Problems of Fall and Redemption

In the *Cleanness* poet's description of the priests attached in fealty to God and in his identification of the second group of guests in the parable with baptized Christians (traditionally the first group are the Jews who refuse Christ), he introduces covenant theology—the pattern of invitation (promise) and response—into his poem and implies that this theology will be central to the poem. This implication is confirmed by the stories from biblical history that the poet presents as types of the reality prophesied in the parable. Noah and Abraham are the first of the Old Testament heroes with whom God establishes his covenant; they correspond to the courteous guests at the feast. Sedecias and Belshazzar break the covenant through their sins: they are types of the tattered and ragged discourteous guest. As I suggested earlier, Lucifer, Adam, and Nebuchadnezzar—whose sins God does not treat like those of the antediluvian men, the Sodomites, Sedecias, or Belshazzar—are analogous to the first guests who refuse God's invitation.

When the *Cleanness* poet turns to his books to verify that "fylþe of þe flesche" makes God angry as nothing else does, he first tells of two sins, Lucifer's and Adam's, that he distinguishes from the ones that make God angry. The vengeance God takes for the sins of Lucifer and Adam is similar to his manner of passing judgment in the parable, where he mildly observes that those who refuse his invitation when "ful dryȝly he carpez" (*C*, 74) have only hurt themselves. Without a qualm, without a hint of anger or anguish, God sends Lucifer to hell as soon as he finishes talking: "Dryȝtyn wyth his dere dom hym drof to þe abyme,/ In þe mesure of his mode, his metz never þe lasse" (*C*, 214–15). I take line 215 to mean that God's spirit (his "mode") is not disturbed nor his mildness upset by the judgment he pronounces: Lucifer's case is straightforward because he willfully and consciously chooses what he gets. Adam's is also an easy case to judge; he openly breaks God's prohibition, so God punishes him and his offspring with death: "Al in mesure and meþe watz mad þe vengaunce" (*C*, 247). In Nebuchadnezzar's case

later in the poem, as in Lucifer's, God pronounces exile on Nebuchadnezzar the moment the king stops speaking and there is no
indication of anger in God's speech (see *C*, 1671–76).

The moderate spirit with which God judges the acts of Lucifer,
Adam, and Nebuchadnezzar in *Cleanness* indicates that these three
are connected to each other and distinct from other sinners in the
poem, but the sins that the poet attributes to these three are not
in every case the same. Lucifer's and Nebuchadnezzar's sins are
sins of pride, in that they claim to be gods; Adam's sin is to fail in
troth, or in the loyalty he owes to God, by eating the prohibited
apple. Penelope B. R. Doob analyzes biblical and commentary
traditions that connect Nebuchadnezzar to Lucifer and Adam in
her study of madness in Middle English literature, *Nebuchadnezzar's Children*; ordinarily, the three are associated by their
common sin of pride, which leads them to declare themselves
gods.[13] In distinguishing these three sinners from those who make
God angry, the *Cleanness* poet follows the standard interpretation
that Lucifer's and Nebuchadnezzar's sins were ones of pride; but
in making Adam's sin a failure in troth, he complicates the implicit theological distinction between these three and the other
sinners in the poem. I shall return to the poet's treatment of Adam,
but first let us consider some aspects of the usual tradition for linking these three. The discussion that follows is a speculative recon-
struction of the theology implicit in *Cleanness*.

Nebuchadnezzar, like Lucifer, refuses to acknowledge that he is
in any way limited by God and asserts instead an equality between
himself and God: "I schal telde up my trone in þe tramountayne,/
And by lyke to þat Lorde þat þe lyft made" (*C*, 211–12). Compare
Nebuchadnezzar's claim to be God's equal as governor and creator:

> "I am God of þe grounde, to gye as me lykes,
> As he þat hyȝe is in heven his aungeles þat weldes.
> If he hatz formed þe folde and folk þerupone,
> I haf bigged Babiloyne, burȝ alþerrychest,

---

13. Doob, *Nebuchadnezzar's Children*, pp 60–66, 69, 90. A midrash,
perhaps known to medieval Christian commentators, connects Nebuchadnezzar to Adam to explain his punishment: "Adam deserved to be spared
the experience of death. Why then was the penalty of death decreed
against him? Because the Holy One, blessed be He, foresaw that Nebuchadnezzar and Hiram would declare themselves gods; therefore was
death decreed against him," *Midrash Rabbah*, vol. 1, *Genesis*, 1.9.5, p. 66.

Stabled þerinne uche a ston in strenkþe of myn armes;
Moȝt never myȝt bot myn make such anoþer." (*C*, 1663–68)

Thomas Aquinas provides us with a way of understanding Nebuchadnezzar's sin when he explains how Lucifer's and Adam's
sins differ from most sins—theirs was the pride that "inordinate
divinam similitudinem appetierit" (coveted God's likeness inordinately).[14] Although Thomas's discussion of Adam's sin does not
account for the way *Cleanness* treats Adam, since the poet regards
Adam's sin as a failure in troth, it does illuminate the way the
poem understands Lucifer's and Nebuchadnezzar's sin. Thomas
distinguishes the sin of pride that takes God for a point of reference from other instances of pride when he treats Adam's sin of
pride separately from other human sins of pride. Adam, Thomas
says, desires a kind of likeness to God that is "similitudo imita-
tionis, qualis possibilis est creaturae ad Deum, inquantum videli-
cet participat aliquid de similitudine ipsius secundum suum
modum" (a likeness of imitation, such as is possible for a creature
in reference to God, in so far as the creature participates somewhat
of God's likeness according to its measure), *ST*, 2–2.163.2. But
Adam, who desires to be like God in the knowledge of good and
evil (*ST*, 2–2.163.2), and Lucifer, who desires to be like God in
power (as Nebuchadnezzar also does in *Cleanness*; see *ST*, 1.63.3),
want to be more like God than they can be, given their dependence
on him. In *Cleanness* Lucifer and Nebuchadnezzar do not acknowledge their subordination to God, which earns them divine punishment; but since their point of reference is God, their desire is
"secundum suam rationem non habet maximam repugnantiam ad
bonum virtutis" (not essentially . . . incompatible with the good of
virtue), *ST*, 2–2.162.6. To the extent that their desire causes them
not to be subject to God, their sin is great and merits the punishment they receive: "These punishments [of Adam and Eve] were
appointed by God, who does all things in number, weight, and
measure" (Wisd. 11:21; quoted in *ST*, 2–2.164.2). There is no suggestion in Thomas that God acts in anger when he punishes these
sins.

In *Cleanness* both Lucifer and Nebuchadnezzar explicitly com-

14. Thomas Aquinas, *Summa theologica* (*Summa Theologica*), 2–2.
163.2 (hereafter cited as *ST*). For a similar interpretation of Lucifer's
sin, see *ST*, 1.63.2–3.

pare themselves to God, which is effectively a claim not to be subject to him. That makes God's decision to punish them an
untroubled one. Similarly, God is untroubled by those who refuse
an invitation to his feast, perhaps because that refusal is at once
an acknowledgment of God and a refusal to be subject to him by
becoming his guests. God respects their choice.

The poet does not represent Adam's sin, which he describes
rather briefly, as an inordinate desire to be like God, but as a
failure in troth. He omits any reference to Satan's role in seducing
Eve, but makes Eve responsible for urging Adam to eat the fruit
of the forbidden tree, an act that "enpoysened alle peplez þat
parted fro hem boþe" (C, 242). This poisoning marks the beginning of human history and presumably also offers a rationale for
the inclusion of the Lucifer and Adam stories, quite apart from
their function as a gloss to Nebuchadnezzar: they explain how
history begins, why men are sinful, and why Christ is necessary.
In disobeying God's express command not to eat the apple, which
was the covenant God made with Adam, Adam loses paradise
(dies). Adam has acted like those who refused God's invitation to
the wedding feast; but because Adam has yet a life to lead and time
to repent, God, as we know from the Bible, promises him the possibility of redemption through Christ, to which the poet alludes
when he says the vengeance on Adam and Eve was "efte amended
wyth a mayden þat make had never" (C, 248). As Jerome was fond
of pointing out, even heretics (also a standard term of identification for those who refuse the wedding feast) ought to be invited to
repent.[15] God was thought, however, to judge those who did not
repent without anger or passion. In Cleanness, both Adam and
Nebuchadnezzar, in the moment of their sins, are like heretics; but
God punishes them so that they may repent. Nebuchadnezzar's
madness, like Adam's death, purges him. Changed into a beast
(the poet imagines the details of this metamorphosis with delight
[C, 1677-98]), Nebuchadnezzar responds to his punishment:

> Erne-hwed he watz [among other things], and al over-
>     brawden;
> Til he wyst ful wel who wroȝt alle myȝtes,
> And cowþe uche kyndam tokerve and kever when hym lyked.
>     (C, 1698-1700)

15. Jerome, In Osee prophetam, 1.2.1.

God then restores Nebuchadnezzar's wits, and Nebuchadnezzar comes to self-knowledge and makes peace with God, loving God and believing in him: "Þenne he loved þat Lorde and leved in trawþe/ Hit watz non oþer þen he þat hade al in honde" (*C*, 1703–4). Nebuchadnezzar's restoration foreshadows Adam's restoration, which is effected by Christ.

What distinguishes Adam's sin, as the *Cleanness* poet presents it, from those sins that later in history make God angry, seems to be Adam's self-consciousness. Presumably, Adam knows when he violates the express and single commandment of God that he is rejecting God's authority (Sedecias, by contrast, does not seem to be aware of his falseness; he is just a little slow in being faithful [*C*, 1171–74]).

Scholastic explanations of why Adam's sin was not the worst of sins do not make the distinction on this ground of self-consciousness; but their arguments do show, in ways that illuminate *Cleanness*, how Adam's sin is related to human history. Generally, Thomas Aquinas argues that Adam's sin was not the most grievous sin. One of his supporting arguments, in which he quotes Origen, asserts that the Fall was a gradual process:

> "Non arbitror quod aliquis ex his qui in summo perfectoque
> constiterint gradu, ad subitum evacuetur aut decidat,
> sed paulatim et per partes defluere eum necesse est." Sed
> primi parentes in summo perfectoque gradu consistebant.
> Non ergo eorum primum peccatum fuit maximum omnium
> peccatorum. ("I think that a man who stands on the
> highest step of perfection cannot fail or fall suddenly: this
> can happen only by degrees and little by little." [Thomas
> concludes:] Now our first parents were established on
> the highest and perfect grade. Therefore their first sin was not
> the greatest of sins.) *ST*, 2–2.163.3

That Adam's sin is not the worst of all sins suggests that the full realization of man's depravity will come later in history (and indeed the Bible does not suggest that God is angry at man until the Flood, Gen. 6). The sins of Lucifer and Adam create the historical conditions under which the worst sins, the hypocrisies of the filthy, discourteous wedding guests, can be committed.

Since, however, the *Cleanness* poet presents Adam's sin as disobedience and a failure to keep troth, Thomas's explanation of that sin as an inordinate desire to be like God cannot have inspired

the poet's conception of Adam; the analysis of Adam's sin by Duns
Scotus is closer to the poet's conception. When Duns Scotus considers Adam's sin and its relationship to natural law—a concept of
considerable importance in *Cleanness*, as the stories of the Flood
and Sodom from the age of the natural law indicate—he proposes
another theory under which Adam's sin may be considered less
evil than transgressions of the natural law. Scotus distinguishes
Adam's sin from transgressions of the ten commandments, which
are the revealed form of the natural law:

> Nunc autem peccatum, quod solum est peccatum, quia
> prohibitum, minus est peccatum formaliter, quam illud
> quod in se malum est, et non quia prohibitum. Nunc autem
> comedere de illo ligno, non plus fuit peccatum de genere
> actus, quam de alio ligno, sed solum quia prohibitum.
> Sed omnia peccata, quae sunt circa decem praecepta, forma-
> liter non tantum sunt mala, quia prohibita, sed quia mala,
> ideo prohibita, quia ex lege naturae oppositum cujuslibet
> fuit malum, et per naturalem rationem potest homo videre,
> quod quodlibet praeceptum ex illis est tenendum. (A sin
> which is a sin only because it is forbidden, is less of a sin
> formally than that which is evil in itself and not because it is
> forbidden. Now to eat of that tree was not more a sin, as
> far as the act was concerned, than to eat of another tree, but
> only because it was forbidden. But all sins which concern
> the ten commandments are formally evil not merely because
> they are forbidden, but because they are evil; therefore
> they are forbidden, since by the law of nature the opposite
> of any commandment was evil, and by natural reason a man
> can see that any of those precepts is to be observed.)[16]

According to Scotus, Adam's sin does not constitute a sin against
the law of nature and is not evil in itself. A consequence of this
interpretation may be that God's wrath is more appropriate to
sins against nature than to sins such as Adam's.

Under Duns Scotus's theory of natural law, all of the biblical
histories in *Cleanness* would be illustrations of the law's trans-
gression. The antediluvian men and the Sodomites commit sexual
sins, including the sin against nature; Sedecias and Belshazzar are

16. Duns Scotus, *Reportata Parisiensia*, 2.22, q. 1.3, in *Opera omnia*,
23:104; for a translation see Frederick Copleston, *History of Philosophy*,
vol. 2, *Mediaeval Philosophy, Augustine to Scotus*, pp. 547–48.

idolaters. Interestingly, when Scotus discusses the Decalogue, he argues that "the first two commandments of the first table [prohibiting idolatry] belong to the natural law in the strictest sense."[17] For Scotus, idolatry is the primary offense against the natural law (it was usual to argue that the Decalogue articulated the law of nature; Scotus's emphasis on idolatry was unusual). As the ages progress from that of nature to that of the written law, the *Cleanness* poet changes the name for the chief offense against God's law from *sexual sin* (stories of the Flood and Sodom) to *idolatry*, which is, by convention, adultery (story of Babylon); the poet may be suggesting that the Decalogue, with its clear prohibition against idolatry, constitutes a historical development in the articulation of the natural law, which was originally observed by fulfilling God's command to "increase and multiply," to procreate. Once the written version of the natural law came into being, the chief way of showing loyalty to God was to keep that law, with its prohibition on idolatry, a sin understood, as we have seen, to be an adultery, a desertion of God the husband for other lovers (other gods). If this line of speculation is correct, then, it explains why, in *Cleanness*, God's anger is directed against the sins that break the natural law and are evil in themselves, rather than against the sins of Lucifer or Nebuchadnezzar, which make God their point of reference, and of Adam, whose disobedience does not violate natural law.

The sinners who arouse God's wrath in *Cleanness* are sexual sinners, idolaters, and murderers: they seem to have no consciousness of God or of God's law and no awareness that their acts are a refusal of God. The anger that God expresses toward them is also anguish; because they have no intellectual understanding of their acts, they deny God by default. Because they are men (hence, unequal to Lucifer, whose ontological superiority to men makes penance, a change of will, impossible to him[18] [see *C*, 229–34]), they are perhaps capable of conversion and reform, a point illustrated by Lot's ineffectual attempt to recall the Sodomites from their sin, which foreshadows Christ's call to mankind to imitate him and turn away from sin. Christ, through his grace, makes a

17. Copleston, *Mediaeval Philosophy*, p. 548; on Duns Scotus's concept of law, see also Efrem Bettoni, *Duns Scotus*, pp. 173–82.

18. For a medieval interpretation of the angels' fall, see John Freccero, "Dante and the Neutral Angels."

conversion through penance possible for the audience of *Clean-ness*: the poet, like Lot, calls on the unselfconscious hypocrites to acknowledge their sins and repent. Christ offers mankind a perfect and more powerful example of cleanness than does Lot, and Christ's ministry shows the power of his love to redeem even the weakest and most corrupt men. Nebuchadnezzar typifies the Christian penitent. He is, like most Christians, a converted gentile; he sins, suffers a penitential madness, and is then restored to spiritual health. Both the punishment and the recovery are unmerited gifts of grace from God. Nebuchadnezzar's recovery is a type of Adam's redemption and a foreshadowing of the spiritual health that results from a renewal of faith and love and from sacramental penance.

Through the sacrament of penance, Christ extends the invitation to the wedding feast to all men in the journey of this life. He offers to take back even those who have violated their covenant with God by their sins against God's law. The *Cleanness* poet chooses sexual sin and the nearly synonymous sin of idolatry to embody literally and directly the sinners' violations of the covenant conceived as a marriage, and the poet makes the vessel a containing form for these sins. Within a poetic universe, the most powerful symbols are those that describe a concrete physical reality and yet are able to carry a further burden of meaning within the conceptual system of that universe. The *Cleanness* poet uses the analogy between a sinful man and a filthy vessel to illustrate Christ's power to purify man as man purifies a vessel. The analogy becomes explicit only in the center of the poem, when the poet presents the Christ-event. There is no need for anyone to fail to arrive at the wedding feast through ignorance or unworthiness, since Christ both clarifies God's will and has the power to redeem every vessel to God. What God does for Nebuchadnezzar, Christ offers to do for every man. The price is obedience to the law of God, now understood to be the law of Christ. The poet fears that he himself and his audience may fail to meet Christ's demands, and his poem is an act of penance for himself and a work of charity toward his audience, an exhortation to all to return to Christ through penance. His stories from history are his means of persuasion. No one knows the day or the hour of Christ's return as judge; but, as the story of the Flood demonstrates, once God has decided on judgment, the time for conversion is past. Penance, then, is urgent, for any who would avoid the fate of Noah's generation, the Sodomites, Sedecias, or Belshazzar.

### The Evidence of History: Noah and the Flood

For violating the central commandment in the law of nature, "to increase and multiply," Noah's generation makes God so angry that he determines to destroy mankind (Gen. 6:6–7). Harsher than the curse on Adam that did not, after all, entirely deprive him of life nor come to him without promise of redemption, the decree against Noah's generation—God says "I will blot out man"—exacts just vengeance for their corruption. Precisely what constitutes that corruption, according to both the Genesis account and the poem *Cleanness,* I will now consider.

To clarify the ignominy of Noah's generation, the poet describes the historical situation of these people. He connects them, the first progeny of the earth, with gardens (he will later stress the para- disiacal settings of Sodom and Babylon), implicitly comparing them to garden blossoms:

> Hit wern þe fayrest of forme and of face als,
> Þe most and þe myriest þat maked wern ever. . . .
> For hit was þe forme-foster þat þe folde bred. (*C,* 253–54, 257)

They had no law but the law of "kynde" (nature) and no obliga- tion but to "kepe to hit, and alle hit cors clanly fulfylle" (*C,* 264). These men, however, failed even in their minimal duty:

> And þenne founden þay fylþe in fleschlych dedez,
> And controeved agayn kynde contrare werkez,
> And used hem unþryftyly uch on on oþer,
> And als with oþer, wylsfully, upon a wrange wyse. (*C,* 265–68)

In contrast to the biblical account of the Flood, the *Cleanness* poet imposes a coherent interpretation on the causes of the Flood by making the sin against nature the initial crime of antediluvian men.

The order of elements in the Genesis story differs from the order the *Cleanness* poet develops.[19] Gen. 6:1–7 says that the sons of God mated with the daughters of men and implies that this union

19. Gen. 6 is confusing; it contains accounts of the Flood from two traditions, 6:9–12 (Priestly), 6:1–7 (Jahwist), 6:13–22 (Priestly and Jah- wist). See E. A. Speiser, trans., *Genesis,* pp. xxii–xxxvii, 44–56.

produced giants;[20] God sees the wickedness of men and vows to destroy what he has made. Medieval commentators understood this mating to be a perverse sexual union and a precondition for God's determination of man's wickedness. The *Cleanness* poet makes this mating the second stage in the increasing depravity of mankind before the Flood, taking his first stage from Gen. 6:9–22, which omits the strange sexual union in giving the preconditions of the Flood:

> And the earth was corrupted before God, and was filled with iniquity. And when God had seen that the earth was corrupted (for all flesh had corrupted its way upon the earth), He said to Noe: The end of all flesh is come before me; the earth is filled with iniquity through them; and I will destroy them with the earth. (Gen. 6:11–13)

In glossing Gen. 6:11–12, Nicholas of Lyra says that the earth was corrupted by carnal sins, specifically fornication and adultery and even sins against nature. Alternatively, Nicholas reads "all flesh" to refer to birds and animals as well as men, and these creatures corrupt the earth by mixing themselves inordinately with those who are not of the same kind or species.[21] His gloss on the preconditions of the Flood makes sexual sin and especially the sin against nature the cause of God's displeasure. *Cleanness*, like Nicholas, interprets corruption (Gen. 6:11) as the sin against nature (*C*, 265–68) and then, going back to Gen. 6:1–7, implies that the strange sexual congress of the sons of God with the daughters of men is a consequence of the sin against nature (*C*, 269–72).

Coherence, significance, and dramatic effectiveness result from the poet's rearrangement of biblical narrative. During the Age of Nature, a sin against the law of nature was the only way that man might irredeemably offend God. By recognizing this, the *Cleanness* poet offers a clear historical perspective on the Flood.

The poet uses the Flood story to exemplify the theory that violation of natural law, which lies at the foundation of all human social order, leads to progressive decay in the social order. Their flesh polluted by sexual sin, the daughters of men are vulnerable

20. See Oliver F. Emerson, "Legends of Cain, especially in Old and Middle English," for more on monstrous beings produced from perverse unions.

21. Nicholas of Lyra, *Postilla super Genesim*, 6:11–12.

to the advances of the fiends (Sons of God or fallen angels) who find them fair. Their matings with the fiends produce giants who measure their greatness in evil. The moral order turns upside down, as the poet observes with biting irony:

> Þose wern men meþelez and maȝty on urþe,
> Þat for her lodlych laykez alosed þay were.
> He watz famed for fre þat feȝt loved best,
> And ay þe bigest in bale þe best watz halden. (*C*, 273–76)

The evils done by Noah's generation are not specified in detail, but fighting (*C*, 275) usually implies its consequence, murder, and the expression "þe maȝty on molde so marre þise oþer" (*C*, 279) may imply murder as well as general injustice to the weak. We see then that the *Cleanness* poet, like the *Queste* author, tends to see dissension and murder as a consequence of sexual sin.

Noah is the one righteous man of his generation, and God excepts him and his family from the judgment he pronounces on the rest of mankind. The story of the Flood, like the parable of the wedding feast, opposes righteousness to unrighteousness. The Flood, as God says, is at once a judgment on evil men and a cleansing of the earth they have corrupted: "For I schal waken up a water to wasch alle þe worlde,/ And quelle alle þat is quik wyth quavende flodez" (*C*, 323–24). By sending the Flood, God restores the earth to make it again a garden where the righteous—Noah and his family—may flourish.

God, whose anger at men makes him talk, or rather rant, to himself (*C*, 284–92), chooses to except Noah from his vengeance because Noah is a man "ay glydande wyth his God" (*C*, 296). He instructs Noah to build an ark, which the poet also calls a "mancioun," a "cofer," and a "kyst," nonbiblical synonyms that emphasize the ark's function as a container. This vessel objectively expresses Noah's internal condition. It is a closed wooden coffer, cleanly planed, sealed on the inside with clay and on the outside with plaster. Is the poet perhaps thinking of the "garden enclosed" of the Song of Solomon? His substitution of *clay* for *bitumine* (pitch), impractical from a shipbuilding point of view, is often explained as the poet's underscoring of the ark's analogical relationship to Noah, a man of clay. As a container for him and his family, the ark becomes an effective sign of the covenant between God and Noah:

Bot my forwarde wyth þe I festen on þis wyse,
For þou in reysoun hatz rengned and ryʒtwys ben ever:
Þou schal enter þis ark wyth þyn aþel barnez
And þy wedded wyf; with þe þou take
Þe makez of þy myry sunez; þis meyny of aʒte
I schal save of monnez saulez, and swelt þose oþer. (*C*, 327–32)

A conversation in the *Queste* between Bors and a hermit demonstrates that a ship (in *Cleanness*, the ark) and the body of a man are comparable vessels: "Li cuers de l'ome si est l'aviron de la nef, qui le meine quel part qu'il veut, ou a port ou a peril"; counseled by the Holy Spirit, the heart guides man to port; enticed by Satan, the heart leads man into peril (*Q*, 165). Noah's ark has no steering equipment (*C*, 417–20), but is driven by the winds, in other words, by God,[22] and "Nyf oure Lorde hade ben her lodezmon, hem had lumpen harde" (*C*, 424). The ark built by Noah expresses and shares Noah's cleanness. God responds to the cleanness of man and vessel by granting them grace to weather the storm.

For Noah and his family the Flood is a comic experience; for everyone else the Flood is rather grim. The *Cleanness* poet is unrelenting in making his audience aware of the menace and the disaster, not only in the first hints of God's anger, but also later in the lengthy account of drowning flesh (*C*, 363–408) that details the effects on all living creatures of the rising waters that "hurled into uch hous" (*C*, 376). People flock to the mountains; the wild creatures of the woods either swim or, like the hares and harts, rush to the high places. They all cry, the animals roaring and the people begging for mercy from God; but God's "mercy watz passed,/ And alle his pyte departed fro peple þat he hated" (*C*, 395–96). Recognizing that they are about to die,

Frendez fellen in fere and faþmed togeder,
To dryʒ her delful deystyne and dyʒen alle samen;
Luf lokez to luf and his leve takez,
For to ende alle at onez and for ever twynne. (*C*, 399–402)

By focusing on friends and lovers, the poet adds a sentimental twist to the exhilaration that those not directly involved—like Noah, like the audience of the poem—feel when witnessing a disaster. Here, mixing sentiment into an epic subject results in a heightening of the drama of the Flood.

22. On the wind as God's agent, see Norman H. Snaith, *The Distinctive Ideas of the Old Testament*, pp. 145–58, 179.

Through the episode of the birds that Noah sends out as messengers to discover whether the earth is again habitable, the *Cleanness* poet foreshadows the pattern of opposition that will reassert itself in history: Noah's treatment of the birds parallels God's judgment on men.[23] Noah curses the raven who "fallez on þe foule flesch and fyllez his wombe" (*C*, 462), so consumed with gluttony that he forgets his mission and his master. The dove returns from her first mission without any sign, but for her loyalty "Noe nymmes hir anon and naytly hir stauez" (*C*, 480).

The dove's second mission confirms the covenant God had made with Noah:

> On ark on an eventyde hovez þe dowve,
> On stamyn ho stod and stylle hym abydez.
> What! ho broȝt in hir beke a bronch of olyve,
> Graciously umbegrouen al wyth grene levez;
> Þat watz þe syngne of savyte þat sende hem oure Lorde. (*C*,
> 485–89)

By his exclamation, the poet-narrator places himself in the poem and invites his listeners to imagine themselves on the ark, watching the returning dove. There is great rejoicing in the ark, and as a fair day dawns, the first day of the first month of the year (March 25, the traditional date for the Annunciation), there is laughter in "þat lome" (*C*, 495). When God gives the sign, Noah opens the door and leads his family first and then the wild creatures out into the world made new.

Noah's first act, upon his release, is to make a sacrifice of one from each of the clean creatures; in response, God renews the covenant of nature:

> "Bot waxez now and wendez forth and worþez to monye,
> Multyplyez on þis molde, and menske yow bytyde.
> Sesounez schal yow never sese of sede ne of hervest,
> Ne hete, ne no harde forst, umbre ne droȝþe,
> Ne þe swetnesse of somer, ne þe sadde wynter,
> Ne þe nyȝt, ne þe day, ne þe newe ȝerez,
> Bot ever renne restlez—rengnez ȝe þerinne!"
> Þerwyth he blessez uch a best, and bytaȝt hem þis erþe. (*C*,
> 521–28)

23. Conventionally, the ark is said to contain the raven and the dove as the Church contains both good and evil; see *Glossa ordinaria*, in *PL* 113:109.

God's intervention in history to save Noah reinforces the covenant
of nature through supernatural revelations to this special man,
but the definition of the covenant does not change. Man's primary
obligation, which he can deduce from the evidence of creation, is
still, as it was for fallen Adam, to procreate his own kind and to
praise the Creator of all things. The account of the Flood ends
with the procession of the creatures back to their natural habitats,
a reestablishment of order that contrasts with the chaos in the
kingdom of wild creatures when the Flood begins.

The *Cleanness* poet makes the point of each of his histories of
judgment explicit at the close of each narrative. In each case, the
point is similar: God destroys men for filth of the flesh and cleanness is a condition of entrance into God's court. The poet does not
allegorize his biblical narratives, but fits his warnings to the stories.
For example, at the end of the Flood story, he says:

> Forþy war þe now, wyӡe þat worschyp desyres . . .
> In þe fylþe of þe flesch þat þou be founden never,
> Tyl any water in þe worlde to wasche þe fayly. (*C*, 545, 547–
> 48)

Even one speck can cause a man to miss "þe syӡte of þe Soverayn"
(*C*, 552). To enforce his point, the poet introduces the images of
the burnished beryl and the "margerye-perle," images of perfection.

## The Evidence of History: Abraham and Lot, Sodom and Gomorrah

To lead into the story of Sodom, the *Cleanness* poet restates the
covenant between God and Noah, in which God promises that he
will never again curse all the earth (*C*, 513–20); this promise affects
the way God can manifest his judgment on Sodom. Restatement
of the covenant gives the poet an opportunity to explore God's
psychology, and he concludes that God felt remorse for the harsh-
ness of his judgment:

> Hym rwed þat he hem uprerde and raӡt hem lyflode,
> And efte þat he hem undyd, hard hit hym þoӡt;
> For quen þe swemande sorӡe soӡt to his hert,
> He knyt a covenaunde cortaysly wyth monkynde þere,
> In þe mesure of his mode and meþe of his wylle,
> Þat he schulde never, for no syt, smyte al at onez,

As to quelle alle quykez for qued þat myȝt falle,
Whyl of þe lenþe of þe londe lastez þe terme. (*C*, 561–68)

To make the didactic point of *Cleanness* (that men should be
clean) convincing, the poet has to make God's actions compre-
hensible and his character trustworthy and lovable; otherwise men
might doubt God's goodness, question the wisdom of relying on
his word, and refuse to acknowledge the desirability of the condition of cleanness. The story of Sodom proves that the gracious
covenant God makes with Noah will last to the world's end, that
nothing men do can bring God to break his word.

At the same time, the story of Sodom illustrates the consistency
of God's judgment by showing again how he hates "harlottrye
unhonest, heþyng of selven" (*C*, 579), which is the sin that leaves
the vessel of the body polluted, the sin by which man commits
sacrilege on himself. The crimes of which the sinners are guilty—
sodomy and intent to murder—and the place in which the crimes
are committed are more specific in this story than in the Flood
narrative. In the last of the biblical narratives, individual sinners,
whose crimes we learn about in even greater detail, will be the
targets of God's vengeance. The progression of the stories in the
poem, then, moves toward a climax as the focus of God's judgment
narrows, from the world to a city to an individual, and as the sins
he curses become more clearly defined.

The poet's admonitions to his audience, which conclude the
Flood story and introduce the story of Sodom, are intended to
make his listeners apply the stories to themselves. As the focus of
God's judgment narrows, the audience is invited to recognize that
eventually it will fall upon each one of them, and each member of
the audience is encouraged to judge himself according to God's
criterion.

In the transition from the story of the Flood to that of Sodom,
the poet exhorts his listeners to respond to the message of these
stories by sardonically addressing himself to "man," a rhetorical
figure that represents the listeners:

Bot savor, mon, in þyself, þaȝ þou a sotte lyvie,
Þaȝ þou bere þyself babel, byþenk þe sumtyme
Wheþer he þat stykked uche a stare in uche steppe yȝe,
Ȝif hymself be bore blynde, hit is a brod wonder;
And he þat fetly in face fettled alle eres,

If he hatz losed þe lysten hit lyftez mervayle;
Traue þou never þat tale, untrwe þou hit fyndez.
Þer is no dede so derne þat dittez his yȝen. (C, 581–88)

This characterization of the judging Creator who knows his work
has its immediate source in Ps. 93:8–9, 11, as Robert J. Menner
notes in his edition of *Cleanness*. The prophetic exemplum of the
potter and his vessel depends on similar assertions of the superiority of the maker to his work:

> Woe to you that are deep of heart, to hide your counsel
> from the Lord! And their works are in the dark, and they
> say: Who seeth us, and who knoweth us? This thought of
> yours is perverse: as if the clay should think against the potter,
> and the work should say to the maker thereof: Thou madest
> me not. Or the thing framed should say to him that fash-
> ioned it: Thou understandest not. (Isa. 29:15–16; cf.
> Jer. 18:2–6)

The poet assures "man" that God will know how to judge, to honor
or to dishonor, "For he is þe gropande God, þe grounde of alle
dedez,/ Rypande of uche a ring þe reynyez and hert" (C, 591–92).

After his rhetorical outburst of prophetic indignation, the poet
relaxes the tension of the poem by turning to the pleasant visit
of the three angels to Abraham, which provides an interlude between the judgment by water and the judgment by fire and allows
the *Cleanness* poet to set forth his most complex human exemplar
of clean behavior. We may compare the three heroic figures in
*Cleanness*, Noah, Abraham, and Daniel, to the three roles of Galahad: Noah corresponds to Galahad as the exemplar of cleanness;
Abraham to Galahad as companion; and Daniel, whose name
means judgment of God, to Galahad as judge of Carcelois. The
*Cleanness* poet reveals Abraham's character through Abraham's
hospitality to the angels, through his marriage to Sara, and
through his charitable attitude toward his neighbors in Sodom.
God renews his covenant with mankind through Abraham in a
way that points directly toward Christ; and Lot, as we will see,
imitates Abraham and also points toward Christ.

Abraham's story resonates with typological implications, some
of which are made explicit by analogies to his story in other parts
of the poem, some of which are present by virtue of the poet's
allusion to conventional typologies of biblical literature. Because

Christianity, like Judaism, demands a constant, lived relationship with God, exemplary narrative is a particularly effective way to interpret requirements of the faith, which are not easy to understand dynamically when they are stated only as principles. Exemplary biblical narratives are particularly significant for interpreting Christianity, not only because they are its basis, but also because they have been so much thought about in Christian commentary. The *Cleanness* poet uses typology to articulate the complexity of his simple message (that a true Christian must be clean and courteous) by writing a series of analogically related narratives, each of which serves to gloss the others. In addition, because they are all biblical stories, they each have a conventional body of interpretation attached to them (the corpus of patristic and medieval exegesis), to which the poet sometimes alludes by the way in which he paraphrases the Bible, by choosing words (such as *clay* rather than *pitch* in Noah's story), adding details (such as Abraham's "clene" cloth [*C*, 634]), or rearranging narrative (as in the beginning of the Flood story).

The *Cleanness* poet confines his presentation of Abraham as exemplar of purity and charity to the story of the visit of the three angels, whose real identity makes their visit a prefiguration of the Christ-event. When Abraham, who has been sitting under the shade of an oak tree, spies three wayfarers on his road, he goes out to greet them as if they were God (*C*, 611) and to invite them to rest a while with him. Gen. 18, the source of this story, suggests that these angels are indeed God, and commentary tradition confirms that they are the three persons of the Trinity, manifesting themselves as angels;[24] in *Cleanness* the poet shifts back and forth from referring to three guests to referring to only one, naming the one guest *God* and the other two *God's messengers* (*C*, 781). The visitors wait under the tree while Abraham fetches water to wash

24. The Abraham story is a standard authority for the common medieval belief that God sometimes manifests himself to man in angelic form. See Augustine, *De civ. Dei*, 10.7–8, 12–13, 15, 16.29; and Gregory the Great, *Moralia in Job*, 19.25.46, in *PL* 76:126–27, for comment on the visit of the three angels to Abraham. The three angels are ordinarily read as a manifestation of the Trinity; see Ambrose, *Cain and Abel*, 1.8.30, CSEL 32:365; and Rupert of Deutz, *De Trinitate et operibus ejus: Commentariorum in Genesim*, 5.37–38, in *PL* 167:400–404, who bases the use of singular and plural in reference to the angels on a distinction between their appearance as God (sing.) and their role as guests (pl.).

their feet, which is an act of hospitality,[25] and while Abraham arranges with Sara and his servant to have a feast prepared.

Historically, according to the interpretation implicit in *Cleanness*, this feast foreshadows the sacrament of the Mass, the communion of God with man; within the poem it echoes the exemplum of the priests at the altar that opens the poem and is the first analogue to the wedding feast.[26] Making a picnic for the angels, Abraham brings a "clene cloþe" (*C*, 634) to lay on the grass; then he serves the angels unleavened cakes and butter, places between them measures of milk, and serves them soup and stew "in plater honest" (*C*, 638). Abraham's posture before the angels, "al hodlez, wyth armez upfolden" (*C*, 643), is suitable to a priest celebrating the Mass. Like the good priests in the prologue of *Cleanness*, Abraham has clean cloths and clean vessels with which to offer his feast to the angels, and the angels treat him as their friend, accepting his service as graciously as he gives it (*C*, 641–42). In the early days of the Church, the congregation usually brought offerings of bread to the Mass, over which the priest spoke in Christ's behalf his words of consecration, "this bread is my body." The Mass, then, is a mutual offering: Christ reciprocates the gifts of man through the gift of his Body.[27] The offering the communicant brings to the Mass was often interpreted to be his heart, contained in the clean vessel of his body.[28] Abraham's offering of food in clean vessels to

25. See Ambrose, *De Spiritu Sancto*, bk. 1, prologue 15, CSEL 79:21–22; and Augustine, *De civ. Dei*, 16.29.

26. Traditionally, another event in Abraham's life, the Melchisedech episode (Gen. 14:18), foreshadows the Eucharist; this seems to have inhibited many commentators from associating the visit of the three angels with the Eucharist. Occasionally, however, the banquets of Abraham and Lot with the angels are read as types of the Eucharist; for Abraham, see John Lydgate, *Minor Poems*, pp. 35ff., and Ambrose, *Cain and Abel*, 1.8.30; for Lot, see Rupert of Deutz, *De Trinitate et operibus ejus: Commentariorum in Genesim*, 6.7, in *PL* 167:408. The *Cleanness* poet, by implying that the Abraham-Lot banquets are types of the Eucharist, fills out the pattern of types of the sacraments of baptism (Noah), Eucharist (Abraham-Lot), and penance (Nebuchadnezzar), with which the poem is otherwise concerned.

27. Jungmann, *Mass of the Roman Rite*, 1:71, 189–90; 2:1–15. Augustine discusses the reciprocal nature of the sacrifice of the Mass in *De civ. Dei*, 10.5–6, 19–20.

28. See Chap. 2, n. 4, and Jungmann, *Mass of the Roman Rite*, 1:24, 27, 175–95.

the angels prefigures the offerings made by communicants in the Eucharist; in the Abraham story the "plater honest" is the objective sign of Abraham's spiritual condition.

As a type of the Eucharist, Abraham's story is not fulfilled until Christ comes to offer his Body in return. As we have already seen through the Grail masses in the *Queste*, the Eucharist is the celebration that confirms a fellowship among the priest and the communicants in the feast and, at the same time, it is a celebration that signifies the betrothal of man to God. As a type of the Eucharist, the feast Abraham hospitably offers to the three angels is accepted as a demonstration of the friendship, of a society of peace, among the angels and Abraham.

God, under the form of the three angels, confirms his friendship with Abraham by renewing his covenant with mankind through the marriage of Abraham and Sara:

> "And þenne schal Sare consayve and a sun bere,
> Þat schal be Abrahamez ayre, and after hym wynne
> Wyth wele and wyth worschyp þe worþely peple,
> Þat schal halde in heritage þat I haf men ȝarked." (*C*, 649–52)

God confirms the meaning of this announcement when he decides, in conversation with himself, to tell Abraham about the fate to befall Sodom, "Syþen he is chosen to be chef chyldryn fader" (*C*, 684).

The promise to Sara that she will conceive a son is a type of the Annunciation. By fathering this son (whom he calls Isaac, or "promise," a fact the poet does not mention), Abraham becomes the natural father of the chosen people. Although Isaac is to be conceived by natural means, through human sexual intercourse, the intervention of God is necessary to make the human act fruitful because Sara is old and barren. Sara laughs when she hears the angels' promise and madly (irrationally) talks to herself, expressing her disbelief. The angels reprove her not for laughing, but for denying her laughter. They accept that her faith is not strong enough to guide her reason to understand the reasonableness of a divine miracle; they reprove her for untruthfulness. Sara's denial is an act of courtesy—misguided, as it happens—toward her husband's guests; she means to avoid antagonizing them, so she conceals her scorn and disbelief. Her behavior at once emphasizes the miraculousness of her conception and contrasts both with

Abraham's faith and with the faith and humility of the Virgin Mary, who accepts without doubting the angel's annunciation to her.

God's promise to Abraham also has typological implications beyond the Christ-event because it foreshadows the foundation of the Church, the spiritual family in Christ. By referring to Abraham as the "chef chyldryn fader," the *Cleanness* poet alludes to this concept of Abraham's fatherhood of the Church. In effect, then, the promise to Abraham is to the poet's audience as well. Paul interprets this promise of a son (Isaac-Christ) as a sign that Christians are the children of promise, that is, of faith, and the heirs of God:

> He, therefore, who giveth to you the Spirit and worketh miracles among you; doth he do it by the works of the law or by the hearing of the faith? As it is written: Abraham believed God; and it was reputed to him unto justice. Know ye, therefore, that they who are of faith, the same are the children of Abraham. . . . Christ hath redeemed us from the curse of the law, being made a curse for us (for it is written: Cursed is every one that hangeth on a tree); that the blessing of Abraham might come on the Gentiles through Christ Jesus; that we may receive the promise of the Spirit by faith. . . . To Abraham were the promises made and to his seed. He saith not: And to his seeds, as of many; but as of one: And to thy seed, which is Christ. . . . For you are all the children of God, by faith in Christ Jesus. . . . There is neither Jew nor Greek; there is neither bond nor free; there is neither male nor female. For you are all one in Christ Jesus. And, if you be Christ's, then are you the seed of Abraham, heirs according to the promise. (Gal. 3:5-7, 13-14, 16, 26, 28-29; cf. Rom. 9:3-9)

The *Cleanness* poet illustrates Abraham's spiritual paternity through an account of Abraham's response to God's intention to destroy Sodom for her sins. Abraham bargains with God on behalf of the citizens of Sodom, to whom Abraham feels a kinship based on their common humanity. God responds to Abraham's humble and courteous display of charity by agreeing to save Sodom if he finds even ten righteous men there. In parting, Abraham reminds God of his poor servant Lot, Abraham's natural kinsman who lives in Sodom.

Through Abraham, the *Cleanness* poet shows his audience what is demanded of them. Abraham's faith in the promise of a son demonstrates the faith in the promise of Christ required of all Christians. The picnic banquet he offers to the angels illustrates his cleanness and courtesy and prefigures the Mass in which each Christian offers himself to God. The Christian, through his clean offer of hospitality to Christ, receives Christ in the sacrament of the Mass, thus effecting a spiritual marriage with Christ; and this fellowship is prefigured in Abraham's companionable talk with God on the way to Sodom. In the *Psychomachia*, Prudentius recounts Abraham's life, including the sacrifice of Melchisedech, the visit of the three angels, and the promise of a son, and then makes explicit, in imagery associated with the paradigm of the vessel, the spiritual implications of such a life of faith:

> mox ipse Christus, qui sacerdos verus est.
> parente inenarrabili atque uno satus,
> cibum beatis offerens victoribus
> parvam pudici cordis intrabit casam,
> monstrans honorem Trinitatis hospitae.
> animam deinde Spiritus conplexibus
> pie maritam, prolis expertem diu,
> faciet perenni fertilem de semine,
> tunc sera dotem possidens puerpera
> herede digno Patris inplebit domum.
> (Then Christ himself, who is the true priest, born of a
> Father unutterable and one, bringing food for the blessed
> victors, will enter the humble abode of the pure heart and
> give it the privilege of entertaining the Trinity; and
> then the Spirit, embracing in holy marriage the soul that has
> long been childless, will make her fertile by the seed eternal,
> and the dowered bride will become a mother late in life
> and give the Father's household a worthy heir.)[29]

A model of faith, Abraham enjoys the privilege of companionship with God; he sets a standard of cleanness and courtesy for Christians to match. The Christian significance that Prudentius discovers in Abraham seems to me to be implicit in *Cleanness*'s account of Abraham as well.

When God speaks to Abraham about the sin of Sodom, he compares the practice of the Sodomites to the office of matrimony (to man and woman joined in sexual intercourse). God's speech reflects back on the promise to Abraham: Abraham and Sara have fulfilled the singularly dear ordinance of the natural law that constitutes man's fitting response to God's creation; and God, in response, has promised them fertility.

God's speech is remarkable for its high and unqualified praise of human sexual love, that is, of marriage under the natural law:

> "I compast hem a kynde crafte and kende hit hem derne,
> And amed hit in myn ordenaunce oddely dere,
> And dyȝt drwry þerinne, doole alþerswettest,
> And þe play of paramorez I portrayed myselven;
> And made þerto a maner myriest of oþer,
> When two true togeder had tyȝed hemselven,
> Bytwene a male and his make such merþe schulde come,
> Wel nyȝe pure paradys moȝt preve no better,
> Ellez þay moȝt honestly ayþer oþer welde;
> At a stylle stollen steven, unstered wyth syȝt,
> Luf-lowe hem bytwene lasched so hote,
> Þat alle þe meschefez on mold moȝt hit not sleke.
> Now haf þay skyfted my skyl and scorned natwre,
> And henttez hem in heþyng an usage unclene.
> Hem to smyte for þat smod smartly I þenk,
> Þat wyȝez schal be by hem war, worlde wythouten ende."
> (C, 697–712)

Just as Noah's ark had no human guidance (C, 417–24), so sexual union is "unstered wyth syȝt," it is accomplished in darkness but ordained and ordered by God. Through this speech, the *Cleanness* poet makes it clear that natural human marriage is the way back to paradise under the natural law, or, to be more precise, that it offers a way, under the law of nature, to approach paradise. Human marriage is the foundation for the concept of the divine marriage between Christ and man, the marriage that ends in paradise regained, the celestial wedding feast, and the vision of God.

With the story of the angels and Lot and the Sodomites, the *Cleanness* poet returns to the pattern of opposition between clean and unclean. Lot behaves as Abraham has toward the angels: like Abraham, he is an exemplar of cleanness. As he is standing on the porch of his palace near the city gates, Lot sees the angels coming and runs out to greet them. He invites the angels to "lyȝt at my loge and lenge þerinne" (*C*, 800) and offers to fetch them "a fatte yor fette forto wasche" (*C*, 802). Persuaded by the graciousness of his invitation, the angels accept. This gesture, inviting the angels to come into his house, parallels in literal terms the spiritual hospitality that men offer to God when they make a clean lodging for him in their hearts. Even when the lecherous Sodomites threaten to kill Lot, he refuses them entry into his house (where the angels are safely ensconced), just as he has refused to let the sinful desires of the Sodomites into his heart. Like Noah's ark, Lot's house becomes identified with its owner's cleanness.

Like Abraham, Lot arranges a feast for the angels; this feast foreshadows the Church Militant and echoes the portraits of the guests at the wedding feast in the introductory part of *Cleanness*. Lot's wife and his daughters make the angels welcome and prepare food for the feast, but despite Lot's instructions, his wife puts salt in the stew broth. Her disobedience, as we know, will have different consequences from Sara's laughter (which is not a deliberate act of discourtesy but a sign of less than perfect faith); Lot's wife is a type of the discourteous guest at the wedding feast because she deliberately disregards the requirements of obedience and indulges her whims. She and Lot, then, typify the membership of the Church Militant, which includes both the reprobate and the elect. The angels, nevertheless, enjoy the feast: "Þenne seten þay at þe soper, wern served bylyve,/ Þe gestes gay and ful glad, of glam debonere" (*C*, 829–30).

The hospitality of Lot cannot be compared to that of the other Sodomites, whose designs on Lot's guests are grossly sinful. The other Sodomites, filthy with sexual sin that God describes as homosexual (*C*, 694–96; the poet seems to echo Rom. 1:26–27 in these lines), also see the angels as they enter the city, and the Sodomites do not forget the angels' beauty. Indeed, to impress their beauty on his audience, the poet admires the angels as they enter the city:

> Bolde burnez were þay boþe, wyth berdles chynnez,
> Royl rollande fax, to raw sylk lyke,
> Of ble as þe brere-flor where so þe bare schewed;
> Ful clene watz þe countenaunce of her cler yȝen;
> Wlonk whit watz her wede and wel hit hem semed.
> Of alle feturez ful fyn and fautlez boþe. (*C*, 789–94)

This beauty arouses the people of Sodom. That night they come
to Lot's house, and clattering on the walls they shout:

> "If þou lovyez þy lyf, Loth, in þyse wones,
> ȝete uus out þose ȝong men þat ȝore-whyle here entred,
> Þat we may lere hym of lof, as oure lyst biddez,
> As is þe asyse of Sodomas to seggez þat passen." (C, 841–44)

The "grete soun of Sodomas," the rumor that has come to God's
ears (C, 689–92), is confirmed.

The poet's exclamatory response to the Sodomites' proposal
treats their words as metaphors for their intentions:

> Whatt! þay sputen and speken of so spitous fylþe,
> What! þay ȝeȝed and ȝolped of ȝestande sorȝe,
> Þat ȝet þe wynd, and þe weder, and þe worlde stynkes
> Of þe brych þat upbraydez þose broþelych wordez. (C. 845–
> 48)

Vessels of filth, all that the Sodomites can produce out of their
mouths is "brych" (vomit). This vomit reveals the evilness of their
intentions and pollutes the wind and the earth, making them stink.
The stench of the Sodomites' intentions directly contrasts with
the sweet savor of the sacrifice that Noah makes to God, a savor
that metaphorically represents Noah's intentions (C, 509–11). God
responds to Noah by renewing the covenant of nature; he responds
to the Sodomites by destroying them. The harsh sounds of line
848—note the rhyme and alliteration in "brych-broþlych"—rein-
force the attitude God's words express.

Charitable like Abraham, Lot tries, even at the last minute, to
remedy the evil intentions and the corrupt ways of the rowdy
Sodomites and lead them back to God's plan by offering them, instead of the angels, his two fair daughters:

> "Bot I schal kenne yow by kynde a crafte þat is better:
> I haf a tresor in my telde of tow my fayre deȝter, . . .
> Hit arn ronk, hit arn rype, and redy to manne;
> To samen wyth þo semly þe solace is better.
> I schal biteche yow þo two þat tayt arn and quoynt,
> And laykez wyth hem as yow lyst, and letez my gestes
> one." (C, 865–66, 869–72)

As his reference to the natural "crafte" of lovemaking (C, 865),
shows, Lot is offering the Sodomites an opportunity to convert

from their evil ways and to enter into the covenant of nature, which requires that men couple with women. They reject Lot's offer.

The Sodomites' proud and truculent response to Lot shows that the *Cleanness* poet again, and this time explicitly, considers murder an inevitable consequence of sexual sin. The Sodomites do not recognize Lot as a fellow citizen, even though he came to Sodom as a boy and is now a rich man (*C*, 878): they call him an "outcomlyng, a carle," and they threaten to cut off his head (*C*, 876).

The Sodomites' desire to seize the angels and assault them sexually parodies the true quest for the vision of God. Neither God nor his messengers, whom the Sodomites do not recognize as angels of God, can be possessed in such a fashion. The angels repay the Sodomites' limited and carnal vision with blindness, a physical disability that literally expresses their lack of spiritual vision or understanding (cf. the distinction between inner and outer darkness in commentary on the wedding feast parable, e.g., Bede, *In Matthaei evangelium expositio*, 3.22, in *PL* 92:96). In effect, the Sodomites interpret the wedding feast in a perverse and carnal sense. As a result, they will neither see God nor know the bliss of the divine marriage. Their condition is like Lancelot's when he sees the Grail as a physical object but cannot respond to its spiritual significance. The difference between them and Lancelot lies in Lancelot's response to the divine vessel: he converts from his evil ways through penance and eventually is granted a glimpse, a foretaste of the celestial wedding feast and the vision of God.

To honor Abraham's request and Lot's courtesy and cleanness, the angels show Lot and his family a way to escape judgment. They tell Lot to leave Sodom quickly and climb to a high place without looking back. The storm of destruction begins as Lot and his daughters are climbing, but they do not look back until they have reached safety. Lot's wife, on the other hand, can obey this command no better than she could the earlier one Lot imposed on her. She looks over her left shoulder to see the storm,[30] and in that moment God turns her into a pillar of salt "and so ho ʒet standez" (*C*, 984). Lot's salvation prefigures the resurrection, he is allowed to keep his life. But his wife, who also welcomed the angels and

30. On this passage, see Hartley Bateson, "Looking Over the Left Shoulder."

seemed to have been part of Lot's holy household, cannot resist looking back, an intentional gesture that reveals that her heart lies in the ungodly city of the world; she loses her life as the sexual sinners do and becomes, as her heart already is, a stone (cf. the curse on Lancelot, *Q*, 61, 67–68).

The effect of divine judgment is to make things seem what they are. The blindness that afflicts the Sodomites is the effect of God's judgment on them. They have also polluted the land with their filth, and the destruction visited upon Sodom makes the place seem what it is, a devastated land. God calls the winds, which fly up and wrestle together; then the rain falls, carrying down with it sparks of fire and flakes of sulphur. This storm, with its rushing wind and foul rain, should be read as God's response to the stinking vomit cast up by the Sodomites' "broþelych wordez"; just such an image is associated with God's judgment in Lev. 18:25–28, which follows an enumeration of sexual offenses, and in Jer. 25:27 ff., which links vomit of sinners and the storm of God's judgment. In the storm and earthquake Sodom and Gomorrah and all the cities of the plain sink into hell and the valley fills with the pitchy water of the Dead Sea.[31]

Sodom was once the fairest place on earth, a dependency of paradise. Significantly, the poet's reference to Sodom "as aparaunt to paradis þat plantted þe Dryȝtyn" (*C*, 1007) echoes God's speech describing heterosexual love as near paradise: "Bytwene a male and his make such merþe schulde come,/ Wel nyȝe pure paradys moȝt preve no better" (*C*, 703–4). Men's failure to come "wel nyȝe pure paradys" in the natural way entails their loss of the paradisiacal land. The corruption of human sexuality violates all of nature, which implies that all aspects of nature, including human sexuality and the earth and the things that grow on the earth, are one. Because God's justice destroys irony, all nature in Sodom must give evidence of the injury by becoming ruined. What is left of Sodom is extraordinarily horrible, the unnaturally blasted landscape and some seductive trees. The trees, a symbol that memorializes but also diminishes the Sodomites, grow the fairest and most colorful fruit found anywhere: "Bot quen hit is brused, oþer broken, oþer byten in twynne,/ No worldez goud hit wythinne,

31. Mandeville's *Travels* supplies the poet with details for his account of Sodom; see Carleton F. Brown, "Note on the Dependence of *Cleanness* on the *Book of Mandeville*."

bot wyndowande askes" (*C*, 1047–48). With this image of desolation, the poet concludes the story of Sodom.

## The Christ-event: The Center of History

A narrative (like the *Queste*) or a structure of narratives (like *Cleanness*) that invites a typological reading can, by implicitly or explicitly using Christ, the Type of types, as its center of reference, convey more effectively than can any other literary form the simultaneously incarnate and spiritual nature of the Christian vision of man and history. Like sermons and biblical commentaries, such narratives are glosses on the Word of God, on Christ and the Holy Scripture, whose presence in these narratives valorizes them. Christ fulfills all the stories told in *Cleanness*; he both reveals and confirms their significance. This interpretation is conventional in the medieval biblical commentary that is the source for these stories, and it is exploited by the poet in his presentation of the Christ-event in several ways. By placing the Christ-event in the midst of his biblical stories, the poet suggests that Christ is the center of history, the source of its meaning, and the focus through which its meaning can be read. As judge, mediator, and bridegroom, Christ determines meaning, reveals himself as the way to meaning, and offers himself to mankind as a partner in the quest for meaning. Christ offers himself as a bridegroom to man in history to give man a foretaste of the pleasure inherent in a condition of meaningfulness. He offers himself to man in eternity as the consummation of meaning. He is first and last the bridegroom; in between he is mediator and judge.

The presence of the Christ-event in *Cleanness* completes the other biblical stories in the poem, just as, in the Christian theology of history, Christ fulfills Old Testament history, for when God in the person of Christ assumes human flesh and undertakes to live in the natural world, he offers mankind an assurance of the significance of life in history and affirms the value of the body as well as of the soul. Through his earthly life of cleanness and courtesy, the incarnate Christ reveals the standards by which men's lives are judged. The stories of biblical history in *Cleanness* are balanced around the Christ-event. After the opening part of the poem, the poet offers two judgment stories, separated by the story of Abraham. After the Christ-event, the poet offers two more judgment stories, those of Sedecias and Belshazzar, which are separated by a description of the Temple vessels. Christ is the man-vessel toward which both Abraham and the Temple vessels point—the candelabrum (C, 1272–75, 1477–92) is a type of Christ,[32] the drinking vessels are types of the Christian believer—so that before and after meet in Christ. The poet relates the standard of judgment to the concept of marriage, which lies at the center of the definition of the covenant in all three ages of history (the Ages of Nature, Written Law, and Grace). As we have seen, man fulfills his covenant with God in the Age of Nature through obedience to the commandment to procreate, through practicing "þe kynde crafte" devised by God for sexual intercourse. In the Age of the Written Law, as we will see in the story of Sedecias, the covenant between God and his chosen people is, metaphorically, a marriage. This covenant demands obedience to the written law and to the law's prescribed rites and avoidance of idolatry with its associated sexual sins. With the Incarnation of Christ, the analogy of human sexual intercourse to the relationship between God and his chosen is transformed into an immediate participation of man in the divine through Christ. Under the law in the Age of Nature, God condemns those who fail to fulfill that law through human marriage and thus fail to foreshadow the Christian believer in his espousal to Christ; and God saves Noah, Abraham, and Lot, whose lives are a fulfillment of that law.

The *Cleanness* poet introduces Christ into the poem when he is exhorting his listeners at the end of the Sodom story. He urges them to relate themselves to Christ in order to avoid the fate of the Sodomites. Here, as in the poet's moral interpretation of the wedding feast parable, he reiterates the goal of his listeners, which is to be members of the court of heaven, to see their Savior face to face (cf. C, 176–78, 189–92 with C, 1053–56). To feed forever on this vision of God is the consummation of the spiritual marriage between Christ and his Church.

Fittingly, since to go to the wedding feast as a bride of Christ is the goal of the poet's listeners, the poet gives them advice appropriate to a lover. God, the poet says, loves "clene layk" (clean sport or play), C, 1053. To explain what "clene layk" is, the poet takes Jean de Meun's advice to the lover in pursuit of his lady in

32. Rupert of Deutz, *De Trinitate et operibus ejus: Commentariorum in Exodum*, 4.8, in PL 167:705–7.

the *Roman de la Rose* and applies it to the relationship of man to Christ.[33] This advice is a traditional feature of Christian contemplative or mystical writing. Origen, for example, had long ago adapted it for the bride in his commentary on the Song of Solomon.[34] In referring this advice to Jean, the *Cleanness* poet is following his usual pattern of analogizing from secular situations to spiritual ones, as he does in presenting first the feast of a worldly prince and then the parable account of the heavenly king's wedding feast. Jean tells the lover to observe his lady, how she bears herself and what she likes, and to make himself like her, from which the *Cleanness* poet concludes: "If þou wyrkkes on þis wyse, þaȝ ho wyk were,/ Hir schal lyke þat layk þat lyknes hir tylle" (*C*, 1063–64). Similarly, man can express his love for God by taking Christ for his beloved:

> If þou wyl dele drwrye wyth Dryȝtyn, þenne,
> And lelly lovy þy Lorde, and his leef worþe,
> Þenne conforme þe to Kryst, and þe clene make,
> Þat ever is polyced als playn as þe perle selven. (*C*, 1065–68)

In both this passage and God's speech on marriage (*C*, 699), the poet chooses to signify *love* by the word *drwry*, a word denoting in a human context the active expression of affection in courtship and sexual intercourse. This word is also used figuratively for the love of man and God; for example, the *Ancrene Riwle* defines married love as "driwerie" in speaking of the spiritual marriage: "Uor þe deore driwerie þet he haue to his deore spuse, þet is to þe clene soule."[35] To alliterate with *drwry* the *Cleanness* poet chooses the words *doole* (share or portion) and *dele* (to share or participate in, from OE n. *dæl, dāl*; v. *dǣlan*). Depending on the context in which they are used, the words *drwry, doole*, and *dele (wyth)* signify sexual intercourse.[36] Although in lines 699 and 1065

33. The *Cleanness* poet supplies an *in bono* allegorical interpretation for Amis's advice to Amant on how to win favor with Bel Accueil and hence access to the Rose, *Roman de la Rose*, lines 7719–36, 3:54. Menner attributes these lines to Raison, a rather significant error. See also Ovid, *Ars amatoria*, 2.198–202, in Ovid, *The Art of Love and Other Poems*, trans. J. H. Mozley, Loeb Classical Library (London: Heinemann, 1939), pp. 78–79.

34. Origen, *Commentarius in Cantica canticorum*, pp. 73–75.

35. *Ancrene Riwle* (MS. Cotton Nero A.xiv), p. 330.

36. See *Sir Gawain and the Green Knight*, line 2449, p. 67.

of *Cleanness* none of these words bears that precise signification, the poet seems to have chosen his vocabulary deliberately to yield an overtone of sexual intimacy: compare "I ... dyʒt drwry þerinne, doole alþerswettest" (*C,* 699) to "If þou wyl dele drwrye wyth Dryʒtyn, þenne" (*C,* 1065). That the poet's advice to his listeners echoes God's speech to Abraham on marriage serves to connect the two passages and to establish the typological relationship between the "clene layk" of human love and the love of Christ for his clean and loyal beloved. Divine love validates human love, which is an imitation and a shadow of the divine marriage. The playful language the poet uses to describe these love relationships —"a maner myriest of oþer," "merþe," "play," and "layk"—has a perfectly serious end in view. He wants to convince his listeners that they will find in the spiritual nuptials a freedom, a joy, and a fulfillment that is beyond any pleasure known on earth and yet is foreshadowed in the earthly delights of sexual intercourse.

The nuptials to which Christ refers in his parable of the wedding feast actually begin with the Incarnation, when the uterus of the Virgin Mary becomes the marriage chamber for the wedding of God and man.[37] Because she is spiritually an appropriate vessel for him, Christ makes Mary his first bride. Through the sacrament of the Eucharist other Christians imitate her action, receiving the body of Christ into the marriage chambers of their hearts. As the model for other Christians, Mary became, by virtue of the Incarnation, a figure of the Church, the body of all the Christian faithful. The *Cleanness* poet suggests the spiritual relationship of Mary to Christ through his account of her motherhood, when she literally becomes the vessel bearing Christ:

> For loke fro fyrst þat he lyʒt wythinne þe lel Mayden,
> By how comly a kest he watz clos þere,
> When venkkyst watz no vergynyte, ne vyolence maked,
> Bot much clener watz hir corse, God kynned þerinne. (*C,*
> 1069–72)

37. Rabanus Maurus, *Commentarius in Matthaeum,* 6.22, in *PL* 107: 1053–54. After noting that the Father made a marriage for his Son in this way, that he joined Holy Church to his Son through the mystery of the Incarnation (see also Bede, *In Matthaei evangelium expositio,* 3.22, in *PL* 92:95; Christianus Druthmarus, *Expositio in Matthaeum evangelisticam,* 52, in *PL* 106:1439), Rabanus says: "Uterus autem virginis genitricis hujus sponsi thalamus fuit." Thomas Aquinas repeats the point in similar language in *Catena aurea in quator Evangelia,* 1:317.

Mary and Christ are joined together physically, the container and the contained, in a union that has spiritual consequences for Mary and becomes the exemplary union for all Christians.

That the literal union of Christ and Mary is an example for men to imitate spiritually is a commonplace that Gregory the Great implies through a witty use of vessel imagery. In glossing the verse, "Wisdom hath builded her a house" (Prov. 9:1), he applies it to the Incarnation and its miraculous consequences, using the images of house and temple to describe both the Incarnation and the union of man to God made possible by it:

> Sapientia quippe domum sibi condidit, cum unigenitus
> Dei Filius in semetipso intra uterum Virginis . . . humanum
> sibi corpus creavit. Sic quippe corpus Unigeniti domus
> Dei dicitur, sicut etiam templum vocatur; ita vero, ut unus
> idemque Dei atque hominis filius ipse sit qui inhabitat,
> ipse qui inhabitatur. (For Wisdom in truth built her a
> house, when the Only-Begotten Son of God . . . created
> Himself a human body within the womb of the Virgin. For
> the body of the Only-Begotten is called the house of God,
> just as it is also called a temple; but so, that that one and the
> same Son of God and Man, is Himself the Inhabitor,
> Himself the Inhabited.)[38]

Christ is first the inhabiter of Mary—literally—and then the inhabiter of men through grace; but since his body is the Church, he is also the inhabited, the house into which the faithful are gathered. Gregory's image of the joining of man's and Christ's houses so that each is within the other expresses the divine marriage union.

The God-man, Christ, because his nature is both human and divine, perfectly mediates between God and man. Through the Church, which is his body, and the sacraments of baptism, penance, and the Eucharist, Christ invites men to bear God in their bodies so that they, like the Virgin, may become cleaner through his presence. This new love union of God and man is the beginning of the marriage that the eschatological wedding feast celebrates as a fulfilled and eternal union.

Since the poet has advised his audience to make themselves conform to Christ if they would be his beloveds ("Þenne conforme þe

38. Gregory the Great, *Moralia in Job* (*Morals on the Book of Job*), 33.16.32, in *PL* 76:693.

to Kryst" [C, 1067]), he must show them what Christ is like, show them Christ's cleanness and courtesy, so that they will know the standard by which they will be judged: this is an instance of the poet's method of explicating major concepts in *Cleanness* through the Christ-event. Man was created in the image and likeness of God, according to Gen. 1:26, a text that received much attention from biblical commentators. These commentators usually distinguished between image and likeness: every man, even after the Fall, is born with the image of God in him; and by his choice he can fulfill that image and make himself, with the aid of grace, into the likeness of God.[39] When the *Cleanness* poet speaks of conformity to Christ, he is implicitly referring to the traditional distinction between image and likeness; he is interested in encouraging his audience to fulfill the image of God in them by converting themselves to the likeness of Christ. The poet selects two events from the life of Christ to show the audience what in him they must imitate to make themselves like him: he uses the story of the Advent to prove Christ's cleanness and the story of his ministry to show his courtesy.

The miraculous nature of Christ's conception and birth makes his purity manifest. God lifts the curse of Eve—the pain of childbirth—from Mary, the "mayden þat make had never" (C, 248), through whom he amends the judgment on Adam and Eve and their progeny: implicitly, the poet acknowledges that Mary is free from Original Sin. Her purity guarantees the purity of Christ. Unfolding the story of this miracle in an attitude of wonder, the poet makes the poor and humble cow's stall seem like the court of heaven itself by describing it as a blissful bower, brighter than a tapestried castle and filled with angelic music. He emphasizes the painless joy of the virgin birth:

> Ne non so glad under God as ho þat grone schulde.
> For þer watz seknesse al sounde þat sarrest is halden,
> And þer watz rose reflayr where rote hatz ben ever,
> And þer watz solace and songe wher sorȝ hatz ay cryed;
> For aungelles wyth instrumentes of organes and pypes,
> And rial ryngande rotes, and þe reken fyþel,

39. For a study of the distinction between image and likeness, see Gerhard Ladner, *The Idea of Reform*, pp. 83–107. For a treatment of this theme in art, see Adelheid Heimann, "Trinitas Creator Mundi," esp. plate 8(d).

And alle hende þat honestly moȝt an hert glade,
Aboutte my Lady watz lent, quen ho delyver were. (*C*, 1077–
84)

At the moment of delivery, the infant Christ appears "burnyst so clene" (like the "beryl bornyst" of line 554) that the ox and the ass, traditionally figures of the Old and New Testaments, worship him at once: "Þay knewe hym by his clannes for Kyng of nature,/ For non so clene of such a clos com never er þenne" (*C*, 1087–88). The poet alludes to groaning, sickness, rot, and sorrow (*C*, 1077–80) to remind us of the pain of ordinary childbirth and to emphasize by contrast the miracle of Christ's birth.

The transition the poet makes from the Advent to the ministry plainly refers to the principle that cleanness is the precondition for the doing of good works: "And ȝif clanly he þenne com, ful cortays þerafter" (*C*, 1089). *Courtesy*, in the language of the *Cleanness* poet, is a name for the attitude and the acts of charity. The poet uses the word to describe what priests ought to have (*C*, 13) and to characterize God's covenant with Noah (*C*, 512); he exemplifies the word through the stories of Abraham and of Lot, who hopes to chasten the harlots of Sodom with his "hendelayk" (a synonym for courtesy [*C*, 860]).

Christ's ministry bears a double significance in *Cleanness*: it both exemplifies the courtesy that men ought to practice and explains how men find the power, in the grace Christ offers to them, to imitate him. Christ's courtesy is illustrated by his hospitality to all who come to him to be healed:

Ȝet comen lodly to þat Lede, as lazares monye,
Summe lepre, summe lome, and lomerande blynde,
Poysened, and parlatyk, and pyned in fyres,
Drye folk, and ydropike, and dede, at þe laste—
Alle called on þat Cortayse and claymed his grace.
He heled hem wyth hynde spech of þat þay ask after. (*C*,
1093–98)

The poet chooses healing as the act of mercy with which to show Christ's charity because Christ is, through the sacraments, the physician to mankind. His graciousness to all the "lodly" who come to him suggests that man must do no less than to help even the least of his neighbors.

The catalogue of those who seek Christ's aid echoes part of the nobleman's guest list for the wedding:

> What-kyn folk so þer fare, fechez hem hider;
> Be þay fers, be þay feble, forlotez none,
> Be þay hol, be þay halt, be þay on-yȝed,
> And þaȝ þay ben boþe blynde and balterande cruppelez,
> Þat my hous may holly by halkez by fylled. (C, 100–104)

The subjunctive grammatical phrase, "be þay," which introduces the short elements in the parable guest list, is transformed in the ministry catalogue into "summe," and this shift in grammatical construction shows the change from potentiality to actuality, from invitation to response. The one list is not an exact reproduction of the other, but a comparison of lines 103 and 1094 shows the resemblance clearly: "boþe blynde and balterande cruppelez" becomes "summe lome, and lomerande blynde." The cripples are blind, the blind are crippled. The adjectives and nouns exchange places, but rhythm and substance remain almost identical. The first passage, in mentioning the "hol" along with the "halt," displays the openness of the invitation. The second focuses exclusively on the "halt" to draw attention to the apparent paradox that the deformed and the diseased, some of whom are marked as unclean under the Old Law, under the New Law come to Christ and find him hospitable to them.

The pattern of judgment, of contrast between clean and unclean, dominates the exempla and biblical narratives in *Cleanness* until the poet introduces the Christ-event into the poem; after he describes the Christ-event, through an account of Christ's ministry, the poet explains how a man can change from the category of the unclean to the category of the clean. Although Christ, the model of cleanness, will not touch "Oȝt þat watz ungoderly oþer ordure watz inne" (C, 1092), he responds to the claims of loathesome men on his grace and heals them by his gracious speech: "For what so he towched, also tyd torned to hele,/ Wel clanner þen any crafte cowþe devyse" (C, 1099–1100). The speech of Christ, the Word of God, is an example of perfect intentionality; his words create what they intend, in this case, purity. In contrast to the speech of the Sodomites that pollutes the earth, Christ's speech touches men and purifies them. His grace is contagious.

The poet uses the word *crafte* several times in *Cleanness*, often associating it quite clearly with the covenants God makes with man. A comparison of these instances demonstrates the changing nature of man's way of fulfilling his covenant with God. In line 1100 the word introduces the poet's wittily complex description of the sacraments of penance and the Eucharist. In the Abraham story God calls sexual intercourse between a man and his mate "a kynde crafte" and requires them to practice this art. In the story of the Temple vessels, the poet describes these vessels as having been wrought "wyth so curious a crafte" (*C*, 1452) because Solomon had brought to their making all the wisdom God granted him. Under the law of Moses, the holy vessels are the vehicles for carrying out the prescribed ritual through which man expresses his relationship to God. Under the law of grace, holy vessels continue to express symbolically man's offering to God, but the principle vessel under the Christian dispensation is man himself. In the opening lines of *Cleanness* the poet accuses the bad priests of counterfeiting "crafte" because they are not like Christ and not fit to touch him. In each of these instances, the word refers to the action man takes to signify his fulfillment of his covenant with God. In line 1100 the poet uses the word *crafte* to refer to Christ's healing powers, which are greater than any "crafte"—any medical art of healing—could devise. Christ's superhuman "crafte," the benefits of which he offers to man, is a response to man's "crafte," the results of which man offers to God: the works of "crafte," human and divine, are media through which the covenant is expressed.

The poet describes the divine "crafte" of Christ in a startling passage that obliquely describes the sacraments of penance and the Eucharist:

> So clene watz his hondelyng uche ordure hit schonied,
> And þe gropyng so goud of God and man boþe,
> Þat for fetys of his fyngeres fonded he never
> Nauþer to cout ne to kerve wyth knyf ne wyth egge;
> Forþy brek he þe bred blades wythouten,
> For hit ferde freloker in fete in his fayre honde,
> Displayed more pryvyly when he hit part schulde,
> Þenne alle þe toles of Tolowse moȝt tyȝt hit to kerve. (*C*, 1101–8)

Grammatically, the comparison of the skill of Christ's fingers to a knife in lines 1103–4, which concludes the poet's allusion to pen-

ance in lines 1101–2, is attached to lines 1105–8, where the poet
alludes to the Eucharist and again concludes with a comparison
of Christ's skill to a knife. The *Cleanness* poet's comparison of
Christ's more than human "crafte" of "hondelyng" and "gropyng"
to the work of a knife is an image curiously appropriate both to
penance and the Eucharist.

Christ touches the sinner so cleanly that he avoids handling the
ordure of sin; his "crafte" in handling sin, that is, in penance, is
as miraculous as his birth. As the poet has made clear in line 1098,
Christ heals by his words. That Christ's Word or the words of the
Spirit are like a sword is a biblical idea:

> For the word of God is living and effectual and more
> piercing than any two-edged sword and reaching unto the
> division of the soul and the spirit, of the joints also and the
> marrow; and is a discerner of the thoughts and intents
> of the heart. (Heb. 4:12)

The *Cleanness* poet compares the skill in Christ's fingers to a knife
or an edge (of a knife or sword blade) in lines 1103–4; and later,
when the fingers of God write on a wall at Belshazzar's feast and
cause the king's joints to strain (*C*, 1533–40), the poet shows that
Christ's fingers can destroy like a sword as well as heal like a surgeon's knife.

Robert Pullen is said to have introduced the image of a knife
into twelfth-century theological arguments about the significance
of the power of the keys, which was an issue in the developing theology of penance.[40] Some argued that there were two keys, one for
the power of discernment (or knowledge), the other for the power
of binding and loosing. This interpretation of the first key con-
flicted, however, with the evident ignorance of some priests who,
nevertheless, had the power of the second key. Robert Pullen offered a way out of this dilemma by arguing that there is only one
key but that it is spoken of in the plural to signify its two powers of
binding and loosing. The key is fitted into a handle, just as a knife

40. The image and the argument connected to it do not occur in
Robert Pullen's extant work: several other writers  of the twelfth and
early thirteenth centuries report what they take to be Pullen's theory,
explicitly attributing it to him. Hence, the assumption that he is the
perpetrator of it. See Paul Anciaux, *La Théologie du sacrement de pénitence au XII<sup>e</sup> siècle*, p. 338; and John W. Baldwin, *Masters, Princes, and
Merchants*, 1:52.

blade is; the handle represents the power of discernment and is necessary for the proper use of the keys. Peter the Chanter records Robert Pullen's argument succinctly:

> Magister Robertus, ut dicitur, dicebat, quod scientia est quasi manubrium, potestas vero ligandi et solvendi sicut lamina cultelli. Et sicut lamina manum incidit, cum tenetur sine manubrio sciendendum panem, ita potentia ledit sine scientia, que est quasi temeramentum lamine. (Master Robert, as it is said, said that knowledge is like a handle, the power of binding and loosing like the blade of a knife. And just as a blade cuts the hand, when it is held without a handle for cutting bread, so power injures without knowledge, which is like a temperance for the blade.)[41]

Peter did not accept Robert's theory, but he and others quote it;[42] Peter does, however, introduce bread as the thing cut by the knife, apparently because the mention of bread adds a familiar and homely detail. If the *Cleanness* poet had happened to see this particular passage, it might well have suggested to him the conflation of the two sacraments of penance and the Eucharist through the knife image; it is more likely that he might have seen some other reference to Robert Pullen's theory, in which the knife with its handle and blade becomes an image for the spiritual "crafte" of the priest confessor. As canons 21 and 22 of the Fourth Lateran Council[43] and penitential literature from the twelfth century on show, the "crafte" of a priest-confessor is a spiritual form of the physician's craft. The priest is the surgeon of the soul, cutting from it, through his words, the filth of sin.

When the *Cleanness* poet speaks of "þe gropyng . . . of God and man boþe" (*C*, 1102; the latter phrase is a periphrastic name for

41. Quoted in Anciaux, *Théologie*, p. 338, n. 3. My translation.

42. See Anciaux, *Théologie*, p. 338, nn. 1–2, for two references by unidentified authors; pp. 541–42 for Odon d'Ourscamp, who accepts Pullen's theory; p. 555 for lines 23–27 of a quotation from Peter the Chanter's work (no mention here of Pullen, only his theory); p. 569 for lines 8–15 of a quotation from Robert de Courçon's work: he refers to "magister Polanus et eius sequaces," suggesting that the theory was widely known through adherents to it.

43. Joannes Dominicus Mansi, ed., *Sacrorum conciliorum, nova et amplissima collectio*, 22:1007–12.

Christ[44]), he refers to the division of the body of Christ in the
Eucharist. Christ's manner of breaking bread with his disciples
was the sign by which they recognized him at Emmaus after the
Resurrection:

> And it came to pass, whilst he was at table with them, he
> took bread and blessed and brake and gave to them. And
> their eyes were opened; and they knew him. And he vanished
> out of their sight. . . . And they told what things were
> done in the way; and how they knew him in the breaking
> of the bread. (Luke 24:30–31, 35)

The dividing of the bread is a miraculous act: though the bread is
divided, each communicant in the Lord's table receives not merely
a piece of Christ's Body, but the whole of it; the whole is divided
into many parts, each of which, paradoxically, is equal to the
whole. No knife from Toulouse (or Toledo; see *C*, 1108) can make
such a division.

The knife image is sometimes explicitly associated with Christ's
breaking of the bread at Emmaus: "Et cognoverunt eum, in modo
fractionis panis, assuetam eius consuetudinem videntes: sic enim
frangebat panem sola manu ac si scienderetur cum cultello" (And
seeing his usual custom, they knew him in his manner of breaking
bread: for thus he broke bread by his hand alone but as if it were
cut by a knife).[45] In other versions of the Emmaus story, the disciples recognize Christ because the bread he breaks with his fingers
look as if it were cut (implicitly, the knife image is there). For example, in the play *Thomas of India* from the Towneley cycle of
Corpus Christi plays, Peter tells Thomas about the supper at
Emmaus:

> Ihesu, goddis son of heuen/ at sopere satt betweyn;
> Ther bred he brake as euen/ as it cutt had beyn.[46]

44. On this aspect of the poet's art, see John W. Clark, "Paraphrases
for 'God' in the Poems Attributed to the Gawain-Poet."

45. Ludolph of Saxony, *Vita Christi Domini Salvatoris*, 2.76. My translation. I am indebted to Thomas J. Hill of Cornell University for this
reference.

46. *Thomas of India*, lines 264–65, in *The Towneley Plays*, p. 348
(hereafter cited in the text by line). Gollancz cites the Towneley play in
his edition for its knife imagery and notes that Toulouse is probably a
mistake for Toledo, a center of knife manufacture. For knife imagery in
the Emmaus story, see *Le Livre de la Passion, poème narratif du XIV*<sup>e</sup>

Because the Towneley play *Thomas of India* treats the sacraments of penance and the Eucharist in a straightforward way, using the knife image and the word *groping*, the play illuminates the complex wit of lines 1101–8 of *Cleanness* and suggests that the source of the wit lies in medieval paraphrases of the appearances of the Resurrected Christ. The play offers, then, an analogue to the poem. In the play the appearances of Christ serve a two-fold purpose: to persuade the disciples (and hence the audience of the play) that Christ lives and to confer upon them their mission. In the first of these appearances (based on Luke 24:39), Christ commands the disciples: "Grope and fele flesh and bone/ and fourme of man well wroght" (line 98). The disciples, Christ's first priests, "grope" his body, an action parallel to that of later priests who handle the bread of his Body in celebrating the Mass as Christ himself does at the Emmaus feast. The commission Christ gives to the disciples, after urging upon them the necessity of cleanness (lines 112–15), charges them:

> The folk that ar with syn lame/ preche theym to repentance,
> fforgif syn in my name/ enioyne theym to penance. (lines
> 146–47; cf. Luke 24:47)

He breathes upon them the spirit that grants them the power of binding and loosing and says:

> Whom in erth ye lowse of syn/ in heuen lowsyd shall be
> And whom in erthe ye bynd ther-in/ In heuen bonden be he.
> (lines 150–51; cf. John 20:23)

Thomas joins the disciples later and refuses to believe their account of the living Christ, but Christ appears again (John 20:26–29) and allays his doubt. The dramatic repetition of Christ's appearances serves a didactic purpose: the disciples, as ordinary men would, doubt the Resurrection miracle and then by the evidence of Christ's appearance become convinced; the audience of the play is invited to join in the doubt and to follow in the conversion of the disciples. *Thomas of India* combines the same themes that are contained in lines 1098–1108 of *Cleanness*: the breaking of bread, the groping of God, the preaching of penance, and the

---

*siècle*, lines 2252–55, p. 75; and Gustave Cohen, *Le Livre de conduite du régisseur et le compte des dépenses pour le "Mystère de la Passion" joué à Mons en 1501*, p. 436, column 1 and n. 5. Thomas J. Hill called the latter references to my attention.

remission of sins. A paraphrase of the Emmaus story and of the
other appearances of Christ connected with that story must have
been one of the sources from which the *Cleanness* poet developed
his treatment of Christ's "crafte"; a version of Robert Pullen's
comparison of the power of discernment to a knife handle may
also lie behind these lines in *Cleanness*.

To summarize the argument of lines 1101–8 in *Cleanness*, the
contrast of Christ's healing art to a knife and of his breaking of the
bread to the capacity of a knife of Toulouse to cut bread emphasizes the "crafte" in Christ's fingers, which cut sin out of the soul
of man and cut the body of God into parts that are whole. The
*Cleanness* poet uses the knife image associated with penance as
well as with the Eucharist to emphasize the miraculous nature of
Christ's "crafte," exercised through his marvelous medicines, his
words, and the bread of his body, which he offers through the sacraments to every man to cleanse and sustain him.

Having obliquely introduced the sacrament of penance, the poet
explicitly develops its relevance to his listeners. He asks them the
question that, after the stories of the Flood and Sodom, ought to
be troubling them:

> Hou schulde þou com to his kyth bot if þou clene were?
> Nou ar we sore and synful and souly uch one,
> How schulde we se, þen may we say, þat Syre upon throne?
> (*C*, 1110–12)

He answers: "þou may schyne þurȝ schryfte, þaȝ þou haf schome
served,/ And pure þe with penaunce tyl þou a perle worþe" (*C*,
1115–16). The pearl, an image of perfection, has the further characteristic of preserving its integrity even under neglect:

> And if hit cheve þe chaunce uncheryst ho worþe,
> Pat ho blyndes of ble in bour þer ho lygges,
> No-bot wasch hir wyth worchyp in wyn, as ho askes,
> Ho by kynde schal becom clerer þen are. (*C*, 1125–28)

Clearly the pearl is an image of the human soul that lies in the
"bour" of the body. By advising that it should be washed in wine,
the poet may be encouraging his audience to communicate in the
Mass: "These are they who are come out of great tribulation, and
have washed their robes and have made them white in the blood

of the Lamb" (Apocalypse 7:14b). The poet again tells his audience that "he may polyce hym at þe prest, by penaunce taken,/ Wel bryȝter þen þe beryl oþer browden perles" (*C*, 1131–32). He warns them, however, that to fall back into sin after having reconciled and consecrated themselves to God makes God angrier than if they had never undergone penance.

The poet's warning makes explicit the analogy between men and vessels, another instance of his strategy of making manifest the assumptions of his poem in the context of the Christ-event. The prediction of God's anger echoes the message of the parable of the wedding feast, which asserts that God reserves his wrath for the discourteous guest, the unclean man in tattered garments. The ragged man is the figure for the sinful Christian, for the hypocritical priest, for the one who offers himself to God and then withdraws the gift of himself by falling back into sin:

> For when a sawele is saȝtled and sakred to Dryȝtyn,
> He holly haldes hit his, and have hit he wolde;
> Þenne efte lastes hit likkes, he loses hit ille,
> As hit were rafte wyth unryȝt, and robbed wyth þewes. (*C*,
> 1139–42)

The poet compares God's outrage at the loss of a man to his anger when a vessel dedicated to him is polluted:

> Þaȝ hit be bot a bassyn, a bolle, oþer a scole,
> A dysche, oþer a dobler, þat Dryȝtyn onez served,
> To defowle hit ever upon folde fast he forbedes,
> So is he scoymus of scaþe þat scylful is ever. (*C*, 1145–48)

The story of the Temple vessels, which follows, proves the poet's claim.

### The Evidence of History: Sedecias and Belshazzar as Polluted Vessels

The last biblical narrative in *Cleanness* is a story from the Age of the Written Law; as I have already pointed out, it has special significance for the poet's audience since it prefigures Christian history and understands the covenant in a way similar to the way it is understood in Christian covenant theology. The concept of marriage remains at the center of covenant theology through

all the ages, a sign of the continuity of history; but there is a disjunction from age to age in the way marriage is understood. The
covenant of nature understands marriage as the sexual union of
male and female for the purpose of procreation: unnatural sexual
acts are sins against the covenant and are "fylþe of þe flesche." As
God reveals more of himself to man through the written law, the
concept of marriage is spiritualized: in the covenant of the written
law, marriage is the union of God to his chosen people, who fulfill
their role as wife of God by keeping the law, much of which is concerned with detailing the proper forms of worship. When the idea
of marriage is spiritualized, so is the sin against it, "fylþe of þe
flesche": adultery, idolatry, and sacrilege are the sins against the
covenant marriage. The Christian idea of the covenant marriage
is similar to that of the written law, but it is personalized: through
the sacraments, man literally and spiritually makes himself the
bride of Christ. Since Christ is absolutely and radically clean, so
must his bride be: finally, under the Christian covenant, any sin
pollutes the sinner and becomes, therefore, "fylþe of þe flesche."

The story of the Temple vessels begins with an account of the
idolatry of Sedecias and his people and the destruction of Jerusalem through God's agents. Having been neglected by the Jews,
the Temple vessels are taken to Babylon by Nebuchadnezzar, who
treats them with honor and has Daniel explain them to him. This
part of the story prefigures the Jews' rejection of Christ and the acceptance of him by the gentiles. It corresponds to the *Queste* story
of Joseph of Arimathea, a Jew like Daniel, who takes the Grail to
Sarras and then Logres and uses the Grail to convert Mordrain,
Nascien, and the inhabitants of Logres. Just as the company of
Joseph, who are a remnant of the Jews, accept Christ, so in the
story of the Temple vessels Daniel and the three children, a holy
remnant, accompany the Temple vessels and explain them to Nebuchadnezzar, who accepts the Hebrew God. As we learn from
Daniel, Nebuchadnezzar sins and, through divine grace, repents;
Nebuchadnezzar's actions foreshadow the trials of Christians in
the Age of Grace and their reformation through penance.

In the opening lines of the story of the Temple vessels, the poet
accuses the Israelites of "fayth . . . untrwe" to God, whom they
had promised "to halde . . . ever" (*C*, 1161–62). This diction echoes
the Christian betrothal promise: "Here I take the . . . to haue and
to holde, . . . tyll dethe us departe, and thereto I plyght the my

trouthe."[47] In response to the promise the Israelites make to him, God hallows the people to be his, and the help he gives is his blessings (see Deut. 28:1–14, the chapter of blessings and curses). The people, however, falsify their faith by following other gods. Their idolatry is an adultery, because it breaks the covenant marriage between themselves and God. The language that the poet uses in lines 1161–74 reflects the language of the prophets and the Deuteronomic reviser, who interpret God's covenant with Israel as a marriage; obedience to the Law as a sign of fidelity to that marriage covenant; and idolatry, which is also adultery (loving other gods), as a sign of infidelity. Israel's sin makes God so angry "Þat he fylsened þe faythful in þe falce lawe/ To forfare þe falce in þe faythe trwe" (C, 1167–68). God's blessing turns into a curse in response to the Israelites' idolatry because they have shown themselves to be even worse than the heathen who, although they have only a false law, are at least faithful to it.

Although Solomon is long since dead by the time of the Babylonian invasion of Jerusalem, the memory of him constantly impinges on the present time of the story. The throne on which the idolatrous king of Judea, Sedecias, sits is Solomon's throne, and the holy vessels that Sedecias has abandoned are Solomon's work. Solomon is the figure of faithfulness to the covenant of the law against whom contemporary kings are measured: "He sete on Salamones solie, on solemne wyse,/ Bot of leaute he watz lat to his Lorde hende" (C, 1171–72). Implicitly contrasted to Solomon, Sedecias, the representative of his sinful people, seems as abominable as the "abominaciones of idolatrye" that he uses.

God sends the Chaldeans, led by "Nabigodenozar" (Nebuchadnezzar), as a scourge and a judgment on Jerusalem. Hunger forces the Jews out of the besieged city, but their attempted escape is foiled by the Chaldean army. Sedecias is captured, and his punishment reveals the fruits of idolatry. His sons are slain before his eyes to show that he is a barren man in the eyes of God. Then his eyes are "holkked out" (dug out), C, 1222; like the Sodomites he has no spiritual vision. Finally, he is sent to Babylon to lie in a dungeon, and this last torture recalls the tattered guest whom God

---

47. *Manuale et processionale ad usum insignis ecclesiae Eboracensis* (York Manual), p. 27, cf. 19\*. On *trawþe*, which Menner sees as a major theme in *Cleanness*, see J. A. Burrow, *A Reading of Sir Gawain and the Green Knight*, pp. 42–46.

expels from the wedding feast and casts into the dungeon that is
hell (*C*, 153–60). With Sedecias and the Jewish army neutralized,
the Chaldean general Nabuzardan sweeps through the city hor-
ribly slaughtering the inhabitants (*C*, 1245–52), capturing those
who escape the sword, despoiling the Temple, and burning it and
the houses. The terrible ruin that Jerusalem suffers is no mere
accident of fortune: God grants victory to the Chaldeans because
Jerusalem has forsaken him (see *C*, 1167–68, 1175–76, 1225–32).

The *Cleanness* poet treats the destruction of Jerusalem as a national judgment, but he also recounts the personal fate of Sedecias.
By singling out Sedecias, and later Belshazzar, to show how God
judges them personally, the poet points forward to the Christian
dispensation when all judgments of God will be made on individual persons as well as on whole peoples (that, at least, is the way
medieval writers represent God's judgments).

The history of the Temple vessels stands at the center of the
narrative of the last story in *Cleanness*; the actions of men become
part of the story only as they relate to the vessels. To hold the vessels in the center of the narrative, the poet makes them the chief
witness to God's greatness, a function they do not serve in biblical
accounts of the Babylonian captivity, a function usually fulfilled
by holy and righteous men. In the biblical story, before his madness comes him, Nebuchadnezzar twice praises God, once
after Daniel interprets his dream (Dan. 2:47) and again after the
three youths survive the fiery furnace (Dan. 3:95–96). The *Cleanness* poet mentions by name the prophets' children (Daniel and
the three youths [*C*, 1301–2]), who are among the captives Nabuzardan presents to Nebuchadnezzar, the conqueror of Judea.
It is not they, however, but rather the vessels of the Temple that
inspire Nebuchadnezzar to praise the Hebrew God:

> Bot þe joy of þe juelrye so gentyle and ryche,
> When hit watz schewed hym so schene, scharp watz his
>   wonder;
> Of such vessel avayed þat vayled so huge,
> Never ȝet nas Nabugodenozar er þenne.
> He sesed hem wyth solemnete, þe Soverayn he praysed
> Þat watz aþel over alle, Israel Dryȝtyn;
> Such god, such gomes, such gay vesselles,
> Comen never out of kyth to Caldee reames. (*C*, 1309–16)

In displacing Nebuchadnezzar's reaction to men with his response to the holy vessels, the poet makes *Cleanness* a counterpoint to the Bible narrative and suggests the metaphorical relationship between men and vessels. Nebuchadnezzar, now the king whom God favors, becomes the guardian of the holy vessels, whose honor he preserves, setting them reverently in a special place in his treasury. Tutored by Daniel, the great king recognizes the principle of the Hebrew law, "þat alle goudes com of God" (*C*, 1326). All reigns must end, and when Nebuchadnezzar dies, his idolatrous son, Belshazzar, takes his place as emperor and king of Babylon (actually, Belshazzar was not the son of Nebuchadnezzar, as the Vulgate suggests, nor did they hold the empire in sequence).

The *Cleanness* poet uses the holy vessels to develop a contrast between the idolatry of Belshazzar and the worship he should be giving to God. Establishing this difference is a primary intention of the poet, and he accomplishes it through his descriptions of the Temple vessels and through his character sketch of Belshazzar. To put the point simply, idolatry is self-reflexive but the worship of God involves man in a relationship with the Other. Idolatry leads to chaos; the worship of God leads to order.

The poet describes the nature of divine worship not through any explicit sacrifice—he has already shown Noah's sacrifice at the end of the Flood—but through accounts of Solomon's making of the holy vessels. The first account precedes and parallels the episode of Nebuchadnezzar's conversion. It occurs in the context of Nabuzardan's sack of the Temple:

> Now hatz Nabuzardan nomen alle þyse noble þynges, . . .
> Þat Salomon so mony a sadde ӡer soӡt to make,
> Wyth alle þe coyntyse þat he cowþe, clene to wryke,
> Devised he þe vesselment, þe vestures clene;
> Wyth slyӡt of his ciences, his Soverayn to love,
> Þe hous and þe anornementes he hyӡtled togedere. (*C*, 1281, 1286–90)

Here, the poet describes the making of the vessels, and of the Temple itself, as an expression of Solomon's love for God. The vessels are a physical expression of a spiritual intention toward God. In the story of Nebuchadnezzar's conversion, the holy vessels are again an intermediate between man and God: their extraordinary beauty leads Nebuchadnezzar to praise the God for whom they were made.

The second account of the making of the vessels occurs in the midst of the episode of Belshazzar's feast and explains that Solomon's wisdom, according to which he designed the vessels, was the gift of God:

> Salamon sete him seven ȝere and a syþe more,
> Wyth alle þe syence þat hym sende þe soverayn Lorde,
> For to compas and kest to haf hem clene wroȝt. (C, 1453–55)

God, the great geometer—whose creation of the universe (itself traditionally considered a vessel of God) is sometimes described iconographically by a picture of God with a compass tracing the circle of the universe—grants Solomon the grace to imitate his creation. Henri de Lubac summarizes the traditional analogies that connect the universe, the Temple, the human body, and the mystical body:

> En vertu de la transposition, opérée par les Pères, de
> l'antique doctrine qui voyait dans l'univers à la fois un
> temple et un corps, et dans chaque temple à la fois le corps
> humain et l'univers, les miroirs cosmique et liturgique,
> se répondant entre eux, répondent aux miroirs historique
> et biblique. L'église matérielle est à l'image de l'Homme
> parfait, étant "la projection géométrique du Fils de l'homme
> sur la croix" [E. de Bruyne], et comme le Temple de
> Salomon elle est également, si l'on songe au mystère qui s'y
> célèbre, à l'image du corps mystique: "Rex Salomon fecit
> templum/ Quorum instar et exemplum/ Christus et Ecclesia
> [Solomon made a temple whose figure and pattern is Christ
> and the Church—Adam of St. Victor]."[48]

As God created order through his design of the universe, so Solomon, aided by the grace of God, expresses on a lesser scale the order of God through the beauty and nobility of the design of the Temple vessels. The holy vessels, then, like the words of the law for whose ritual they were made, are the medium of God's descent

48. de Lubac, Exégèse médiévale, vol. 1, pt. 1, p. 155. For God as geometer, see Otto von Simson, The Gothic Cathedral, p. 35 and n. 37; and Otto Pächt, C. R. Dodwell, and Francis Wormald, The St. Albans Psalter, p. 51 and n. 2.

to man and the way by which man returns to God under the covenant of the law.

The *Cleanness* poet alludes to the circle of divine worship that
he describes through Solomon's making of the vessels in a lament
for the vessels, which are about to be desecrated:

> Þe jueles out of Jerusalem wyth gemmes ful bryȝt, . . .
> Þat hade ben blessed bifore wyth bischopes hondes,
> And wyth besten blod busily anoynted,
> In þe solempne sacrefyce þat goud savor hade,
> Bifore þe Lorde of þe lyfte in lovyng hymselven,
> Now is sette for to serve Satanas þe blake. (*C*, 1441, 1445–49)

The bishop's blessing represents the descent of God's grace into
the vessels, the priests then use the vessels to make sacrifices having
good savor (sacrifices that are acceptable) to express their love for
God. Although Noah's sacrifice involves no vessels, only clean
beasts and a hallowed altar, that act of thanksgiving also participates in the circle of divine worship:

> When bremly brened þose bestez, and þe breþe rysed,
> Þe savor of his sacrafyse soȝt to hym even
> Þat al spedez and spyllez; he spekes wyth þat ilke
> In comly comfort ful clos and cortays wordez:
> "Now, Noe, no more nel I never wary
> Alle þe mukel mayny no molde for no mannez synnez." (*C*,
> 509–14)

Noah offers the beasts that God made for man's use to express love
and praise to God, who responds to the sweet savor of the sacrifice
by renewing his covenant with Noah.

As the concept of marriage at the center of the covenant changes,
so does the medium through which man expresses his love for God.
Under the covenant of nature, Noah presents beasts to God. When
under the written law the concept of the covenant marriage is
spiritualized, the medium through which it is expressed becomes
the holy vessels. The vessels are made by man to contain and to
express the formal nature of the covenant marriage with God.
Under the written law, the vessels contain the clean beasts that
are sacrificed to God—a point that the *Cleanness* poet implies (in
line 1446 the vessels are anointed with the blood of animals). In
a sense, the vessels contain the natural world, now ordered by the

written law and engaged to God in a formal way. In the Age of Grace, the holy vessels contain God himself: they become the medium through which direct communication between God and man takes place to effect the sacramental, eschatological marriage of the covenant of grace. Man's offering of his heart to God through the holy vessels, and God's offering of himself to man in the consecrated bread and wine in the holy vessels, establish the beginning of the nuptials of man with Christ the bridegroom. Under the covenant of grace, the earlier covenants are fulfilled: human sexual union of the covenant of nature is transformed under the written law into a spiritual marriage, and in the Age of Grace marriage becomes both a physical and a spiritual union. In the Age of Grace the Christian must identify himself with the holy vessel that bears Christ in order to be himself the vessel of Christ, as the exemplum of the priests at the beginning of *Cleanness* and the role of the Virgin in the Christ story show. The *Queste* and the *Sankgreal* show that under grace man must identify himself with the holy vessel if he is to use it.

As I pointed out earlier, holy vessels play an important part, both ritually and symbolically, in Christian worship, even though the most important vessel is the Christian himself. By choosing to make the Temple vessels the reason for Nebuchadnezzar's conversion, the *Cleanness* poet insists on the necessity of intermediary things—the Law, the vessels—to express the covenant under the written law. These intermediaries remain under the Christian dispensation because they are necessary for Christian ritual and for an understanding of the Christian covenant; but, as the poet makes clear in his description of the Christ-event, the new covenant of grace makes immediate participation in the divine possible to man through the sacraments. Like the Virgin Mary, the faithful Christian becomes, literally, a dwelling place for God. The poet, in his handling of the Temple vessels and of the story of Mary expresses both the sameness and the difference of the dispensations of law and grace. At the same time, the poet is probably also reflecting the great interest of his age in beautiful church vessels in the lengthy and loving descriptions of the Temple vessels.[49] But the

49. See catalogues of recent exhibitions: Musée National du Louvre, *L'Europe gothique, XIIe–XIVe siècles* (Paris: Reunion des Musées Nationaux, 1968); Konrad Hoffmann, ed., *The Year 1200* (for the Metropolitan Museum Exhibition, 1970); and Peter Brieger and Philippe Verdier,

*Cleanness* poet, however much he may have liked beautiful things and beautiful verse, is not given to allowing these things for their own sake; rather, he uses them in the service of God, as the expression of a spiritual intention.

Characterizing Belshazzar as an idolater whose act of worship is self-reflexive, the *Cleanness* poet says that the king began his reign from the greatest palace on earth or, as he thinks, in heaven, with all the glory left to him by his father; but Belshazzar "honored . . . not hym þat in heven wonies" (*C*, 1340). The poet first describes Belshazzar's worship of idols, which I will discuss in a moment, and then his general way of life, as if the latter followed from the former. Pride and vanity, lust and lechery and injustice are Belshazzar's way of life. The poet interprets Belshazzar's idolatry through an account of his favorite things:

> In þe clernes of his concubines and curious wedez,
> In notyng of nwe metes and of nice gettes,
> Al watz þe mynde of þat man on misschapen þinges,
> Til þe Lorde of þe lyfte liste hit abate. (*C*, 1353–56)

The poet's conclusion that Belshazzar sets his mind—that is, aims his desires—on "misschapen þinges" argues that the king's concubines, meat, and clothes are his real gods. He is a lecher and a glutton; all his thoughts are turned upon satisfying his sensual appetites and feeding his pride. Yet, as the poet ironically indicates through his diction, Belshazzar is fastidious about his "misschapen þinges." He chooses "clere" (fair, radiant, or even pure) concubines, "curious" (exquisite) clothes, and "nice" (not only foolish, but also dainty) devices or fashions. Put to the service of God, Belshazzar's sense of propriety could have made him a model of faithful adherence to the Law, but instead his concern for good things merely demonstrates his obsession with himself.

The king reveals his character by the idols he chooses to worship, just as men who use holy vessels reverently express their internal condition through their overt acts. Belshazzar does not worship God,

---

eds., *Art and the Courts/L'Art et la Court* (Ottawa: National Gallery of Canada, 1972). From A. Bartlett Giamatti's characterization of the Christian Latin paradise (see *The Earthly Paradise*, p. 71), we may infer that the bejeweling of vessels makes them fit ornaments of the Church-Temple as garden-paradise.

Bot fals fantummes of fendes, formed with handes
Wyth tool out of harde tre, and telded on lofte,
And of stokkes and stones he stoute goddes callz
When þay are gilde al with golde and gered wyth sylver,
And þere he kneles and callez, and clepes after help.
And þay reden him ryȝt, rewarde he hem hetes,
And if þay gruchen him his grace to gremen his hert,
He cleches to a gret klubbe and knokkes hem to peces. (C,
    1341–48)

These idols compare badly to the elaborate and beautiful vessels
of Solomon: the poet grants to Belshazzar's gods no nobility of
design or construction. "Fals fantummes of fendes," they are
monuments to man's chaotic and selfish will; and, in fact, Belshazzar takes a club and knocks them to bits whenever his desires
are not satisfied.

Biblical and medieval writers respect the pagan notion that
strange gods or demons—Belshazzar's fiends, whom he commemorates in sticks and stones—exist, and yet the writers also argue that
the fiends have neither life nor power. These two theories of devils
are contradictory and yet coexistent.[50] The episodes involving
demonic temptation of the knights in the Queste—the black lady's
temptation of Perceval, for example—and the copulation of fiends
with daughters of men before the Flood in Cleanness give evidence
of the medieval belief in the real existence of devils. Notably, however, in fiction the devils assault a man only when his reason is in-
operative, when he is already disposed to evil, or at least not on
guard against it; if he makes the sign of the cross or calls on Christ,
the devils evaporate. In the Flood story the daughters of men do
not copulate with fiends until after mankind has fallen into the
sin against nature. This sexual union of devils and men is a literal
one; Belshazzar's idolatry corresponds to it on a spiritual level in
that the worship of idols, according to the Old Testament, is fornication, an illicit union. The notion of the real existence of devils
or pagan gods, besides being evident in the Queste and Cleanness,
underlies the biblical conception of idolatry: "And they shall no
more sacrifice their victims to devils, with whom they have committed fornication. It shall be an ordinance for ever to them and
to their posterity" (Lev. 17:7; cf. Deut. 32:17). The ambivalence

50. See Otto of Freising, Chronicon, 1.26, for a typical medieval account of the power and the powerlessness of demons.

in medieval attitudes toward the reality of the devil-gods can be
resolved, as it was by the theologians, by recognizing that the
fiend, of which the idol is an image, and the idol, as the product
of man's imagination, both represent the selfish will, which compared to God is powerless and lifeless. For that reason, it does not
matter to a poet whether the idol is considered as an image of a
fiend and hence possibly a means of contact with supernatural
evil, or whether the idol is considered exclusively as the product
of man. Under both interpretations, the idol is a monument to
the self-indulgent will, human or demonic.

Belshazzar regards himself as the source of authority, as his relationship to his idols demonstrates; and he completes his role
as god of Babylon by offering a feast that parodies God's wedding
feast. He holds the feast to impress his nobles and to claim their
adoration; they are "to reche hym reverens, and his revel herkken,/
To loke on his lemanes and ladis hem calle" (*C*, 1369–70). His
guest list includes all the great men of his empire, and they all
accept. The feast is held in Belshazzar's great "palayce of pryde
passande alle oþer" (*C*, 1389); none sit on the high dias "'bot þe
dere selven [Belshazzar],/ And his clere concubynes in cloþes ful
bryȝt" (*C*, 1399–1400). The food for the feast is subtly ornamented
with paper canopies, which are decorated with monkeys, beasts,
and birds enameled in azure and india (dark blue or black).[51]
Chaucer condemns just such a display of food in the *Parson's Tale*
when he rebukes pride of the table:

> Pride of the table appeereth eek ful ofte; for certes, riche
> men been cleped to festes, and povre folk been put awey and
> rebuked./ Also in excesse of diverse metes and drynkes,
> and namely swich manere bake-metes and dissh-metes,
> brennynge of wilde fir and peynted and castelled with papir,
> and semblable wast, so that it is abusioun for to thynke./
> And eek in to greet preciousnesse of vessel and curiositee
> of mynstralcie, by whiche a man is stired the moore to delices
> of luxurie,/ if so be that he sette his herte the lasse upon
> oure Lord Jhesu Crist, certeyn it is a synne; and certeinly
> the delices myghte been so grete in this caas that man myghte

51. See *Sir Gawain and the Green Knight*, lines 801–2: Hautdesert
looks to Gawain like a paper decoration. For the parodic implications of
these passages, see Robert W. Ackerman, "'Pared Out of Paper': *Gawain*
802 and *Purity* 1408."

lightly falle by hem into deedly synne. (*Parson's Tale*, lines 443–46)

The *Cleanness* poet follows the Parson's recipe for a banquet of pride in the description of Belshazzar's feast. The music accompanying his feast is not like that in the parable of the wedding feast, "mynstrasy noble" (*C*, 121), rather it is chaotic sound:

> And ay þe nakeryn noyse, notes of pipes,
> Tymbres and tabornes, tulket among;
> Symbales and sonetez sware þe noyse,
> And bougounz busch batered so þikke. (*C*, 1413–16)

The noise of Belshazzar's feast is an indication of the chaos of Belshazzar's will, which it celebrates, and a contrast to the order and harmony of God's feast.

In a fit of drunken and lecherous inspiration, Belshazzar sends his retainers to bring in the Temple vessels so that he may do reverence to his concubines by serving them, rather than God, with these incomparably beautiful things:

> "Bryng hem now to my borde, of beverage hem fylles,
> Let þise ladyes of hem lape—I luf hem in hert!
> Þat schal I cortaysly kyþe, and þay schin knawe sone
> Þer is no bounte in burne lyk Baltazar þewes." (*C*, 1433–36)

The poet interrupts his account of the feast to describe again the Temple vessels (*C*, 1439–92; see also *C*, 1271–80) and to lament their misuse: he commemorates the last moment before Belshazzar takes the vessels. The poet also comments to his audience on God's displeasure: "Leve þou wel þat þe Lorde þat þe lyfte ʒemes,/ Displesed much at þat play in þat plyt stronge" (*C*, 1493–94). Belshazzar's retainers, however, carry out his orders. They bring the holy vessels, Belshazzar cries "Wassayl!," and the retainers serve all the company from the Temple vessels. To complete the outrage, the Babylonian company praise their own gods as they drink from Solomon's vessels:

> So long likked þise lordes þise lykores swete,
> And gloryed on her falce goddes, and her grace calles,
> Þat were of stokkes and stones, stille evermore—
> Never steven hem astel, so stoken is hor tonge;
> Alle þe goude golden goddes þe gaulez ʒet nevenen,
> Belfagor, and Belyal, and Belssabub als,

Heyred hem as hy3ly as heven wer þayres,
Bot hym þat alle goudes gives, þat God þay forзeten. (*C*, 1521–
28)

The incapacity of the idols to speak demonstrates their powerlessness; it is another way of proving that they are the inventions of
men, at the disposal of men's wishes, and unavailing against the
Hebrew God, whose independent Word creates what it intends.

God's response to Belshazzar's sacrilege comes speedily in the
form of the words written on the wall, which are interpreted to
Belshazzar by Daniel, whose very name, meaning "judicium Dei,"
predicts the nature of his role.[52] As Belshazzar watches the fist
with a pen in its hand write on the wall, such dread fills him

Þat al falewed his face and fayled þe chere;
Þe stronge strok of þe stonde strayned his joyntes,
His cnes cachches to close, and cluchches his hommes,
And he wyth plattyng his paumes displayes his lers,
And romyes as a rad ryth þat rorez for drede. (*C*, 1539–43)

The words of God turn Belshazzar into the beast that he is. Re-
covering a little, he calls for his Chaldean soothsayers, but since
they cannot read the inscription Belshazzar curses them as he
curses his gods. In her chamber, the "chef quene" (Belshazzar's
wife, possibly his "worþelych quene" of line 1351) hears his rant-
ing, comes to the banqueting hall, and with all humility reminds
Belshazzar of Daniel, who "hatz þe gostes of God þat gyes alle
soþes" (*C*, 1598) and who had advised Nebuchadnezzar. Daniel,
his soul full of wisdom, is brought to Belshazzar, who promises
him great honor if he can read the inscription. Before Daniel reads
the inscription, however, he recounts the history of Nebuchadnezzar's madness, which was a plague from God and a chance for
the emperor to do penance for his claim to be as powerful as God.
After accusing Belshazzar of failing to heed the example of his
father (*C*, 1709–12), Daniel interprets "mane," "techal," and
"phares" as indicating, first, that God has counted up the Babylonian kingdom and that it is at an end (perhaps a suggestion that
there were only a limited number, "a clene noumbre" [*C*, 1731],

52. For a discussion of the function of onomastics in Old English
poetry, with attention to Daniel, see Roberta Frank, "Some Uses of
Paronomasia in Old English Scriptural Verse." See also *Daniel and
Azarias*.

of generations granted to it); second, that God has weighed Belshazzar's reign and found it wanting in "fayth-dedes" (C, 1735);
and, third, that Belshazzar's kingdom will be taken by the Medes
and the Persians. In spite of the terrible significance Daniel puts
on the inscription, Belshazzar honors him with the third highest
position in the kingdom.

Belshazzar draws upon himself the judgment of God by committing sacrilege on the holy vessels: polluted himself, he spreads
his pollution to the vessels by touching them and drinking from
them. He is both an idolater and an adulterer, as the poet has
made clear; he abandons God and honors instead idols and concubines. But Belshazzar knew the Hebrew God's power from the
example of his father, and his failure to dedicate himself to God
cannot be excused. This is the point of Daniel's account of Nebuchadnezzar's madness and the justification for Daniel's harsh
words to Belshazzar for ignoring God's power. Long before Belshazzar profanes the vessels of the Temple, he has desecrated himself, a potential and, through Nebuchadnezzar's conversion, a
promised vessel of God. Belshazzar, then, is a type of the Christian
who, although promised to God, pollutes himself with sin and
invites the wrath of God upon himself.

Just as the Sodomites pollute their city by sin, the sacrilege Belshazzar commits upon himself and then upon the Temple vessels
extends also to the land. The poet claims a paradisiacal setting
for Babylon, a claim that links it with other once unspoiled lands:

> For þe borʒ watz so brod and so bigge alce,
> Stalled in þe fayrest stud þe sterrez anunder,
> Prudly on a plat playn, plek alþerfayrest. (C, 1377–79)

Belshazzar's palace of pride is already an offense to the natural
landscape, but through God's judgment on the king the land becomes actually polluted. The judgment prophesied by Daniel
comes the very night of Belshazzar's banquet; the Medes and the
Persians slip into the city and murder the drunken and sleeping
Chaldeans in their houses. They find Belshazzar in his bed; the
poet has ironically remarked that "Baltazar to his bedd with blysse
watz caryed,/ Reche þe rest as hym lyst, he ros never þerafter" (C,
1765–66). In the indignity of his death, Belshazzar's corpse, spilling
brains and blood, is cast out, to be a pollution on the land:

> Baltazar in his bed watz beten to deþe,
> Þat boþe his blod and his brayn blende on þe cloþes;
> The kyng in his cortyn watz kaȝt bi þe heles,
> Feryed out bi þe fete, and fowle dispysed,
> Þat watz so doȝty þat day and drank of þe vessayl;
> Now is a dogge also dere þat in a dych lygges. (*C*, 1787–92)

As I have already suggested, Belshazzar is a type of the impenitent Christian and of the discourteous guest at God's wedding feast. Like the dungeon the ragged guest is thrown into, Belshazzar's ditch is an image for hell (see Luke 6:39; Matt. 15:14). The poet concludes his story of Belshazzar by pointing out that the king is cut off forever from worldly honor; then the poet dryly comments that he believes Belshazzar is also kept from the delights of heaven, from the vision of God. In the pattern of judgment there are only two alternatives, and whoever misses heaven is destined for hell.

Announcing to his audience that the last of his three biblical exempla is complete, that the design of the poem has been fulfilled, the *Cleanness* poet reminds them of the message of his stories: uncleanness provokes God to wrath and vengeance; but God loves cleanness and wisdom, "and þose þat seme arn and swete schyn se his face" (*C*, 1810). Here, seemliness and sweetness are synonyms for cleanness and courtesy, for purity and good works; and in each case the latter condition is a function of the former.

The poet's closing prayer asks that he and his audience may be found acceptable to God:

> Þat we gon gay in oure gere þat grace he uus sende,
> Þat we may serve in his syȝt þer solace never blynnez.
> Amen. (*C*, 1811–12)

*Cleanness* ends with a prayer for grace, for cleanness and courtesy, which are symbolized under the image of "gay ... gere," an image reminiscent of the angels' "wedez ful bryȝt" (*C*, 20). The poet's work, his act of courtesy and charity, is his poem; in effect, he asks God through his grace to accept him and his work and the listeners who share his work. The poet is, like Abraham, concerned for his neighbors and, like Solomon, a maker of a beautiful thing. His poem, like the vessels of Abraham and Solomon, expresses his desire and love for God.

# 5

## Epilogue

The author of the *Queste* and the *Cleanness* poet sought to engage their audiences in something more than an aesthetic response. They rooted their stories in Christian themes, in biblical and traditional ways of understanding human life and history; and, using literature as a means of witnessing to their faith, they called upon their audiences to repent, to prepare for judgment and the end of history.

Both authors make the parable of the wedding feast the controlling model for their narratives. As Augustine uses the parable of the prodigal son to interpret his early life, so these authors use the parable of the wedding feast to interpret the Arthurian world and Old Testament history and, by extension, the lives of their audiences. "Many are called, but few are chosen" (Matt. 22:14), because few respond. Nothing less than a totally committed affirmative response will do, and the first stage of response must be contrition and faith. Then, through penance and the Eucharist, through cleanness and courtesy, a man or woman may move with the assurance of faith and grace toward death and God, who is life and eternal bliss. There, celebrating the heavenly wedding feast, the resurrected souls remain forever distinct and forever in a perfect relationship to their true lover, who is Christ, the lover who never betrays, who never fails to satisfy his beloved.

The urgent need to cry abroad the call to penance justifies these authors, and Malory, too, in spending their time and talent on making works of fiction, and at the same time it justifies the texts themselves: their didactic message is unmistakable. To make their message more broadly applicable to the audiences they address, these authors develop a pattern of judgment; that is, they show a number of typical cases of those merely called and of those chosen, so that the audiences may better understand how the call applies to them. In the view of these medieval writers, the history of men through the ages and men's personal histories are not, as twentieth-century thinkers often despairingly or bemusedly suggest, meaningless or insignificant, rather they are purposeful. In time, in the adventures in this wasteland of a fallen world, God tests man: he offers him access to grace and an invitation to the eschatological wedding feast. To accept or not is man's choice, but halfhearted acceptance is worse than refusal. Like refusal, halfhearted acceptance leads to personal and social chaos in this world and the next, but the halfhearted are always surprised by God's rejection. God's curse shocks them, and that curse of damnation, now and in death, is isolation, alienation, meaninglessness. So Hector stands alone, outside the Grail castle, denied admission, alienated even from his natural brother, Lancelot; and the tattered guest at the prince's table finds himself cast out from the festivities, alone, separated from cheer.

The paradigm of the vessel, implicit in the *Queste* and *Cleanness*, defines more clearly than does the parable of the wedding feast the basis for God's judgments. What does it mean to have tattered clothes, and how does one get rid of them? The *Queste* and *Cleanness* propose an apparently more specific answer than does Langland in *Piers Plowman* for Hawkyn's dirty coat, which is a sign of his sins generally, or than does the similar first explanation of the ill-clothed wedding guest in *Cleanness*. If the covenant with God is marriage, then the failure to keep it is adultery, which is at the same time idolatry. Sexual sin becomes, then, the chief figure for sin generally; and, since in sexual intercourse men and women pollute themselves with semen, sexual sin is a particularly apt figure for the ontological condition of uncleanness. Contaminated in themselves, sexual sinners (and sinners generally) cannot limit the effects of their uncleanness but, willy-nilly, spread their inward contamination into the social order by quarreling and murdering, until the order becomes disorder, the pollution effects a sacrilege on the land, and the very earth itself becomes a wasteland. To halt the spread of infection, the sinner has only one alternative: to cure his own disease, to clean his own stained and bloody garments, which he cannot do by himself but may do with God's help (or grace) through the sacrament of penance, which involves ritual purification. Then, if he perseveres and remains steadfast, as Bors does and as Lancelot strives to do, he will find adventures, chances to express his newfound state of cleanness in works of charity and courtesy. The social harmony that his condition of cleanness permits him to advance finds expression in the fellowship of the altar and in the shared meal of the Eucharist, which at the same time renew his strength. Galahad's red and white armor and visage signify charity and cleanness, the *Cleanness* poet's bright and gay clothes make them suitable to be filled, as the Grail or chalice is filled, with God.

Finally, the *Queste* proposes that the true food of the wedding feast is the unmediated vision of God. This vision is foreshadowed in the bread and wine of the Eucharist and in the words of Scripture; and, in the life after resurrection, it consummates the marriage of man and God in a never-ending consummation. As the *Cleanness* poet implies, this spiritual consummation is more playful, more delightful, more joyful than its nearest equivalent in physical, bodily experience, the consummation of sexual intercourse. The sexual sinner ought to give up his transient pleasure for the much greater spiritual reward, in the view of the *Queste* author and the *Cleanness* poet, who cannot leave men to persist in sin, but call them to repentance.

The paradigm of the vessel gives these authors a theoretical model through which to display the significance of the stories they tell. This model serves not only to interpret individual stories, but even history itself. The impulse that moved the authors of the *Queste* and *Cleanness* to include all of history comes in part from their having chosen judgment as their major theme: the Christian God, whose criteria for judgment they have set out to explain, has intervened in history in order to reveal what he requires of his faithful, and his actions make a consistent pattern. By including in their works the full sweep of history and of God's acts of judgment upon history, these authors at once lend the full authority of tradition to their interpretations of particular stories and implicitly or explicitly call upon their audiences to recognize that the pattern of God's judgment will be brought to bear on their own cases. The theoretical model, the paradigm of the vessel as an image of man, serves as an analytical lens through which to see whether a man or a nation has chosen sin and death or cleanness and life.

In Chaucer's *Man of Law's Tale*, individuals and nations reveal their choice by their response to Constance, whose function in the

tale closely resembles the function of the Temple vessels in the
*Cleanness* poet's account of the judgments on Jerusalem and Babylon: respect or reverence for the vessel (Constance, the Temple
vessels) leads to conversion and life; sexual sin or idolatry leads to
judgment and death. Unlike the authors of the *Queste* and *Cleanness*, Chaucer does not offer a paradigm of history in the *Man of
Law's Tale*, although he does associate Constance typologically
with a variety of biblical figures. Constance's journeys do, however, reflect one of the historical patterns in the *Queste*: Joseph of
Arimathea moves westward with the Grail to Sarras and then
Logres, effecting conversions to Christianity, and Galahad and
the Grail companions return the Grail from Logres to Sarras,
where the nature of Galahad and the Grail is clearly revealed;
similarly, Constance moves from Rome to the East to effect a temporary conversion of Islam, then from the East to the West (North-
umberland) to effect a conversion of Britain, then finally back to
Rome where her reunion with her son, her husband, and her father
confirms and celebrates the success of her mission as a vessel of
faith. Sarras or Rome is the center to which the faithful bride of
Christ returns for reunion banquets with father and husband, in
Constance's case natural reunions that reflect the pattern of spiritual reunion that Galahad achieves.

In her purity and innocence and in her capacity for fellowship
(and natural marriage), Constance embodies the positive aspects
of the paradigm of the vessel. She is obedient but not entirely willing when she sets out to marry the sultan, whose mother rejects
the effects of baptism and at her feast murders all the Christians,
both the Romans and her son and his companions, all except Constance. The sultaness makes a sacrilege of the Christian sacraments
of purification and fellowship (baptism and the Eucharist) and,
as we learn at the end of the tale, receives the judgment of death
from the Roman emperor, who avenges his daughter Constance
(an analogue of God's vengeance on those who reject Christ). A
figure of the remnant, Constance, set in a rudderless ship that will
be steered by Christ, henceforth freely wills her obedience to God:
the ship is an image of her internal condition. In *Cleanness* the
Temple vessels move Nebuchadnezzar to convert, and in the *Man
of Law's Tale* Constance moves Hermengild and Alla to convert.
Twice, lecherous men attack her; by virtue of Constance's role as
a figure for the Church (a vessel of faith), their adulterous inten-

tions are idolatrous and bring the judgment of death upon them.
A British knight, thwarted in his lecherous desire for Constance,
murders Hermengild and frames Constance. In the trial before
Alla, the British king is moved by Constance's innocence to convert to her faith and to marry her; the lecherous knight, forced to
swear Constance's guilt on the Gospels, earns death. The hand of
God strikes the knight's neck so that his eyes burst out of his head,
and the voice of God condemns him; this judgment resembles the
judgment on Belshazzar, when a hand writes the word of God on
the wall and makes Belshazzar's knees knock with fear. Alla puts
the British knight to death, just as the Medes and the Persians
complete God's judgment on Belshazzar. Constance bears Alla a
son, a natural sign of her spiritual fertility, but again an idolatrous
mother-in-law intervenes to persecute her by driving her away.
Constance and her son, however, return on her little ship to Rome,
again with Christ as steersman, and there her husband, Alla, re-
joins her and reunites her and her son with her father, whose acceptance of her foreshadows the reception that will be hers in
heaven (so the tale implies).

There are, of course, other ways of analyzing the *Man of Law's
Tale*. To discover the paradigm of the vessel in it says nothing of
its relation to folklore or to direct literary sources and does not
account for the narrator's strategies in presenting his tale, but the
paradigm of the vessel does help to make sense of the events that
befall Constance.

The theoretical model of the paradigm of the vessel also allows
us as readers to see clearly the anthropology of a work that it gov-
erns. For example, in discussing the difference between the *Queste*
and Malory's *Sankgreal*, I have pointed to the greater indepen-
dence of Malory's characters. The *Queste* tends to present man's
choice of death or life as a psychomachy in which God and the
Devil contest the right to inhabit a man's soul (for example, Lancelot's). By expressing his vision in the form of a quest romance, the
*Queste* author is, however, insisting that man actively chooses to
contain either God or the Devil. His allegorization of the quest as
a psychomachy defines that choice to be between marriage to God
(in which man contains Christ's Body and Blood) and fornication
with the Devil (as a result of which man contains filth or sin). The
sexual metaphors used to describe these unions function to preserve the identities of the personalities involved and, like the quest

form itself, insist on the importance of choice in a man's decision to enter into union with either God or the Devil.

Malory eschews the psychomachy interpretation of the quest by simply omitting references to the Devil and his cosmic struggle with God. The result is a more complex view of human psychology that places the conflict of desires in the human psyche instead of objectifying it as between God and the Devil. Malory tends to make Lancelot stand by himself in the landscape of the romance world, as a subject without an object; the tendency clearly is a relative one, however, since Malory in fact removes only one of the objects, the Devil, and not the other, God. The *Queste* assumes that man can, if he wishes, know the content he chooses to contain; and if he chooses God, the meaning of life in the world becomes clear to him. In the *Sankgreal*, because Malory reduces the internal glossing of events that are fully elaborated in the *Queste*, the events remain in part a mystery. For example, in dropping the psychomachical allegorization of the quest from the hermit's discourses, Malory withholds from Lancelot the full explanation of the alternatives between which he must choose.

When Renaissance writers use the paradigm of the vessel as a model through which to see their worlds, their tendency to set man adrift from sure knowledge of God or the Devil is even more pronounced than it is in Malory. Shakespeare's *Hamlet*, for example, contains the model: the analogy of man to vessel at the dramatic climax of the play (the cup of poison for the corrupt king and queen); the adulterous love of Claudius for Gertrude and for the Kingdom of Denmark; the murder of King Hamlet; the imagery of Gertrude as a ruined garden and of Ophelia as a garden that Prince Hamlet will never possess. Prince Hamlet recognizes the corruption that infects his kingdom and yet resists taking any action because he has no certain way of confirming his mission. His problem is essentially epistemological: he must be the agent of divine vengeance, just as Galahad is at Carcelois, but he has none of Galahad's advantages. His father's ghost does not come from heaven. His first act miscarries and results in the death of Polonius. His own journey by ship does not grant him the sword of Solomon and David or confirm him in an Edenic state of justification. He brings not life but death to two of those who should be his companions, Ophelia, his would-be bride, and Laertes, her brother. Everything we know about the conditions in Denmark suggests that Hamlet does what he must do, that the role of avenger is rightly his. The play's end brings us not, however, to an assumption of Hamlet's soul into heaven, which is Galahad's fate, but to Horatio's prayer of petition: "And flights of angels sing thee to thy rest." These differences between Galahad and Hamlet make a perfect illustration of the distinction we ordinarily draw between medieval and Renaissance culture: in the Renaissance man is no longer a pawn in a cosmic struggle; rather, he stands alone, comparatively insecure, with no one to sanction his choices.

The paradigm of the vessel is so deeply rooted in the theme of judgment that we should not expect it to appear in literature unconcerned with judgment, except perhaps in attenuated form. An understanding of the interrelationship of ideas in the paradigm, however, may increase the resonance of our response even to brief allusions to those ideas. For example, in Dante's encounter with Pope Nicholas III in *Inferno* 19, Dante accuses him and Boniface of fornication and idolatry; their infidelity to the Church, their bride, dooms them to stand forever upside down, like Satan, divorced from God. The pattern of adultery and murder, or of adultery, idolatry, and murder, runs through the disharmonious worlds of Elizabethan and Jacobean revenge tragedy, which seldom see a penitent or glimpse a vision of an ordered world, of fellowship or true marriage, human or spiritual. I think, for example, of John Webster's *The White Devil*, which makes a world of the negative part of the paradigm of the vessel, or of John Marston's *The Malcontent*, a happier vision that, though it does not explicitly use vessel imagery, opposes sin to righteousness by embodying major concepts of the paradigm of the vessel: adultery (as idolatry), murder, and hell contrast with penitence, chaste marriage, and the virtue aimed to heaven.

Milton uses the paradigm of the vessel more fully in *Paradise Lost*, particularly in his interpretation of history: the pattern of sexual sin and murder that first appears in Satan's encounter with Sin and Death (book 2) recurs in books 11 and 12, where Milton, like the *Cleanness* poet, distinguishes the Age of Nature with its sexual sins (book 11) from the Age of the Written Law with its adulteries and idolatries. Balanced against this vision of the effects of sin is Milton's portrayal of Adam and Eve's marriage in paradise, of the harmony that they must work to recover in the wilderness of the world, seeking to make "a paradise within . . . happier far." This harmony depends not on man's willingness to contain God, as in the sacramental theology of the *Queste* or *Cleanness*, but on his knowledge of "what this vessel can containe," that is, on language, the medium through which Adam knows himself, his history, God, and Satan. Adam's task is to use language properly; man as vessel in *Paradise Lost* contains words, not the Word. In theory, then, the "paradise within" that Milton's Adam must strive to create is far more subjective than the one Galahad and his companions find on Solomon's ship and in the vision of the Grail.

The *Queste* and *Cleanness*, embodying as they do the full scope of the paradigm of the vessel, focused as they are on the pattern of God's judgment in history, provide us with central visions of medieval anthropology. They belong among the most serious and representative artistic achievements of the High Middle Ages. With consummate literary skill, their authors portray for us the coherence of the medieval view of the world, a world in which man has clear choices to make and in which the choices he does make have both immediate and ultimate consequences.

# Bibliography

*For abbreviations used in the bibliography, see "List of Abbreviations,"*
*p. vi.*

## I. Reference Works

*An Anglo-Saxon Dictionary.* Edited by Joseph Bosworth and T.
Northcote Toller. 1898. Reprint. London: Oxford University
Press, 1954.
*An Anglo-Saxon Dictionary: Supplement.* Edited by T. Northcote
Toller. Oxford: Clarendon, 1921.
*Dictionnaire de l'ancienne langue française.* Edited by Frédéric
Godefroy. 10 vols. 1881–1902. Reprint. Paris: Librairie des sci-
ences et des arts, 1937–1938.
*Dictionnaire de théologie catholique.* Edited by A. Vacant and E.
Mangenot. 15 vols. Paris: Letouzey et Ané, 1903–1950.
Du Cange, Charles Du Fresne. *Glossarium ad Scriptores mediae et
infimae latinitas.* Rev. ed., by G. A. L. Henschel. 10 vols. Graz,
Austria: Akademische Druck-U. Verlagsanstalt, 1954.
*Französisches etymologisches Wörterbuch.* Edited by Walther von
Wartburg. Bonn and Leipzig: B. G. Teubner et al., 1922–.
*A Greek-English Lexicon of the New Testament and Other Early
Christian Literature.* Edited by William F. Arndt and F. Wilbur
Gingrich. Chicago: University of Chicago Press, 1957.
*Lexicon latinitatis medii aevi.* Edited by A. Blaise. CCCM (1975).
*Middle English Dictionary.* Edited by Hans Kurath, Sherman M.
Kuhn, and John Reidy. Ann Arbor: University of Michigan
Press, 1954–.
*New Catholic Encyclopedia.* 15 vols. New York: McGraw-Hill,
1967.
*Nouveau Dictionnaire étymologique.* Edited by Albert Dauzat,
Jean Du Bois, and Henri Mitterand. Paris: Larousse, 1964.
*The Oxford English Dictionary.* Edited by James A. H. Murray.
13 vols. Oxford: Clarendon, 1933.
*A Patristic Greek Lexicon.* Edited by G. W. H. Lampe. Oxford:
Clarendon, 1961.
*Prompta bibliotheca canonica, juridica, moralis, theologica.* Edited
by Lucius Ferraris. 8 vols. Paris: Migne, 1861–1863.

*Theological Dictionary of the New Testament.* Edited by Gerhard Kittel and Gerhard Friedrich. Translated by Geoffrey W. Bromiley. 8 vols. Grand Rapids, Mich.: Eerdmans, 1964–1976.

*Thesaurus linguae latinae.* Edited by F. Vollmer, et al. Leipzig: B. G. Teubner, 1900–.

*Tobler-Lommatzsch, Altfranzösisches Wörterbuch.* Edited by Adolf Tobler. Berlin: Weidmannsche Buchhandlung, 1925–1943; Wiesbaden: F. S. Verlag, 1951–.

## II. Primary Sources

*Acta sanctorum.* Edited by Jean Bolland. 69 vols. Paris: V. Palmé, 1863–1940.

Aelred of Rievaulx. *Speculum caritatis.* Edited by C. H. Talbot. CCCM, vol. 1 (1971).

Alain de Lille. *The Complaint of Nature.* Translated by Douglas M. Moffat. Yale Studies in English, vol. 36. New York: Henry Holt, 1908.

———. *Liber poenitentialis.* Edited by Jean Longère. Analecta mediaevalia namurcensia, vol. 17. Louvain: Nauwelaerts, 1965.

———. *De planctu naturae.* Edited by Thomas Wright. In *Anglo-Latin Satirical Poets of the Twelfth Century,* vol. 2. Rolls Series, 59. London: 1872.

Alexander of Hales. *Summa theologica.* Edited by Bernardine Klumper. Vol. 3. Florence: Quaracchi, 1930.

Amalarius of Metz. *Opera liturgica omnia.* Edited by John Michael Hanssens. 3 vols. Studi e testi, 138–40. Vatican City: Biblioteca apostolica vaticana, 1948–1950.

Ambrose. *Cain and Abel.* Edited by Karl Schenkl. CSEL, vol. 32, pt. 1 (1897), pp. 337–409.

———. *De excessu fratris.* Edited by Otto Faller. CSEL, vol. 73 (1955), pp. 207–325.

———. *De mysteriis.* Edited by Otto Faller. CSEL, vol. 73 (1955), pp. 87–116.

———. *De obitu Theodosii.* Edited by Otto Faller. CSEL, vol. 73 (1955), pp. 369–401.

———. *De obitu Valentiniani.* Edited by Otto Faller. CSEL, vol. 73 (1955), pp. 327–67.

———. *De sacramentis.* Edited by Otto Faller. CSEL, vol. 73 (1955), pp. 13–85.

———. *De Spiritu Sancto.* Edited by Otto Faller. CSEL, vol. 79 (1964).

———. *Theological and Dogmatic Works.* Translated by Roy J.

Deferrari. Fathers of the Church, vol. 44. Washington, D. C.: Catholic University of America, 1963.

*Analecta hymnica medii aevi.* Edited by G. M. Dreves, C. Blume, and H. M. Bannister. 55 vols. in 32. Leipzig: O. R. Reisland, 1886–1922.

*Ancrene Riwle.* Edited and translated by James Morton. Camden Society, no. 57. London: Camden Society, 1853.

*Ancrene Wisse.* Edited by J. R. R. Tolkien. EETS, o.s. 249 (1962).

*Appendix Vergiliana.* Edited by R. Ellis. 1907. Reprint. Oxford: Clarendon, 1957.

Aquinas, Thomas. *Catena Aurea: Commentary on the Four Gospels.* 4 vols. in 8. n.trans. Oxford: John Henry Parker, 1841–1845.

———. *Catena aurea in quator Evangelia.* Edited by Angelico Guarienti. 2 vols. Turin: Marietti, 1953.

———. *Summa theologica.* Edited by Institut d'études médiévales, Ottawa. 5 vols. Ottawa: Studii Generalis O.P., 1941–1945.

———. *Summa Theologica.* Translated by Fathers of the English Dominican Province. 3 vols. New York: Benziger Bros., 1947.

Augustine. *Augustine: Later Works.* Translated by John Burnaby. Library of Christian Classics, vol. 8. Philadelphia: Westminster, 1955.

———. *The City of God.* Translated by Marcus Dods. Modern Library. New York: Random House, 1950.

———. *De civitate Dei.* Edited by Bernard Dombart and Alphonse Kalb. CCSL, vols. 47–48 (1955).

———. *Commentaire de la première épître de S. Jean (Tractatus in epistolam Joannis ad Parthos).* Edited by Paul Agaesse. SC, vol. 75 (1961).

———. *Confessiones.* Edited by Martin Skutella (1934) et al. Stuttgart: Teubner, 1969.

———. *The Confessions of St. Augustine.* Translated by John K. Ryan. Garden City, N.Y.: Doubleday, 1960.

———. *De doctrina christiana.* Edited by Josef Martin. CCSL, vol. 32 (1962).

———. *De Genesi ad litteram.* Edited by Joseph Zycha. CSEL, vol. 28, pt. 1 (1894).

———. *On Christian Doctrine.* Translated by D. W. Robertson, Jr. New York: Bobbs-Merrill, 1958.

Baldwin of Ford, Archbishop of Canterbury. *Le Sacrement de l'autel (Tractatus de sacramento altaris).* Edited by J. Morson. Translated by E. de Solms. SC, vols. 93–94 (1963).

Bede. *De tabernaculo.* Edited by D. Hurst. CCSL, vol. 119A (1969), pp. 1–139.

———. *De templo.* Edited by D. Hurst. CCSL, vol. 119A (1969), pp. 141–234.

Bernard of Clairvaux. *Cantica canticorum: Eighty-six sermons on the Song of Solomon.* Translated by Samuel J. Eales. London: Elliot Stock, 1895.

———. *Sermones super Cantica canticorum.* In *Opera,* edited by J. Leclercq, C. H. Talbot, and H. M. Rochais, vols. 1, 2. Rome: Editiones Cistercienses, 1957–1958.

———. *On the Song of Songs, 1–46.* Translated by Kilian Walsh. In *Works.* Cistercian Fathers, nos. 4, 7. Kalamazoo, Mich.: Cistercian Publications, 1976.

*Book of Vices and Virtues.* Edited by W. Nelson Francis. EETS, o.s. 217 (1942).

Brady, Ignatius, trans. *The Legends and Writings of Saint Clare of Assisi.* St. Bonaventure, New York: Franciscan Institute, 1953.

Caesarius of Arles. *Sermones.* Edited by D. Germain Morin. 2d ed. CCSL, vols. 103–4 (1953).

Catherine of Siena. *The Dialogue of . . . St. Catherine of Siena.* Translated by Algar Thorold. London: Kegan Paul, Trench, Trübner, 1896.

———. *Libro della divina dottrina.* Edited by Matilde Fiorilli. Bari, Italy: Gius, Laterza & Figli, 1912.

Chaucer, Geoffrey. *Works.* Edited by F. N. Robinson. 2d ed. Boston: Houghton Mifflin, 1957.

*Daniel and Azarias.* Edited by R. T. Farrel. London: Methuen, 1974.

Dante Alighieri. *Il Convivio.* Edited by Maria Simonelli. Testi e Saggi di letterature moderne, 2. Bologna: Riccardo Pàtron, 1966.

———. *The Divine Comedy.* Edited by Giorgio Petrocchi (1966–1968). Revised and translated, with commentaries, by Charles S. Singleton. 6 vols. Bollingen Series, vol. 80. Princeton: Princeton University Press, 1970–1975.

Duns Scotus, *Reportata Parisiensia.* In *Opera omnia,* edited by Observantine Franciscan Fathers, 2d ed., vols. 22–24. Paris: Vives, 1894.

Gratian. *Decretum.* In *Corpus iuris canonici,* edited by Emil Friedberg, vol. 1. Leipzig: Bernhard Tauchnitz, 1879.

Gregory the Great. *Morals on the Book of Job.* Library of Fathers, vols. 18, 21, 23, 31. Oxford: J. H. Parker, 1844–1850.

Guillaume de Lorris and Jean de Meun. *Roman de la Rose.*

Edited by Ernest Langlois. 5 vols. La Société des anciens textes français. Paris: Champion, 1914–1924.

Hauréau, B. *Notices et extraits de quelques manuscrits latins de la Bibliothèque Nationale*. Vol. 4. Paris: C. Klincksieck, 1892.

Hugh of St. Victor. *On the Sacraments of the Christian Faith*. Translated by Roy J. Deferrari. Mediaeval Academy of America, no. 58. Cambridge: Mediaeval Academy of America, 1951.

———. *Selected Spiritual Writings*. Translated by a Religious of C.S.M.V. London: Faber and Faber, 1962.

Ilarino da Milano. *L'Eresia di Ugo Speroni nella confutazione del Maestro Vacario: Testo inedito del secolo XII con studio storico e dottrinale*. Studi e testi, 115. Vatican City: Biblioteca apostolica vaticana, 1945.

*Jacob's Well*. Edited by A. Brandeis. Part 1. EETS, o.s. 115 (1900).

Jerome. *Commentarii in Matheum*. Edited by D. Hurst and M. Adriaen. CCSL, vol. 77 (1969).

———. *In Osee prophetam*. Edited by M. Adriaen. CCSL, vol. 76 (1969).

———. *Lettres*. Translated and edited by Jérôme Labourt. 8 vols. Paris: Les Belles Lettres, 1949–1963.

*Le Livre de la Passion, poème narratif du XIVᵉ siècle*. Edited by Grace Frank. CFMA, 64. Paris: Champion, 1930.

Lombard, Peter. *Sententiarum libri quatuor*. Edited by J. P. Migne. Paris: Migne, 1846.

Ludolph of Saxony. *Vita Christi Domini Salvatoris*. Nuremberg: Anton Koberger, 1495.

Lydgate, John. *Minor Poems*. Vol. 1. Edited by Henry Noble MacCracken. EETS, e.s. 107 (1911).

Mansi, Joannes Dominicus, ed. *Sacrorum conciliorum, nova et amplissima collectio*. Vol. 22, *1166–1225*. Venice: Antonium Zatta, 1767.

*Manuale et processionale ad usum insignis ecclesiae Eboracensis* (York Manual). Edited by W. G. Henderson. Surtees Society, vol. 63 (1874).

*Middle English Sermons*. Edited by W. O. Ross. EETS, o.s. 209 (1960 [1938]).

*Midrash Rabbah*. Translated by H. Freedman and Maurice Simon. 10 vols. London: Soncino Press, 1939.

Nicholas of Lyra. *Moralia super totam biblium*. Strassburg: Georg Husner, 1478 [?].

———. *Postilla super Genesim*. Nuremberg: Anton Koberger, 1493.

Origen. *Commentarius in Cantica canticorum*. In *Werke*, edited by W. A. Baehrens, vol. 8. Die griechischen christlichen Schriftsteller der ersten drei Jahrhunderte, vol. 33. Leipzig: J. C. Hinrichs, 1925.

———. *The Song of Songs: Commentary and Homilies*. Translated by R. P. Lawson. Ancient Christian Writers, vol. 26. Westminster, Md.: Newman, 1957.

Otto of Freising. *Chronicon*. In *Opera*, edited by Roger Wilmans, vol. 1. Monumenta germaniae historica: Scriptores rerum germanicarum. Hanover: Hahn, 1867.

———. *The Two Cities: A Chronicle of Universal History to the Year 1146*. Translated by Charles Christopher Mierow. Columbia Records of Civilization: Sources and Studies. New York: Columbia University Press, 1928.

*Patrologia latina*. Edited by J. P. Migne. 221 vols. Paris: 1844–1900.

Powicke, F. M., and Cheney, C. R., eds. *Councils and Synods, with Other Documents Relating to the English Church*. Vol. 2, *1205–1313*. Oxford: Clarendon, 1964.

Prudentius. *Prudentius*. Vol. 1. Translated by H. J. Thomson. Loeb Classical Library. 1949. Reprint. Cambridge: Harvard University Press, 1962.

Ralph of Coggeshall. *Chronicum Anglicanum*. Edited by Joseph Stevenson. Rolls Series, 66 (London: 1875).

Robert de Boron. *Le Roman de l'estoire dou Graal*. Edited by William A. Nitze. CFMA, 57. Paris: Champion, 1927.

Robert Mannyng of Brunne. *Handlyng Synne*. Edited by F. J. Furnivall. EETS, e.s. 119 (1901).

Seton, Walter. "The Letters from Saint Clare to Blessed Agnes of Bohemia." *Archivum franciscanum historicum* 17 (1924): 509–19.

*Sir Gawain and the Green Knight*. Edited by J. R. R. Tolkien and E. V. Gordon. 2d ed., edited by Norman Davis. Oxford: Clarendon, 1967.

Tertullian. *De pudicitia*. Edited by E. Dekkers. CCSL, vol. 2 (1954).

*The Towneley Plays*. Edited by George England and Alfred W. Pollard. EETS, e.s. 71 (1897).

*Vices and Virtues*. Edited by F. Holthausen. EETS, o.s. 89 (1888).

Wakefield, Walter W., and Evans, Austin P., eds. and trans. *Heresies of the High Middle Ages*. Records of Civilization: Sources and Studies, vol. 81. New York: Columbia University Press, 1969.

Walter, Daniel. *Life of Ailred of Rievaulx.* Edited by F. M. Powicke. New York: Oxford University Press, 1951.

William of Saint-Thierry. *Exposé sur le Cantique des Cantiques.* Edited by J.-M. Déchanet and translated by M. Dumontier. SC, vol. 82 (1962).

———. *Exposition of the Song of Songs.* Translated by Mother Columba Hart. Cistercian Fathers, no. 6. Kalamazoo, Mich.: Cistercian Publications, 1970.

William of Shoreham. *Poems.* Edited by M. Konrath. EETS, e.s. 86 (1902).

## III. Secondary Works

Ackerman, Robert W. *Backgrounds to Medieval English Literature.* New York: Random House, 1966.

Al-Hamdani, Betty. "The Burning Lamp and Other Romanesque Symbols for the Virgin that Come from the Orient." *Commentari* 16 (1965): 167–85.

Allbright, William Foxwell. *From the Stone Age to Christianity: Monotheism and the Historical Process.* 2d ed. Garden City, N.Y.: Doubleday Anchor, 1957.

Allen, Judson Boyce. *The Friar as Critic: Literary Attitudes in the Later Middle Ages.* Nashville: Vanderbilt University Press, 1971.

Alphandéry, Paul. *La Chrétienté et l'idée de croisade.* Texte établi par Alphonse Dupront. Paris: A. Michel, 1954.

Anciaux, Paul. *The Sacrament of Penance.* n.trans. London: Challoner, 1962.

———. *La Théologie du sacrement de pénitence au XIIᵉ siècle.* Ph.D. dissertation, University of Louvain, ser. 2, vol. 41. Louvain: É. Nauwelaerts, 1949.

Anderson, Bernhard W. *Understanding the Old Testament.* 2d ed. Englewood Cliffs, N. J.: Prentice-Hall, 1957.

Arnould, E. J. *Le "Manuel des péchés": Étude de la littérature religieuse anglo-normande.* Paris: Droz, 1940.

Artonne, André. "Les Statuts synodaux diocésains français du XIIIᵉ siècle au concile de Trente." *Revue d'histoire de l'église en France* 36 (1950): 168–81.

Auerbach, Erich. "Figura." In *Scenes from the Drama of European Literature,* translated by Ralph Manheim. New York: Meridian Books, 1959.

———. *Literary Language and Its Public in Late Latin Antiquity and in the Middle Ages.* Translated by Ralph Manheim. Bollingen Series, vol. 74. New York: Pantheon Books, 1965.

Baldwin, John W. *Masters, Princes, and Merchants: The Social Views of Peter the Chanter and His Circle.* 2 vols. Princeton: Princeton University Press, 1970.

Bateson, Hartley. "Looking Over the Left Shoulder." *Folk-Lore* 34 (1923): 241–42.

Bettoni, Efrem. *Duns Scotus: The Basic Principles of His Philosophy.* Translated by Bernardine Bonasea. Washington, D.C.: The Catholic University of America Press, 1961.

Bloch, Marc. *Feudal Society.* Translated by L. A. Manyon. 2 vols. London: Routledge & Kegan Paul, 1961.

Bloomfield, Morton W. *Piers Plowman as a Fourteenth-Century Apocalypse.* New Brunswick: Rutgers University Press [1962].

———. *The Seven Deadly Sins.* East Lansing: Michigan State College Press, 1952.

Bloomfield, Morton W., and Reeves, Marjorie E. "The Penetration of Joachism into Northern Europe." *Speculum* 29 (1954): 772–93.

Boblitz, Hartmut. "Die Allegorese der Arche Noahs in der frühen Bibelauslegung." *Frühmittelalterliche Studien* 6 (1972): 159–70.

Boman, Thorleif. *Hebrew Thought Compared with Greek.* Translated by Jules L. Moreau. Rev. ed. London: SCM Press, 1960.

Borroff, Marie. *Sir Gawain and the Green Knight: A Stylistic and Metrical Study.* Yale Studies in English, vol. 152. New Haven, Conn.: Yale University Press, 1962.

Brieger, Peter, and Verdier, Philippe, eds. *Art and the Courts/ L'Art et la Court.* Ottawa: National Gallery of Canada, 1972.

Brody, Saul Nathaniel. *The Disease of the Soul: Leprosy in Medieval Literature.* Ithaca, N.Y.: Cornell University Press, 1974.

Buddensieg, Tilman. "Gregory the Great, the Destroyer of Pagan Idols: The History of a Medieval Legend Concerning the Decline of Ancient Art and Literature." *Journal of the Warburg and Courtauld Institutes* 28 (1965): 44–65.

Büchler, A. *Studies in Sin and Atonement in the Rabbinic Literature of the First Century.* London: Oxford University Press, 1928.

Burrow, J. A. *A Reading of Sir Gawain and the Green Knight.* London: Routledge & Kegan Paul, 1965.

———. *Ricardian Poetry: Chaucer, Gower, Langland and the "Gawain" Poet.* London: Routledge & Kegan Paul, 1971.

Charity, A. C. *Events and Their Afterlife: The Dialectics of Christian Typology in the Bible and Dante.* Cambridge: Cambridge University Press, 1966.

Cheney, C. R. "The Earliest English Diocesan Statutes." *English Historical Review* 75 (1960): 1–29.

Chenu, M.-D. *Nature, Man, and Society in the Twelfth Century: Essays on New Theological Perspectives in the Latin West.* Translated by Jerome Taylor and Lester K. Little. Chicago: University of Chicago Press, 1968.

———. *La Théologie au douzième siècle.* Études de philosophie médiévale, vol. 43. Paris: J. Vrin, 1957.

Cheyette, Frederic L. Review of *The Medieval Manichee*, by Steven Runciman. *Speculum* 48 (1973): 411–15.

Cohen, Gustave. *Le Livre de conduite du régisseur et le comptedes dépenses pour le "Mystère de la Passion" joué à Mons en 1501.* Paris: H. Champion, 1925.

Cohn, Norman. *The Pursuit of the Millennium: Millennarians and Mystical Anarchists of the Middle Ages.* Rev. ed. New York: Oxford University Press, 1970.

Copleston, Frederick C. *Aquinas.* Baltimore: Penguin, 1955.

———. *A History of Philosophy.* Vol. 2, *Mediaeval Philosophy, Augustine to Scotus.* 2d ed. Westminster, Md.: Newman, 1950.

Cullman, Oscar. *Christ and Time: The Primitive Christian Conception of Time and History.* Translated by Floyd V. Filson. 3d. ed. London: SCM Press, 1962.

Curtius, Ernst Robert. *European Literature and the Latin Middle Ages.* Translated by Willard Trask. Bollingen Series, vol. 36. New York: Pantheon, 1953.

Daniélou, Jean. *The Bible and the Liturgy.* n.trans. University of Notre Dame Liturgical Studies, vol. 3. Notre Dame, Ind.: University of Notre Dame Press, 1956.

———. *From Shadows to Reality: Studies in the Biblical Typology of the Fathers.* Translated by Wulfstan Hibberd. London: Burns & Oates, 1960.

———. *The Lord of History: Reflections on the Inner Meaning of History.* Translated by Nigel Abercrombie. London: Longmans, Green, 1958.

Davies, W. D. *Paul and Rabbinic Judaism: Some Rabbinic Elements in Pauline Theology.* Rev. ed. New York: Harper and Row, 1967.

de Lubac, Henri. *Corpus Mysticum: L'Eucharistie et l'église au moyen âge.* Paris: Aubier, 1944.

———. *Exégèse médiévale: Les Quatre Sens de l'écriture.* Études ... de la faculté de théologie S. J. de Lyon-Fourvière, nos. 41, 42, 59. 2 parts in 4 vols. Paris: Aubier, 1959–1961.

Dobiache-Rojdestvensky, Olga. *La Vie paroissiale en France au*

*XIIIe siècle d'après les actes épiscopaux.* Paris: Alphonse Picard, 1911.

Doob, Penelope B. R. *Nebuchadnezzar's Children: Conventions of Madness in Middle English Literature.* New Haven, Conn.: Yale University Press, 1974.

Douglas, Mary Tew. *Purity and Danger: An Analysis of Concepts of Pollution and Taboo.* London: Routledge & Kegan Paul, 1966.

Dumoutet, Édouard. *Le Christ selon la chair et la vie liturgique au moyen-âge.* Paris: Beauchesne, 1932.

————. *Le Désir de voir l'hostie et les origines de la dévotion au saint-sacrement.* Paris: Beauchesne, 1926.

Ehlers, Joachim. "*Arca significat ecclesiam*: Ein theologisches Weltmodell aus der ersten Hälfte des 12. Jahrhunderts." *Frühmittelalterliche Studien* 6 (1972): 171–87.

Eisenhofer, Ludwig, and Lechner, Joseph. *The Liturgy of the Roman Rite.* Translated by A. J. and E. F. Peeler. 6th ed. London: Nelson, 1961.

Emerson, Oliver F. "Legends of Cain, especially in Old and Middle English." *PMLA* 21 (1906): 831–929.

Evans, Joan. *Art in Medieval France, 987–1498.* 2d ed. Oxford: Clarendon, 1969.

Favez, Charles. *La Consolation latine chrétienne.* Paris: J. Vrin, 1937.

Ferguson, A. B. *The Indian Summer of English Chivalry.* Durham, N.C.: Duke University Press, 1960.

Folliet, G. "La Typologie du sabbat chez St. Augustine." *Revue des études augustiennes* 2 (1956): 371–90.

Foreville, Raymonde. *Latran I, II, III et Latran IV.* Histoire des conciles oecuméniques, no. 6. Paris: Éditions de l'Orante, 1965.

Frank, Roberta. "Some Uses of Paronomasia in Old English Scriptural Verse." *Speculum* 47 (1972): 207–26.

Freccero, John. "Dante and the Neutral Angels." *Romanic Review* 51 (1960): 3–14.

————. "Dante's Prologue Scene." *Dante Studies* 84 (1966): 1–25.

————. "The River of Death: *Inferno* II, 108." In *The World of Dante,* edited by S. Bernard Chandler and Julius A. Molinari, pp. 25–42. Toronto: Toronto University Press, 1966.

Freccero, John, ed. *Dante: A Collection of Critical Essays.* Twentieth Century Views. Englewood Cliffs, N.J.: Prentice Hall, 1965.

Giamatti, A. Bartlett. *The Earthly Paradise and the Renaissance Epic.* Princeton: Princeton University Press, 1966.

Gray, John. *Archaeology and the Old Testament World*. London: Nelson, 1962.

Grundmann, Herbert. *Bibliographie zur Ketzergeschichte des Mittelalters, 1900–1966*. Sussidi eruditi, 20. Rome: Edizioni di storia e letteratura, 1967.

Hardison, O. B., Jr. *Christian Rite and Christian Drama in the Middle Ages: Essays in the Origin and Early History of Modern Drama*. Baltimore: The Johns Hopkins University Press, 1965.

Heimann, Adelheid. "Trinitas Creator Mundi." *Journal of the Warburg and Courtauld Institutes* 2 (1938–1939): 42–52.

Heschel, Abraham. *The Prophets*. New York: Harper and Row, 1962.

*Histoire de l'Église, depuis les origines jusqu'à nos jours*. Edited by Augustin Fliche and Victor Martin. Paris: Bloud and Gay, 1934–.

Hoffmann, Konrad, and Deuchler, Florens. *The Year 1200*. The Cloisters Studies in Medieval Art, vols. 1–2. New York: The Metropolitan Museum of Art, 1970.

Hontoir, Camille. "La Dévotion au Saint Sacrement chez les premiers Cisterciens (XII<sup>e</sup>–XIII<sup>e</sup> siècles)." In *Studia Eucharistica*, edited by E. P. St. Alexis et al., pp. 132–56. Antwerp: De Nederlandsche Boekhandel, 1946.

Jungmann, Joseph A. *The Mass of the Roman Rite: Its Origins and Development (Missarum sollemnia)*. Translated by Francis A. Brunner. 2 vols. New York: Benziger Brothers, 1955.

Kaske, R. E. "Dante's *Purgatorio* XXXII and XXXIII: A Survey of Christian History." *University of Toronto Quarterly* 43 (1974): 193–214.

Kennedy, V. L. "The Date of the Parisian Decree on the Elevation of the Host." *Mediaeval Studies* 8 (1946): 87–96.

———. "The Moment of Consecration and the Elevation of the Host." *Mediaeval Studies* 6 (1944): 121–50.

Kerns, Joseph E. *The Theology of Marriage: The Historical Development of Christian Attitudes Toward Sex and Sanctity in Marriage*. New York: Sheed and Ward, 1964.

Kessler, H. L. "*Hic Homo Formatur*: The Genesis Frontispieces of the Carolingian Bibles." *Art Bulletin* 53 (1971): 143–60.

Köhler, Wilhelm. "Leo (the Great) Bible." In *Die karolingischen Miniaturen*, vol. 1, *Die Schule von Tours*. Berlin: Deutscher Verein für Kunstwissenschaft, 1933.

Kolve, V. A. *The Play Called Corpus Christi*. Stanford: Stanford University Press, 1966.

Ladner, Gerhard. *The Idea of Reform: Its Impact on Christian*

*Thought and Action in the Age of the Fathers*. Rev. ed. New York: Harper and Row, 1967.

Lea, Henry Charles. *A History of Auricular Confession and Indulgences in the Latin Church*. 3 vols. Philadelphia: Lea Brothers & Co., 1896.

Leclercq, Jean. *Recueil d'études sur Saint-Bernard et ses écrits*. Vol. 3. Storia e letteratura, no. 114. Rome: Storia e letteratura, 1969.

Leclercq, Jean; Vandenbroucke, François; and Bouyer, Louis. *The Spirituality of the Middle Ages*. Translated by Benedictines of Holme Eden Abbey, Carlisle. A History of Christian Spirituality, vol. 2. London: Burns & Oates, 1968.

Leff, Gordon. *Heresy in the Later Middle Ages: The Relation of Heterodoxy to Dissent, c.1250–c.1450*. 2 vols. Manchester, Eng.: Manchester University Press, 1967.

Le Goff, Jacques, ed. *Hérésies et sociétés dans l'Europe pré-industrielle 11e–18e siècles*. Civilisations et sociétés, no. 10. Paris: La Haye, 1968.

Lerner, Robert E. *The Heresy of the Free Spirit in the Later Middle Ages*. Berkeley: University of California Press, 1972.

Leyerle, John. "The Interlace Structure of *Beowulf*." *University of Toronto Quarterly* 37 (1967): 1–17.

Lourdaux, W., and Verhelst, D., eds. *The Concept of Heresy in the Middle Ages (11th–13th C.)*. Mediaevalia Lovaniensia, series 1, studia 4. Louvain: Louvain University Press, 1973.

McGarry, Loretta. *The Holy Eucharist in Middle English Homiletic and Didactic Verse*. Washington, D.C.: The Catholic University of America Press, 1936.

Mandonnet, Pierre. *St. Dominic and His Works*. Translated by Mary Benedicta Larkin. London: B. Herder, 1945.

Manselli, Raoul. *Spirituali e Beghini in Provenza*. Istituto Storico Italiano per il Medio Evo, Studi Storici, fasc. 31–34. Rome: Istituto Storico Italiano per il Medio Evo, 1959.

Mays, James Luther. *Hosea: A Commentary*. London: SCM Press, 1969.

Michaud-Quantin, Pierre. *Sommes de casuistique et manuels de confession au moyen âge (XII–XVI siècles)*. Analecta medievalia namurcensia, vol. 13. Louvain: Nauwelaerts, 1962.

Musée National du Louvre. *L'Europe gothique, XIIe–XIVe siècles*. Paris: Réunion des Musées Nationaux, 1968.

Newman, F. X. "St. Augustine's Three Visions and the Structure of the *Commedia*." *Modern Language Notes* 82 (1967): 56–78.

Noonan, John T., Jr. *Contraception: A History of Its Treatment* by the Catholic Theologians and Canonists. Cambridge: Harvard University Press, 1966.

Oakley, Thomas Pollock. *English Penitential Discipline and Anglo-Saxon Law in their Joint Influence*, Studies in History, Economics and Public Law (Columbia University), vol. 107, no. 242. New York: Longmans, Green and Co., 1923.

Olson, Glending. "Deschamps' 'Art de dictier' and Chaucer's Literary Environment." *Speculum* 48 (1973): 714–23.

———. "The Medieval Theory of Literature for Refreshment and its Use in the Fabliau Tradition." *Studies in Philology* 71 (1974): 291–313.

Owst, G. R. *Literature and Pulpit in Medieval England*. 2d. ed. 1961. Reprint. Oxford: Basil Blackwell, 1966.

———. *Preaching in Medieval England: An Introduction to Sermon Manuscripts of the Period c. 1350–1450*. Cambridge: Cambridge University Press, 1926.

Pächt, Otto; Dodwell, C. R.; and Wormald, Francis. *The St. Albans Psalter*. Studies of the Warburg Institute, vol. 25. London: Warburg Institute, 1960.

Payen, Jean-Charles. *Le Motif du repentir dans la littérature française médiévale (des origines à 1230)*. Publications romanes et françaises, 98. Geneva: Droz, 1967.

Pelikan, Jaroslav. *The Shape of Death: Life, Death, and Immortality in the Early Fathers*. New York: Abingdon Press, 1961.

Poggioli, Renato. "Tragedy or Romance? A Reading of the Paolo and Francesca Episode in Dante's *Inferno*." *PMLA* 72 (1957): 313–58. Reprint (abridged). "Paolo and Francesca." In *Dante*, edited by John Freccero, pp. 61–77. Twentieth Century Views. Englewood Cliffs, N.J.: Prentice-Hall, 1965.

Poschmann, Bernhard. *Penance and the Annointing of the Sick*. Translated and revised by Francis Courtney. New York: Herder and Herder, 1964.

Quinn, Esther Casier. *The Quest of Seth for the Oil of Life*. Chicago: University of Chicago Press, 1962.

Rahner, Hugo. "Antenna crucis, III." *Zeitschrift für katholische Theologie* 66 (1942): 196–227.

———. "Odysseus at the Mast." In *Greek Myths and Christian Mystery*, translated by Brian Battershaw, pp. 328–86. New York: Harper and Row, 1963.

Reeves, Marjorie. *The Influence of Prophecy in the Later Middle Ages: A Study in Joachimism*. Oxford: Clarendon, 1969.

———. *Joachim of Fiore and the Prophetic Future*. London: SPCK, 1976.

————. "The 'Liber Figurarum' of Joachim of Fiore." *Medieval and Renaissance Studies* 2 (1950): 57–81.

Reeves, Marjorie, and Hirsch-Reich, Beatrice. *The Figurae of Joachim of Fiore.* Oxford: Clarendon, 1972.

Remy, Paul. "La Lèpre, thème littéraire au moyen âge: Commentaire d'un passage du roman provençal de Jaufré." *Le Moyen Âge* 52(1946):195–242.

Ricoeur, Paul. *The Symbolism of Evil.* Translated by Emerson Buchanan. Religious Perspectives Series, vol. 17. New York: Harper and Row, 1967.

Ringgren, H. *The Prophetical Conception of Holiness.* Upsala universitets årsskrift, 1948, no. 12. Upsala: Lundequistska Bokhandeln, 1948.

Robertson, D. W., Jr. *A Preface to Chaucer: Studies in Medieval Perspectives.* Princeton: Princeton University Press, 1962.

Runciman, Steven. *The Medieval Manichee: A Study of the Christian Dualist Heresy.* Cambridge: Cambridge University Press, 1947.

Schillebeeckx, Edward. *Marriage: Secular Reality and Saving Mystery.* Translated by N. D. Smith. New York: Sheed and Ward, 1964.

Singleton, Charles S. *Dante Studies.* Vol. 2, *Journey to Beatrice.* 1958. Reprint. Cambridge: Harvard University Press, 1967.

Smalley, Beryl. *English Friars and Antiquity in the Early Fourteenth Century.* Oxford: Basil Blackwell, 1960.

————. *The Study of the Bible in the Middle Ages.* Oxford: Basil Blackwell, 1952.

Snaith, Norman H. *The Distinctive Ideas of the Old Testament.* London: Epworth, 1944.

Southern, R. W. *The Making of the Middle Ages.* New Haven, Conn.: Yale University Press, 1953.

————. *Medieval Humanism and Other Studies.* Oxford: Basil Blackwell, 1970.

————. *St. Anselm and His Biographer: A Study of Monastic Life and Thought, 1059–c.1130.* Cambridge: Cambridge University Press, 1963.

Speiser, E. A., trans. and commentator. *Genesis: Introduction, Translation, and Notes.* The Anchor Bible. Garden City, N.Y.: Doubleday, 1964.

Strayer, Joseph R. *The Albigensian Crusades.* New York: Dial Press, 1971.

Tavard, George H. *Woman in Christian Tradition.* Notre Dame, Ind.: University of Notre Dame Press, 1973.

Teetaert, Amédée. *La Confession aux laiques dans l'Église latine depuis le VIIIe jusqu'au XIVe siècle.* Ph.D. dissertation, University of Louvain, series 2, vol. 17. Paris: J. Gabalda, 1926.

Tentler, Thomas N. *Sin and Confession on the Eve of the Reformation.* Princeton, N.J.: Princeton University Press, 1977.

Trexler, R. C. Review of *La Religion populaire au moyen âge: Problèmes de méthode et d'histoire,* by Raoul Manselli. *Speculum* 52 (1977): 1019–22.

Vinaver, Eugène. *Form and Meaning in Medieval Romance.* Modern Humanities Research Association, 1966.

Volpe, Gioacchino. *Movimenti religiosi e sette ereticali nella societa' medievale italiana, Secoli XI–XIV.* Biblioteca storia Sansoni, n.s., vol 37. Florence: G. C. Sansoni, 1961.

von Moos, Peter. *Consolatio: Studien zur mittelalterlichen Trostliteratur über den Tod und zum Problem der christlichen Trauer.* 4 vols. Munich: Wilhelm Fink Verlag, 1971.

von Rad, Gerhard. *Old Testament Theology,* Vol. 2, *The Theology of Israel's Prophetic Traditions.* Translated by D. M. G. Stalker. Edinburgh: Oliver and Boyd, 1965.

von Simson, Otto. *The Gothic Cathedral.* 2d ed. New York: Bollingen Foundation, 1962.

Watkins, Oscar D. *A History of Penance.* 2 vols. 1920. Reprint. New York: Burt Franklin, 1961.

Wetherbee, Winthrop. "The Function of Poetry in the *De planctu naturae* of Alain de Lille." *Traditio* 25 (1969): 87–125.

———. *Platonism and Poetry in the Twelfth Century: The Literary Influence of the School of Chartres.* Princeton: Princeton University Press, 1972.

Woledge, Brian. *Bibliographie des romans et nouvelles en prose française antérieurs à 1500.* Société de publications romanes et françaises, no. 42. Geneva: Droz, 1954.

———. *Bibliographie des romans et nouvelles en prose française antérieurs à 1500: Supplément.* Publications romanes et françaises, no. 130. Geneva: Droz, 1973.

Yedlicka, Leo Charles. *Expressions of the Linguistic Area of Repentance and Remorse in Old French.* Studies in Romance Language and Literature, vol. 28. Washington, D.C.: The Catholic University of America Press, 1945.

## IV. *La Queste del Saint Graal*

A. Texts and translations

*The Quest of the Holy Grail.* Translated by P. M. Matarasso. Baltimore: Penguin, 1969.

*La Queste del Saint Graal.* Edited by Albert Pauphilet. CFMA, 33 (1923). Reprint. Paris: Champion, 1967.
*The Vulgate Version of the Arthurian Romances: Le Livre de Lancelot del Lac.* Edited by H. Oskar Sommer. Vols. 3–5. Carnegie Institution of Washington Publications, no. 74. Washington, D.C.: Carnegie Institution, 1910.

B. Secondary Works

Adolf, Helen. "The Concept of Original Sin as Reflected in Arthurian Romance." In *Studies in Language and Literature in Honor of Margaret Schlauch,* edited by Irena Dobrzycka, Alfred Reszkiewicz, and Grzegorz Sinko, pp. 21–29. Warsaw: Polish Scientific Publishers, 1966.
Bloch, R. Howard. "The Text as Inquest: Form and Function in the Pseudo-Map Cycle." *Mosaic* 8, no. 4 (1975):107–19.
Bogdanow, Fanni. *The Romance of the Grail: A Study of the Structure and Genesis of a Thirteenth-century Arthurian Prose Romance.* New York: Barnes & Noble, 1966.
Bruce, James Douglas. *The Evolution of Arthurian Romance from the Beginnings down to the Year 1300.* Vol. 1. Baltimore: The Johns Hopkins University Press, 1923.
Brunel, C. "Les Hanches du roi pêcheur." *Romania* 81 (1960): 37–43.
Cornet, Luc. "Trois Épisodes de la *Queste del Graal.*" In *Mélanges offerts à Rita Lejeune,* 2: 983–98. Gembloux: J. Duclot, 1969.
de Briel, Henri, and Herrmann, Manuel. *King Arthur's Knights and the Myths of the Round Table.* Collection le Roi Arthur, no. 4. Paris: C. Klincksieck, 1972.
Fisher, Lizette Andrews. *The Mystic Vision in the Grail Legend and in the Divine Comedy.* New York: Columbia University Press, 1917.
Frappier, Jean. *Étude sur La mort le Roi Artu.* Paris: E. Droz, 1936.
———. "Le Graal et la chevalrie." *Romania* 75 (1954): 165–210.
———. "Le Graal et ses feux divergents." *Romance Philology* 24 (1971): 373–440.
———. "Plaidoyer pour l'*architecte,* contre une opinion d'Albert Pauphilet sur le *Lancelot en prose.*" *Romance Philology* 8 (1954–1955): 27–33.
Gilson, Étienne. "La mystique de la grâce dans *La Queste del Saint Graal.*" *Romania* 51 (1925): 321–47. Reprint. In *Les Idées et les lettres,* 2d ed., pp. 59–91. Paris: J. Vrin, 1955.
Hennessy, Helen. "The Uniting of Romance and Allegory in *La*

*Queste del Saint Graal.*" *Boston University Studies in English* 4 (1961): 189–201.

Hynes-Berry, Mary. "Malory's Translation of Meaning: *The Tale of the Sankgreal.*" *Studies in Philology* 74 (1977): 243–57.

Jonin, Pierre. "Un Songe de Lancelot dans la *Queste du Graal.*" In *Mélanges offerts à Rita Lejeune,* 2:1053–61. Gembloux: J. Duclot, 1969.

Locke, Frederick. *The Quest for the Holy Grail.* Stanford Studies in Language and Literature, no. 21. Stanford: Stanford University Press, 1960.

Loomis, Roger Sherman. *The Development of Arthurian Romance.* London: Hutchinson & Co., 1963.

———. *The Grail: From Celtic Myth to Christian Symbol.* New York: Columbia University Press, 1963.

Loomis, Roger Sherman, ed. *Arthurian Literature in the Middle Ages: A Collaborative History.* Oxford: Clarendon, 1959.

Lot, Ferdinand. *Étude sur le Lancelot en prose.* Sciences historiques et philologiques, fasc. 226. Paris: Champion, 1918.

Lot-Borodine, Myrrha. "Les Apparitions du Christ aux messes de l'*Estoire* et de la *Queste del Saint Graal.*" *Romania* 72 (1951): 202–23.

———. *De l'Amour profane à l'amour sacré.* Paris: Nizet, 1961.

———. *Trois Essais sur le roman de Lancelot du Lac et la Quête du Saint Graal.* Paris: Champion, 1919.

Marx, Jean. *La Légende arthurienne et la Graal.* Bibliothèque de l'École des Hautes Études, Sciences religieuses, vol. 54. Paris: Presses universitaires de France, 1952.

———. *Nouvelles Recherches sur la littérature arthurienne.* Bibliothèque française et romane, series C, no. 9. Paris: Klincksieck, 1965.

Micha, Alexandre. "L'Esprit du *Lancelot-Graal.*" *Romania* 82 (1961):357–78.

———. "La Table ronde chez Robert de Boron et dans la *Queste del Saint Graal.*" In *Les Romans du Graal aux XII^e et XIII^e siècles,* pp. 119–33. Paris: Centre national de la recherche scientifique, 1956.

Moorman, Charles. "Malory's Treatment of the Sankgreall." *PMLA* 71 (1956): 496–509. Revised. In Lumiansky, R. M., ed., *Malory's Originality,* pp. 184–204. Revised. In Moorman, Charles, *The Book of Kyng Arthur: The Unity of Malory's "Morte Darthur,"* pp. 28–48. Lexington: University of Kentucky Press, 1965.

Nelli, René, ed. *Lumière du Graal*. Paris: Les Cahiers du Sud, 1951.

Newstead, Helaine. "The Grail Legend and Celtic Tradition." Franco-American Pamphlets, ser. 3, no. 5. New York: American Society of the French Legion of Honor, 1945.

O'Sharkey, Eithne M. "The Influence of the Teaching of Joachim of Fiore on Some Thirteenth-Century French Grail Romances." *Trivium* 2 (1967): 47–58.

Pauphilet, Albert. *Études sur la Queste del Saint Graal*. 1921. Reprint. Paris: Champion, 1968.

Paris, Gaston. *La Littérature française au moyen âge (XIe–XIVe siècle)*. Paris: Librairie Hachette, 1905.

Quinn, Esther Casier. "The Quest of Seth, Solomon's Ship and the Grail." *Traditio* 21 (1965): 185–222.

Savage, Grace Armstrong. "Fathers and Sons in the *Queste del Saint Graal*." *Romance Philology* 31 (1977): 1–16.

Todorov, Tzvetan. "La Quête du récit." In *La Poétique de la prose*, pp. 129–50. Paris: Editions du Seuil, 1971.

Tuve, Rosemond. *Allegorical Imagery: Some Mediaeval Books and Their Posterity*. Princeton: Princeton University Press, 1966.

Vinaver, Eugène. *The Rise of Romance*. Oxford: Clarendon, 1971.

West, G. D. "Grail Problems, II: The Grail Family in Old French Verse Romances." *Romance Philology* 25 (1971): 53–73.

## V. Malory's *Tale of the Sankgreal*

### A. Texts

Malory, Thomas. *Le Morte D'Arthur*. Edited by Janet Cowen. 2 vols. Harmondsworth, Eng.: Penguin, 1969.

Malory, Thomas. *The Works of Sir Thomas Malory*. Edited by Eugène Vinaver. 3 vols. 2d. ed. Oxford: Clarendon, 1967.

### B. Secondary Works

Bennet, J. A. W., ed. *Essays on Malory*. Oxford: Clarendon, 1963.

Benson, Larry D. *Malory's Morte Darthur*. Cambridge: Harvard University Press, 1976.

———. "Sir Thomas Malory's *Le Morte Darthur*." In *Critical Approaches to Six Major English Works*, edited by R. M. Lumiansky and Herschel Baker, pp. 81–131. Philadelphia: University of Pennsylvania Press, 1968.

Brewer, D. S. "The Present Study of Malory." In *Arthurian Romance: Seven Essays*, edited by D. D. R. Owen, pp. 83–97. New York: Barnes & Noble, 1971.

Davies, R. T. "Malory's Lancelot and the Noble Way of the World." *Review of English Studies*, n.s. 6 (1955): 356–64.

———. "Malory's 'Vertuouse Love.' " *Studies in Philology* 53 (1956): 459–69.

———. "The Worshipful Way in Malory." In *Patterns of Love and Courtesy: Essays in Memory of C. S. Lewis*, edited by John Lawlor. Evanston: Northwestern University Press, 1966.

Field, P. J. C. *Romance and Chronicle: A Study of Malory's Prose Style*. London: Barrie and Jenkins, 1971.

Jurovics, Raachel. "The Definition of Virtuous Love in Thomas Malory's *Le Morte Darthur.*" *Comitatus* 2 (1971): 27–43.

Kellogg, Alfred L. *Chaucer, Langland, Arthur: Essays in Middle English Literature*. New Brunswick: Rutgers University Press, 1972.

Kelly, Robert L. "Arthur, Galahad and the Scriptural Pattern in Malory." *American Benedictine Review* 23 (1972): 9–23.

Lambert, Mark. *Malory: Style and Vision in "Le morte Darthur."* Yale Studies in English, vol. 186. New Haven, Conn.: Yale University Press, 1976.

Lewis, C. S. Review of *Sir Thomas Wyatt and Some Collected Studies*, by E. K. Chambers. *Medium Aevum* 3 (1934): 237–40.

Lumiansky, R. M. "Malory's Steadfast Bors." *Tulane Studies in English* 8 (1958): 5–20.

Lumiansky, R. M., ed. *Malory's Originality: A Critical Study of "Le Morte Darthur."* Baltimore: The Johns Hopkins University Press, 1964.

Pochoda, Elizabeth T. *Arthurian Propaganda: "Le Morte d'Arthur" as an Historical Ideal of Life*. Chapel Hill: University of North Carolina Press, 1971.

Reiss, Edmund. *Sir Thomas Malory*. Twayne English Author Series, no. 35. New York: Twayne, 1966.

Tucker, P. E. "The Place of the *Quest of the Holy Grail* in the *Morte Darthur.*" *Modern Language Review* 48 (1953): 391–97.

Vinaver, Eugène. *Malory*. Oxford: Clarendon, 1929.

Whitworth, Charles W. "The Sacred and the Secular in Malory's *Tale of the Sankgreal.*" *Yearbook of English Studies* 5 (1975): 19–29.

Wilson, Robert H. *Characterization in Malory: A Comparison with His Sources*. Chicago: University of Chicago Press, 1934.

## VI. *Cleanness*

### A. Texts and translations

*Cleanness.* Edited by J. J. Anderson. Manchester, Eng.: Manchester University Press, 1977.

*Cleanness.* Edited by Sir Israel Gollancz. Select Early English Poems, vols. 7, 9. London: Humphrey Milford, Oxford University Press, 1921, 1933. Reissued in one vol. with translation by D. S. Brewer. London: D. S. Brewer, 1974.

*Cleanness.* In *The Complete Works of the Gawain-poet,* translated by John Gardner. Chicago: University of Chicago Press, 1965.

*Cleanness.* In *The Owl and the Nightingale; Cleanness; St. Erkenwald,* translated by Brian Stone. Baltimore: Penguin, 1971.

*Cleanness.* In *The Pearl-poet: His Complete Works,* translated by Margaret Williams. New York: Random House, 1967.

*Cleanness.* In *The Poems of the "Pearl" Manuscript,* edited by Malcolm Andrew and Ronald Waldron. North Medieval Texts. London: Edward Arnold, Forthcoming.

*Cleanness.* In *The Works of the Gawain-poet.* Edited by Charles Moorman. Jackson, Miss.: University of Mississippi Press, 1976.

*Purity: A Middle English Poem.* Edited by Robert J. Menner. Yale Studies in English, vol. 61. New Haven: Yale University Press, 1920.

### B. Secondary Works

Ackerman, Robert W. " 'Pared Out of Paper': *Gawain* 802 and *Purity* 1408." *Journal of English and Germanic Philology* 56 (1957): 410–17.

Brown, Carleton F. "Note on the Dependence of *Cleanness* on the *Book of Mandeville." PMLA* 19 (1904): 149–53.

Clark, John W. "Paraphrases for 'God' in the Poems Attributed to the *Gawain*-Poet." *Modern Language Notes* 65 (1950): 232–36.

Cuffe, Edwin Dodge. "Interpretation of *Patience, Cleanness,* and the *Pearl,* from the Viewpoint of Imagery." Ph.D. dissertation, University of North Carolina, 1951.

Foley, Michael M. "A Bibliography of *Purity* (*Cleanness*), 1864–1972," *Chaucer Review* 8 (1973–1974): 324–34.

Fowler, David C. "Cruxes in *Cleanness." Modern Philology* 70 (1973): 331–36.

Kelly, T. D., and Irwin, John T. "The Meaning of *Cleanness*: Parable as Effective Sign." *Mediaeval Studies* 35 (1973): 232–60.

Moorman, Charles. *The Pearl-Poet*. Twayne English Author Series, no. 64. New York: Twayne, 1968.

Morse, Charlotte C. "The Image of the Vessel in *Cleanness*." *University of Toronto Quarterly* 40 (1971): 202–16.

Spearing, A. C. *The Gawain-Poet: A Critical Study*. Cambridge: Cambridge University Press, 1970.

Turville-Petre, Thorlac. *The Alliterative Revival*. Cambridge, Eng.: D. S. Brewer, 1977.

Vantuono, William. "*Patience, Cleanness, Pearl*, and *Gawain*: The Case for Common Authorship." *Annuale mediaevale* 12 (1971): 37–69.

Williams, David J. "A Literary Study of the Middle English Poems *Purity* and *Patience*." Ph.D. dissertation, Oxford University, 1965.

Wilson, Edward. *The Gawain-Poet*. Leiden: E. J. Brill, 1976.

Zavadil, Joseph Benedict. "A Study of Meaning in *Patience* and *Cleanness*." Ph.D. dissertation, Stanford University, 1962.

# Index